Rory O'Connor was born in 1928 near the village of Knocknagoshel, close to where the three counties of Kerry, Cork and Limerick meet. He worked as a journalist at the *Irish Press*, and later as film critic and News Editor at the *Sunday Press*, before going to Radio Eireann as news writer and broadcaster. He was for fifteen years head of Television News Broadcasting at RTE until his retirement in 1993.

'He is a masterly storyteller, evoking what he calls "the wonders of life" with consummate skill. He deals with a past that ranges from the gentle to the murderous, the violent and grim to the humorous and fantastical. *Gander at the Gate* is completely authentic, a gripping feat of memory, a candid, detailed evocation of a lost world. It is a delightful book and a splendid achievement' Brendan Kennelly

'I loved the book. I read it all in one sitting . . . I carried Rory O'Connor's vivid images and phrases around with me in my imagination long after I had finished reading. He seems to have had the type of magical, untrammelled childhood, populated with extraordinary characters, to which we have all aspired' Deirdre Purcell

'Rory O'Connor's book enthralled me. Of course, its time and place was a factor – I was familiar with this world. I believe, however, that it would be even more enthralling to people from the world outside . . . The book depicts an Ireland that has almost vanished, but that was the seedbed of the Ireland we know today' Con Houlihan

'The poet W. B. Yeats desired to produce written work that, while . . . arduously crafted, would appear as immediate and spontaneous as the ordinary spoken words of people. It is a testament to the achievement of Rory O'Connor that he has accomplished just that by writing a memoir that connects closely to the oral tradition . . . It could be hoped, perhaps, that every community – urban and rural – would have a Rory O'Connor among them who would possess the ability of capturing that society in all its vitality, colour and mystery. If that were possible they would – like this present book – make for fascinating reading' *Sunday Business Post*

Gander at
the Gate

Rory O'Connor

review

To Knocknagoshel

First published in Great Britain in 2000
by REVIEW

An imprint of Headline Book Publishing

First published in paperback in 2001

10 9 8 7 6 5 4 3

ISBN 0 7472 6642 5

Printed and bound in Great Britain by
Clays Ltd, St Ives plc.

Headline Book Publishing
A division of Hodder Headline
338 Euston Road
London NW1 3BH

www.reviewbooks.co.uk
www.hodderheadline.com

Contents

– I –

First Dawn

I SHED my first real tears, howling out at life, standing in the cradle my father had made from the wood of an ash tree. I was in the corner of the kitchen, beside the hearth, filled with anger at my imprisonment and striking my hands in fury on the cradle sides that held me in. I longed to break free and walk on the cold stone floor, and go out into the grass and mud and flowers. After many days had gone this is what I did, and pushed my head into wet shrubs, and felt the drops of water run down my neck and back. I looked at the flowers in their beds and beat them with my hands and took up the wet brown earth and flung it about. I saw the white gate and the trees and the sky everywhere, and I fell back in contentment and went to sleep.

It was near the end of winter when I awakened. I was on my mother's back on the way to school for the first time. I was bundled up in a scarf and woollen cap, and my mother bore me along a cold winter road. The road was white and ice crackled beneath her feet.

We journeyed on over a stile and across hard land, and over a small bridge on a river and up a long boreen to a new road. In the schoolroom she placed me on a long narrow bench with other infants next to a small white-faced girl with black hair. I put my arms around her and kissed her. For a long time after, that small girl with the black hair belonged to me.

In the many years after that, the journey to school had many faces as the body grew and the eyes looked farther. The black rain of winter and the treacherous paths over bogland, the benign coming of springtime, and the warm air of summer days. Below our house, the spring well in the tinkers' dingle. The frog-spawn spread over the water, speckled with small black dots of life. The breaking into tadpoles, with monster heads and tails of hair. The growing of the hands and feet into small froglets, and the day they were all gone, driven by instinct into the grasses of wet fields.

The autumn morning full of mist, and through the last boreen to the school. Thorn bushes and whins and wild weeds, covered from end to end with jewels of the night, floating thousands of spider webs, borne in on soft winds, spread out for all to see, still glistening with the tiny droplets of the morning dew.

Through the years the roles were changing until I became the protector of my mother, guarding her against her fears. This last boreen became the scene, on many occasions, of my feats of chivalry. I went ahead to spy out the enemy. A large white she-goat with magnificent horns and a long luxury of beard. An erratic creature, malignant towards those from whom she could smell fear. My mother feared her and was never safe from her charges.

She waited for us, standing guard near the school outside the cottage of the old woman who owned her. I approached her full of trickery and movement until she raised her head from her charging position to have a look. Then I seized her long beard and she was powerless.

The old school was built in 1882. That was the date carved on a stone plaque high up on the front wall. It had two large rooms with high windows on every side. There were two small fireplaces, and at times there were over one hundred pupils. In one room my mother taught low and high infants, and first class; my father took fifth, sixth and seventh. In the next room another woman teacher, Mrs Curtin, had second, third and fourth.

I did not fully understand then that many of the students came from small farms, and were well fed and clad, but many more were the children of the poor. Their clothing was thin, their food meagre. Some had strong shoes and protection against rain and wind. Others had worn-out footwear and cheap ganseys and ragged jackets, seeking shelter in rain from outhouses and walls and bushes along the roads and the fields to school. There was buttered bread and bottles of milk in the satchels of the fortunate. The poor dipped their fingers in their pockets to feel for their unbuttered slices and ate the dry morsels.

I did not know then that a small yearly government grant was sent to the parish priest for heating and cleaning, but rarely reached the teachers and was spent on other causes considered more worthy. The heat came mostly from sods of turf brought each day by the pupils, and they too cleaned the school each evening as a last act before going home.

The fire blazed and the room steamed from the clothing of the miserable. There was no teaching until the wet children were seen to. My mother started a song and the cold raised their voices to race their blood.

There was nothing she could not do for them and with them, this smiling fair-skinned woman with the yellow hair. Smiles and a tin gallon of hard sweets soothed their worries and took away their tears. Small briberies and praise gladdened them. They sought to please her and yearned for her favour.

Their happiness shone in their eyes, with the music and words of Gaelic songs: 'The summer is wafting and moving, now through the island of saints, with brightness the sun is shining, with beauty filling the land. Oh, no matter, for we are returning, going back to the friends of our hearts, good health in our bodies still, as we sail for the green hills of Ireland. The green hills of Ireland, the beauty of the valleys and woods, oh friends, how wonderful it is, at last moving back on the tide. Wind and sun fill our sails, on the rise and fall of the ocean, soon we shall be safe again, at home in the hills of Ireland.'

The small children sang for her in the school and they sang for her each year at small festivals in the field behind the village. They won prizes for her and for themselves. They danced reels and horn-pipes, and sang songs, and played music on their penny whistles. Each time they felt taller within themselves, and the shy came forward and raised their hands.

We loved the first half hour of each day. We talked of God and the Holy Family, of the inn that turned them away, and the search for shelter for the night. We saw the baby Jesus in the manger in his swaddling clothes, and the animals around breathing warmth into his body.

Later from the penny catechism we learned who made the world, and how many gods there were. The Father was God, the Son was God and the Holy Ghost was God. There were three gods but my mother said there was only one. We marvelled at this.

When she was at the other end of the room with my father, we skitted among ourselves. 'Who made the world?' the ringleader asked. 'Two little pigs with their tails curled,' the chorus replied. 'What is sin?' the ringleader asked. 'Catch a flea and break his shin,' the chorus replied. 'I'll tell the teacher what you said,' the little snitch said. She reddened and filled with tears when she saw the eyes that looked at her.

The geranium in the flowerpot on the big gable window looked down on us all, and nodded his red flower over our heads in blessing.

For many years I looked through the big school window at the world outside and saw many things. On a winter morning I looked out over the river on a rising frosty bogland, covered in whirls of white mist shot with rays of bright winter sun. A tall man strode out through the scene, and his dogs moved back and forth around him. He looked like a wraith moving through a heavenly place, and I longed to be with him and to travel with him in freedom, to whatever land he was striding towards.

I had a feeling then that there was magic and mystery everywhere, that I lived in a special place. I felt it even though I did not know then that I lived in the oldest land. I did not know then that ten thousand years ago, when the great ice cap melted and moved south, it left my North Kerry homeland untouched. Was this why the ghosts of time were always moving in my head, the ghosts of the ancient time, the time before the melting ice came down?

— 2 —

Clarke Comes In

FOR WHATEVER REASON our home below the village of Knockna-goshel was the temporary refuge of a number of strange characters who wandered in out of the day or night. The austere demeanour of my father hid a romantic heart. His eyes lit when unusual people came into our kitchen. He sat them down and fed them, and took from them the stories they had to tell. Sometimes they stayed the night, sometimes far longer. This ease and liberality was a constant delight to me, and I looked forward in hope and expectation towards the next voyager to come in.

One of the oldest memories, from the age of three or four, is of a man named Johnny Clarke. I did not know then, nor did I ever learn, the full story of his early life. He looked to be in the nature of a cross between an Arab from somewhere in the East and an Indian from the American plains. He was neither short nor tall, of light build, and quick and active of movement. He had a head of very dark hair of greasy quality, and he wore it fairly long. He had black eyes under black eyebrows, and his upper teeth were long, of a yellowish colour. His nose gave a hawkish impression, set well forward in a face of sallow skin. The word sinister is the most apt that I could apply to him. He looked old to me.

He was reputed to be from Dublin, although I never heard of his giving any account of his early years. He had been living round the village, during the wars in the early twenties. It was said he was involved in running dispatches, although he never had a gun. I was told later in derision that the nearest he came to action was a day he was picked up by the Staters with an empty bullet case in his pocket. It was over ten years later that he wandered into my life and gave me many occasions for fear and wonder. I did not know exactly how he came, except that one day I was aware he was living in the house.

However unprepossessing he was, it was agreed that he knew a lot about motor cars and what made them run. It was agreed that there was no one else in the parish who was better at taking a motor engine apart and putting it together again.

Motor cars appeared to be a fairly important part of our lives at that time and certainly they were important to Johnny Clarke, or Clarke, as my father usually referred to him. Maybe this was their affinity. There were plenty of old, fairly worn-out cars, and these were the only ones that seemed to interest my father, as he was short of money, having just finished building the house by direct labour on a half acre he had acquired from our farmer neighbour, a widow by the name of Delia Keane. Some of the debt still remained to be paid.

A year or so earlier he had cut the entire back off an old car and built on a small timber room with one wooden bed and one window. It was a travelling house, the first that had ever been seen in our village, and was a source of considerable pride to all of us. There was a small cooking area, a bare wooden bench about a foot and a half square, and the main equipment was a small primus stove run on methylated spirits, a kettle and a couple of pots and pans. The mobile home, well before its time, was taken around Kerry and the adjoining counties, to the watering places of Ballybunion, Lisdoonvarna, and Lahinch, and places farther, during the long glorious summers of that time.

Clarke was of the greatest help in this, carrying out the frequent running repairs that were necessary. He was also of considerable assistance, acting as cook, housemaid, and child-minder during the many trips made at weekends and holidays, and during the social visits of my father and mother, at night, to a public house in the village.

They normally had the services of a young woman from the surrounding district, who lived in the house, and who received a stipend of about a pound a month. For some reason or other at this time she was absent for a considerable period, and Johnny Clarke took up her duties, with doubtful enthusiasm.

I looked upon Clarke with not a little suspicion and apprehension, chiefly, I think, because of his unbecoming looks and a certain glint of madness in his eye, like you'd see in the eyes of a dog you couldn't trust. It was always with unease that I saw my father and mother departing for the village in the evening. I was, at the time and for long afterwards, afflicted with atrocious and disturbing nightmares, inhabited by black vicious goblins and other figures of a similar kind that tried to eliminate me from the earth, by the use of knives and spears and swords and other weapons of that kind.

The almost nightly visitations were caused by fear of the dark and an over-active imagination. There was also overreaction to scenes I had witnessed, of the castration of young bonhams and calves by a local farmer, called Charlie O'Donoghue, who was skilled in the use of sharp knives for almost any occasion.

He sat on the ground and held the bonham between his knees, turned on its back. He ignored the screaming, took the scrotum in a small pouch in his hand, and made a neat slice across with a razor. Then he dipped in, took the first testicle between forefinger and thumb, pulled it out, and with one skillful flick severed it from the little body. Within seconds the second testicle was removed in like manner, and Charlie called for the bottle of Friar's Balsam. A good douche and the piglet ran away with quickly diminishing screams. All was silence until the next bonham was brought to the operating table of Charlie's knees.

When he castrated young calves the testicles were not cut off. Each was clamped at the rear with two small pieces of wood, bound tightly together with strong twine. In this way the blood supply was cut off, and after a number of days the testicles withered and fell off.

Another thing that troubled my mind was sending old cows to the factory in Roscrea. I saw the picture of an infernal machine with open maw, and I saw the animals hurled into this, to be turned into masses of blood and pulp.

It was the dark that troubled me most. There was no electricity, and a paraffin oil lamp hung on the wall of the kitchen. The dim yellow light from the two wicks brought little joy to the heart of a fearful child. There were only the shadows it threw into the dark scullery and the hallway, where unknown demons, malicious and horrible, were skulking. Elsewhere in the house there were candles, small white candles with sickly light, standing up, brave as they could, on their tallowed candlesticks.

In this scene and frame of mind I had my first nightmare, during the reign of Johnny Clarke in our house. Mother and Father were gone out, the night was quiet, and first sleep was passing, when the goblins struck. Screams rent the household and the night, until Clarke had to act. He lit a candle and faced upstairs. In a half-crazed state, I saw the light appearing at the opening door, followed by a face of horror. The light on his sallow face, his black hair and eyes, and open yellow mouth, convinced me my last hour had come. Beyond any shadow of doubt, the devil had, at last, come to take me.

*

I heard mention of fellows like Stalin and Hitler and de Valera and Cosgrave and the Blueshirts, but the main conversation between Clarke and my father was about motor cars. Such things as dynamos and sparking plugs and the proper sizes of the gaps, and the best type of sandpaper to clean up the operations. Clarke had still no car of his own, and I'd sometimes see him in front of the house examining my father's old contraption as if he had some plans for it himself.

It happened that at that time word came out that de Valera was going to bring out a new newspaper called the *Irish Press*. As an ex-IRA man who had gone with de Valera, my father was in great delight. Because he had to spend most of each day teaching at the Knockbrack school with my mother, he couldn't be of much use circulating the paper around Knocknagoshel and the surrounding districts. Johnny Clarke, man of no work, was the man.

The day the deal was done was a lovely sunny day, and my mother and father had come back from Mass in the village. Clarke was hanging about when they returned, and before long the discussion got up. The car was started and stopped several times with Clarke making some point or other and holding his head close to the bonnet while the engine was running. Finally Clarke handed over two pound notes into my father's hand. He was the new owner and he was also the new circulation manager for the new paper for Knocknagoshel and surrounding areas.

It was an ill-fated arrangement. The car performed up to specification but Clarke did not. He was circulating for all he was worth. He was out each day in frenetic activity. He said if he ran out of petrol he ran it on paraffin oil. He even declared that one day when there was nothing else to be done he ran it on a bottle of whiskey.

It was strange that I should be the instrument of his downfall. One day, filled with the curiosity of a four-year-old, I secretly entered the door of his new mobile abode and began an inspection. It was unrewarding enough until I turned up the hard mattress on the wooden bed and opened up a scene that could have come out of a fairytale. There before my eyes was an Aladdin's cave of treasure. The bed was covered with silver coins, half-crowns, florins, shillings, sixpences and thruppeny bits. Such intelligence could not be for long kept a secret. I hotfooted to my father to tell him of my new riches. The investigation that followed told all. The revelation was that in the six months he had been district representative, Clarke had never paid a penny back to the *Irish Press*.

It was a sad occasion. Shortly afterwards Clarke ran his motor car down the Board of Works road for the last time. Failure of some kind, which even he could not put right, forced him to abandon it in a field, half a mile below our house. Its remains were there for many years, and there were times when I saw it and felt sorrow for the fate of the unfortunate man.

Clarke was not completely finished yet. His stories about motor cars and what he could do with them became more and more colourful. He had found a dynamo that had been out in the rain for five years, and damaged and rusted to such an extent that no other man in the world would do anything with it. No other man would do anything with it, but use it to hold a swinging gate open, to let cattle pass through; or to stop a horse's car from backing on you while resting the animal with a load on Mall Hill; or holding down one end of a net while making a sweep for salmon in Lyre Hole in the Oweveg river; or last of all, to take it and pitch it into some ditch or quarry hole to melt away there for all time.

He took it and by dint of his own genius and a few bits of copper wiring he got electric current to come out of it again, and in Coffey's forge using Coffey's own tools, meant only for belting out horseshoes or making gates, by the delicacy of his work he was able to build a complete new light housing for it, so that it now rested secure and snug under the bonnet of a motor car that was running every day, and starting at the first swing of the handle.

And in a final flourish of fancy or defiance, he told of his ultimate achievement in his handling of motor cars. 'You know the Mall Hill, it's as steep as you'd find anywhere, going down across Barret's Bridge and then lifting up again the other side by Jimmie Keane's house to the right of Knockane graveyard. I set it up to such a high rate of revs leaving the top crossroads that I knew by the time I was halfway down that something famous was going to happen to me. I flashed through Murphy's cross and she was still picking up speed to such a high degree that – and let God be my judge on this – fifty yards this side of the bridge she left the road into the air, and over the bridge, and picked up the road again on the other side, with no damage being done. The first time in history that a motor car flew.'

Most people laughed out at his story, but a few said that as far as motor cars were concerned, he was capable of anything. Be that as it may, his reign in the O'Connor household at Bunavalla, at the bottom of the parish, was over.

Kitty Cronin, the girl from Drummada, two miles back the Boola road, was coming back. Kitty, who had acted as my second little mother up to a year or two earlier, had been absent for several months, whether through illness or something else I did not know. She was returning to take over the small upstairs room at the back of the house, where Clarke had snored and smoked and coughed for far too long. He had outlived his welcome; the experiment was over.

It must be said that despite his looks and frightening manner, he never did any of us any harm and was friendly with us all for a long time after that.

Clarke had a flourish or two left. He hung round for a few years, doing the odd bit of work, mostly fairly light stuff that wouldn't overtax his delicate frame and genteel propensities. A travelling road show came round to the village, with a main act that astounded us all. The high-point of the show every night was when a handsome man with oiled hair and powdered face swept his black hat to the ground in a most gracious bow, and introduced to us a golden-haired woman of pleasing shape and countenance who incredibly was finished off at her whole rear end with a full-size fish's tail. It always caused a great stir of movement in the audience, and a high degree of clapping and cheering.

Clarke decided to join the road show, as what I do not know, and made off with them. It wasn't long before word came back that he had married the woman with the fish's tail and was living with her in contentment, or so 'twas said.

A few years later he was back. The fishwoman and himself had a falling-out that couldn't be patched up. He lived on for many years after, in a cosy little house on wheels that he built himself on the side of the road, above the forge behind the village. He died at the age of seventy and was buried in Knockane churchyard, among the people he had adopted as his own fifty years before.

− 3 −

Coneen the Boy Bawn

ANOTHER POOR MAN who was a frequent guest in our house and far closer to my heart than Clarke ever could be, was an itinerant labourer called Coneen the Boy Bawn. The name he went by, meaning little Con, the White Boy, told that at one time of his life, when he was young, he was the object of a good deal of care and affection from somebody or other, probably a mother who died young. It was one of few periods of affection he ever experienced during a long and often miserable life. His father had died young also, as when I knew him first, when he was about thirty years of age, he was referred to in conversation as an orphan.

He was a small man, about five foot two in height, and was of a naturally sweet and pleasing nature, only turning sour when he was treated outrageously, which was not an infrequent occurrence. He was completely uneducated, could make no attempt to read or write, and was devoid of critical faculty.

He was eternally restless, going here and going there, staying at one house for a period, and then going on to another and another, as if searching for something that was always eluding him. He treated men with a certain amount of reserve, sometimes even suspicion. But in the presence of a woman, any woman, he became transformed, his face breaking out in smiles, and his body adopting a series of fawning movements, like a little puppy seeking to be loved. He'd move around her at a respectful distance, his arms fully stretched downwards and his fingers moving as if he was playing an imaginary piano. Then, turning his back, his right hand moved slightly back and upwards continuing to play, so that one might think he was not so respectful after all, that is, if one did not know any better.

The farmers he worked for usually paid him no money, except for a few shillings he'd get to go to the Pattern day in the village on the 15th of August. This he always spent on small open packets of five Woodbine cigarettes, at tuppence a packet, and a couple of pints of porter. But as the day and night wore on, the festivities inevitably warmed the hearts and loosened the pockets of others, so that he got plenty of porter, on top of his own, and ended up the night as drunk as a lord, with a sore head the following morning – one of the few sore heads he had in the course of a year. No, he was paid no money but got his bed and board and an odd old trousers or shirt or jacket, or a pair of half-worn shoes.

I often thought that what Coneen was really looking for was some kind of security, so that he wouldn't be always at the mercy of some farmer or other, or of the elements themselves, with the wind and the rain driving into his badly clad figure, often in open country, when he'd be between houses and on the run. He'd usually stay only an average of a few months at any one house, but strange to say the harder a farmer worked him, the longer he'd stay with him. It was as if the very hard work gave him a sense that he was worth something, and was wanted. With a really hard farmer, he could last up to a year.

But I knew nothing of all this when I came across Coneen for the first time. It was a summer's day in the middle thirties, and I was about seven years old. I was sitting one day, looking out the kitchen window, dreaming as usual, when a wonderful thing caught my eye.

'Mama, Mama, do you know what I'm just after seeing. The peak of a cap walking by itself along the top of the ditch outside.'

My mother knew immediately. 'Oh, that's Coneen the Boy Bawn,' she said. 'He must be on the run again.' And of course she was right. Coneen always wore a cap, not of course like a normal man, but with the peak always pointed to the sky.

Coneen never made a straightforward entrance to the house he had chosen for his next period of work. There was a certain ritual to be gone through. After the cap he was not to be seen for a good few minutes. Then the peeping started, a quick dart of his head and cap round the outside pier of the front gate and then back again, repeated until he was sure everybody knew he was there.

I saw this scene repeated many times after that in my all-too-short childhood. Before long, all the children would be out with him, circling round, examining, and asking him how he was and where he was coming from. Ah, sure he'd better come in. But it was not as simple as that. Was the Master in? Where was the Missus? But eventually, all resistance was broken down, and we escorted him in triumph, and pride, into the kitchen. We'd all be smiling at him, making him welcome, and finding a nice chair for him sit on. Maybe not so much my mother. I would always see some kind of concern on her face. But Coneen would be laughing up at her, rubbing his hands, and going into his fawning act, and before long any resistance would be broken down. All right, Coneen could stay, but he'd have to sleep in the small room at the back of the stairs. We'd all be rushing around, getting his bed ready. Mama, what pillow, what blankets, will we give him a sheet? Can we use the rug?

Coneen's coming was nearly as good as the lady with the fish's tail, or the travelling road show 'Murder in the Red Barn', or the one with the mother holding the body of her dead child and wailing, 'Dead, dead, and never called me mother!'. We'd wash his face and comb his hair, and when my mother said he'd have to wash his feet before he'd go to bed in our house, we'd do it for him. A big pan of water on the cement kitchen floor, a bar of Sunlight soap, rubbing his shins and tickling the soles of his feet until he'd be kicking and thumping with his legs, roaring and splashing the water round the place. And then the big fight about who'd dry his feet, sometimes reefing the old towel, with the pulling and tearing, and all ending up in tears, with an ending of patience, and the final punishment, 'Children go to bed at once, at once, I say.'

On a Saturday night we'd really go to town on him. Our parents would be gone to the pub, and we'd all be trying to make Coneen beautiful, as near as we could to a film star, like you'd see in the odd picture that would come to the village dance hall. We'd find a clean shirt for him, and clean him up generally, including cutting his hair. Then I'd get out my instruments, consisting of my father's safety razor, and a new Mac's Smile blade, if one was to be found at all. He had a tough old beard maybe after a week or more but every inch would be done; Coneen would be groaning after an odd cut or two, but his face would be as soft and as pink as the bottom of any baby you ever saw. As a final flourish, the jar of Brylcreem would be located, and after a liberal application and much experimental combing, his hair would be as black and as sleek as any crow that sat and cawed on Delia Keane's ash-tree rookery down below the house.

On one occasion he came to us limping with a sore leg. I examined it carefully as soon as I got the opportunity, and sure enough, halfway up his shin to one side there was a red and ugly-looking sore that was turning black at the edges. I consulted with my father, who besides being a schoolmaster was also a bit of a doctor, and we came to the conclusion that a kind of ulcer had set in, and needed to be treated, and that it might take some time to cure. My father got me a can of Boraccic Powder, with lint and bandages, and it was my job every night to bathe the wound in warm water, apply liberal quantities of powder, and then carefully bandage it up. This went on for a week or more, with me playing nurse and doctor, just as my sisters were playing mammies and housey in their mock-up shop of chainies and bits of broken kitchenware at the corner of the house, except that mine was better, with a real patient and real medicine. The treatment was successful, and the ulcer gradually faded away and Coneen was able to get back to work.

The work that was to be done in our house was not suitable for Coneen. It was all light knicky-knacky kind of work that he was never used to. And the trouble was that he could hardly do any kind of work at all, unless he was fairly closely supervised. And this was not possible during the weekdays, with my father and mother at school.

We had beautiful gardens with flowers and shrubs of many kinds in front of the house, with plenty of weeding to be done from time to time. But Coneen could not be left next or near them. He'd take out plenty of weeds all right, but as sure as God made little apples, out too would come most of the flower plants.

This at times led to hilarious moments. On one occasion my mother asked him to weed and pull the grass around the bases of apple trees and blackcurrant bushes, so that the sunlight and rain-water might more easily get at them. Coneen stuck to his task all day, and by the time my mother returned home he had removed every single blade of grass in the orchard. She didn't say much to him except to blame herself, but by the look on her face I knew she wouldn't be saying too many prayers for him.

He excelled himself on another occasion when she put him washing the cement floor of the kitchen, armed with a big basin of water and a new scrubbing brush, while she went to the village for a message. She returned about half an hour later to find a remarkably fine cleaning job having been done on a few square yards, and the scrubbing brush worn down to the timber.

If it was to save his life, Coneen couldn't turn sods in the back field to plant potatoes in the spring, or master the intricacies of putting down young cabbages with a pikefull or two of cow manure round the roots. All this, I think, played on his mind. He sensed he was not pulling his weight, and this realization eventually made him unhappy and restless. You could see the unease creeping over him, and he'd start looking around him all the time, and pulling the peak of his cap first to one side and then the other, the peak all the while pointing to the sky. This went on for a day or two, and then at a suitable opportunity, when nobody was about, he'd be gone without a word or a warning to anybody.

*

Money or the lack of it never appeared to trouble Coneen too much. He was more concerned with things and events he knew would be coming up as the year went by. He'd say to me when we met on the road or on a nearby farm, 'Rory, are we far from the Pattern Day?' Christmas was the thing that was most on his mind. When the colours of the autumn had left the trees, he'd be interminably asking 'Are we anyway near the 'fourth of Christmas?', or 'Have ye got the coloured candles yet?', or 'Any sign of the bags of raisins?' It was always the 'fourth of Christmas, not Christmas Day. For the 'fourth of Christmas was Christmas Eve, the evening when everything was changed into a blaze of colour and romance in the kitchens of Coneen's life.

There was only one occasion when money brought a period of great trouble and suffering down upon him. The dole had been brought in some time previously, and somebody trying to be helpful got the form and applied for the few shillings to brighten his life. Coneen was delighted. For the first time he felt as good as other men, striding with them into the barracks on a Tuesday and setting down his mark on the sheet in front of the Guard. And then into Mrs Mangan's post office to collect the six shillings. He was staying at Kate Donoghue's farm at the time, and the old woman and her middle-aged sons, Simon and Sean, cousins of mine, tried to persuade him to buy a pair of new hobnailed boots. But it was to no avail. Coneen had other plans for his new riches. No doubt in his mind's eye, he could see that somewhere ahead the Pattern Day was coming up, when he would join the throngs striding up and down the village in full display, and elbow his way into the crowded pubs, and order his drink and pay for it with money that would never run out.

But it was not to be. Coneen had his own banking system. As the weeks went by and the half crowns and shillings mounted up, he changed them into notes and lodged them snug and dry in an empty Fry's Cocoa canister, which he hid in a certain field by a ditch. Some person was spying on him, and one day when he came to make his latest deposit, the canister was gone. Coneen pulled up grass and scraws and stones all round his hiding place, and for days afterwards he would go back and continue the search. They said at the time that it nearly drove him out of his head. So disillusioned was he that he never signed for the dole again.

Coneen lived on through the years going his itinerant way. When I came home on holidays from school in Tipperary he often came to see me to find out how I was, as if to say thanks for the few things I had done for him, and enquiring, in simple ways, about all the family. Was Eileen coming home from England soon, or was Mary still doing the hair? And where was Uncle Jack now, did he still have the screeching, watering, pony?

I always thought he'd die fairly young, with all the difficulties and hardship he'd been through. I was convinced that the kidneys would kill him, as quite often when I'd ask him how he was he'd say, 'I'm alright, but the ould machine is causing me a lot of trouble. I hardly get a wink at times. I have to bring an ould can to bed with me, getting up with water.' He held on for years and years, but inevitably was being worn down, and the health getting worse. At last he could work no more, and was taken to the union in Killarney, twenty-four miles away.

He never had much, but in his heart he had his own place, and his own people. And in the end he tried to come back to them. A couple of years before my father died in the late sixties he was driving from Killarney to Knocknagoshel. It was a dreadful day with the wind blowing and the rain falling heavily. After passing through Castleisland, and about seven miles from home, he saw a small figure trudging along. It was Coneen, wet to the skin, making his last break for freedom. He was brought to Knocknagoshel and dried out. Inevitably, he was sent back to the union, and died shortly afterwards. He was nearly seventy years of age.

– 4 –
Delia

OUR HOUSE was a half mile east of the village, on the side of the valley going down to the river. On days when the Cud Kits, my childhood companions, did not respond to my loud whistling across the Oweveg river I'd be on my own, for there were no other boys of near my own age anywhere round that I could get up to mischief with. I'd usually make my way back the road and down to Delia's farm looking for any adventure I could find. Delia was a widow for the second time. Murphy was her name and she had gone to America as a young girl towards the end of the century, from a small, fairly poor farm below the village. She had various jobs, mostly running house for rich people in New York, and she was not too long there when she got married. I never heard the full story of this, but it was not many years before her husband died and she was left a widow for the first time.

She decided to come home and she met up with a man called Luke Keane, whose forebears were said to have come down from

Ulster some time after the Battle of Kinsale, at the end of the long war that drove the Northern Princes, the O'Neills of Tyrone and the O'Donnells of Donegal, out through Lough Swilly in their wooden ships, into exile for ever. Luke Keane had a nice snug farm of over ninety acres running down to the river, and he was looking for a wife, so the match was made. He was not destined too long for this world, but he lived long enough to father four sons, Simon, Mossie, Luke and Sean, and two daughters, Bridie and Mary.

With all that done, he died suddenly at the age of around forty-five, leaving Delia a widow for the second time. From the time of my first memory of her, when I was about three in the early thirties, Delia was for ever mourning her three children, Simon and Luke and Bridie, that had had to go on the boat to America. Mossie and Mary and Sean, all somewhere in their twenties, were at home help-ing her to run the farm.

Delia was an exceedingly handsome woman, even in her middle age. She was tall and free moving, with a fine physique, a face of nearly classical features, blue grey-eyes, and a fine head of beauti-ful black hair. She had a good singing voice, and I remember her with her head thrown back, singing mournful ballads of lost loves, and at the end the tears filling her eyes from the sentiments of the words she had been singing.

Her kitchen was large and warm, and was white with the bright-ness of whitewashed walls, although the windows were fairly small. I loved the kindly smell of yeast bread, or the aromatic scents that rose from big white oven cakes sprinkled with caraway seeds, or the distinctive smell of currant bread, laced with raisins and spices. And nearer the fire the heavy odour from the big black pot of potatoes, hanging from the black crane, for the pigs, and everywhere the pun-gent smoke from the burning turf and wood. And the soft tones of her voice warning and cajoling me to mind myself from the dangers that lurked everywhere, for a wandering and inquisitive child.

Delia's was my second home, and Delia and Mary two fine extra mothers that I had in the year or so before I went to school at the age of four. I remember one of many days that repeated themselves again and again. My mother and father were gone off to school themselves, bright and early, and it wasn't too long before I was scalding the heart out of Kitty Cronin, the girl that was looking after us at home, parading around her, pulling her skirts and looking up at her with a chorus of 'I want to go to Delia's, I want to go to Delia's.' In the end there was nothing for her to do but march me back the road and down into the yard. Delia saw us coming, and stood by the half door to meet me, like I was a king coming home to his palace.

Her face was bright and smiling, and she raised me up into her arms and kissed me. 'Glory be to God,' she said, 'my little wanderer has come to visit me again.' She took me inside and stood me on the stone floor. She found a big meal-sack and folded it beside the fire, and sat me gently upon it. 'God of Mercy,' she said, 'look at him there like a king on his throne. Sure it brings to my mind the old days passed and gone. Little Simon, and Bridie and Luke, they'd sit in the self-same spot where you are now. And where are they now, mavourneen, but far across the sea, maybe for me never to see them again.' And she sighed, and a mist came on her eyes, and she looked away.

'Yerra, cheer up mother,' Mary said, 'sure you can't be mournful for ever, and as sure as God is in heaven, they'll all be home some day. Things aren't too good in America now, and one day you'll open the door and they'll all come in with the song of the morning.'

'Wisha Mary,' Delia said, 'you were always the one to be hopeful, and I only hope myself that you are right. But it's many the one I saw go away, and many the one I saw that never came back.'

Then the gloom passed and brightness came back into the kitchen again. Delia straightened herself and told Mary to bring in the potatoes and cabbage for the dinner. Then she took down a big flitch of yellow bacon from a hook above the hearth, and cut several fine hunks from it and put them in the small black pot, and half filled it with water from the white enamel bucket. And when she saw me looking at her waiting for her to hang it from the crane, she said: 'I'll let it rest there for a good bit yet, it'll draw the worst of the salt out of it.'

And Mary came in with three round heads of white cabbage, and a half a bucket of potatoes, scrubbed clean and white like polished wood. Then with a butcher's knife, out of the table drawer, she split the heads in two, and she cut the hard white hearts out of each half head, pulled them asunder with her hands, and knifed off the hard spines from the backs of the cabbage leaves. Now everything was ready for the big meal of the day, and it wasn't long before the smell of the boiling bacon began to drift past me on the floor.

It was a fine kitchen, placed in the centre of the long house, big as you could find anywhere, and high up to the roof itself. Behind me was the broad hearth the width of the house. To my left, within the house itself, was a kind of porch with two doors, one leading out the back to the orchard, and the other leading up the house to a big bedroom and through that to a smaller bedroom. Over my head to the left and over the roof of the porch was a big black hole, which led, on the north side, to a dark windowless loft that I had never seen. It gave me a kind of a shiver to look up at it, and more than a shiver to think of what might be inside it. Ghosts and goblins of all kinds came into my mind, and maybe dead bodies stretched out in brown shrouds with their hands crossed in front of them. And big black rats jumping about, and their red eyes shining in the dark.

On the left wall was a small window looking out at the apple trees, and further on again a narrow stairs that led up, and up again, in two flights, to a landing, with a door that opened into the south loft. This had a small window on the far gable, and was used as a bedroom for one of the men. Directly under that was a store-room, filled with all kinds of the things that went with a farm. Twenty-stone meals-sacks folded and piled high, sacks of corn and barley, old bins and boxes, rusty ploughshares and boards and pieces of old harnesses for the horses. It was lit by one small window.

'In the name of the Almighty Himself,' Delia would say to me, 'will you keep away from that lower room, for if you go in you'll bring something down on your head.' It was an admonition that I avoided heeding as often as I could, and before too long, I knew nearly everything that was in the storeroom.

Directly across the kitchen was a big dresser, and on the right of this a door that led to another small bedroom, beside the store-room. By the right kitchen wall was a long table, and just beyond that again, the front door and half door that led to the yard.

It was mid-morning and I was seated again on my sack, after a ramble or two exploring the kitchen. From where I sat, I could see the head of the goose, looking balefully out from her low box under the stairs, where she was sitting on a clutch of eggs. I never had any time for geese, or ganders either, for they had a murderous look about them, and I knew that if I came too near this one she could leave a skelp on the side of my leg as big and as black as a sloe. There was a hen hatching under the dresser. She was harmless and quiet enough, mostly giving out a low gurring sound, and an occasional squawk, maybe when something or other would cross her mind. Once she got up and shouldered herself off the eggs, and took herself out into the yard, on some business or other, maybe to see what the day was like. Before you'd notice it she was back again in the kitchen, on top of the eggs.

It was not long before we had a visit out of the yard by a hen and a clutch of chickens. To look at the hen you'd know she thought she was some sort of queen, strutting along with her head high, and all her attendants behind her, darting around the place as if they were half demented. And sure enough Delia and Mary were up and about her like she was some special friend they had not seen for years.

'I declare to God,' said Mary, 'do you see who's here. It's that Rhode Island Red vagabond that has been straying for a month.'

'All praise to God, and thanks to His Blessed Mother. They have their own way with these poor creatures, and guide them in the end to the right path.'

'I do not know too much about that,' said Mary 'for that Rhode Island was always as contrary as could be from the time she was a chicken herself. I knew she was missing and I knew she was laying out, for I used to hear her back the fields, every couple of days, crowing like a cock to the sky every time she laid an egg. You'd think she was calling me to find her. I searched every clump of briars and ditch, but I couldn't find sight nor light of the nest. I was only hoping she had been with the cock, or 'twould have been a nest of rotten gluggers we'd have found in the end of the day.'

'The ways of God are a mystery, to be sure,' said Delia, 'but she has come back to us now with a fine clutch of chickens, and isn't that as much as we could ask for. Praise be to the Lord.'

Then Delia and Mary got down to it. Delia got the head of a canister and half filled it with some kind of meal and pinhead oatmeal. Mary took down a big saucer and poured water into it from the bucket. These they placed on the floor side by side, and the two of them clucking to the hen to bring over the chickens. But they didn't make too much headway. They were the worst-trained chickens you could wish to see. They ran up and down, hither and thither, cavorting and sidestepping around the canister head and saucer, tripping and dancing through the meal and over the water.

It was no wonder they weren't up to much in this regard, seeing the way the hen was carrying on. 'Twas surely only the luck of the devil that saved half of them from being killed. She'd lift her leg high in the air and stamp it down like she was trying to crack a nut. She'd do it with one leg and then the other. And every time, by some kind of miracle, she missed giving out certain death to the chickens around her. She scratched at the meal, and sent it flying around the floor, and then she stood on the edge of the saucer, and turned it upside down, with not a drop left for man or beast to drink. And then, for a final insult, she did it on the floor, and the smell that was rising would send you to Knockane graveyard for shelter. 'Your soul to the devil', said Mary, 'we'll give them the door', and that's what she did.

Peace again, and me on my meal sack once more, examining the small shafts of yellow sunlight that spilled in through the window curtains from the spring day outside, dappling the grey black flag-stones of the kitchen floor, spread out before me down to the dresser. Delia and Mary were foostering around, and I knew that something was going to happen soon. Before long I heard the chimes of a distant bell ringing, coming in with small rising and falling of sound over the top of the closed half door.

'Merciful God,' said Mary, looking at her mother, 'it's the Angelus, they'll be in any minute, I didn't feel the time passing.' She made to go towards the big plates on the dresser, but Delia made the sign of the cross and said, 'We'll say the prayers girl.' And on the two of them went.

'The Angel of the Lord declared unto Mary, and she conceived of the Holy Ghost. Hail Mary full of Grace, the Lord is with thee … Holy Mary Mother of God … Blessed art thou amongst women, and blessed is the fruit of thy womb, Jesus. Hail Mary … Holy Mary … Behold the handmaid of the Lord, Be it done unto me according to Thy Word. Hail Mary … Holy Mary … And the Word was made flesh, and dwelt amongst us. Hail Mary, Holy Mary.' And then it was all over and Mary made again for the dresser, and heaped the big plates on one another and brought them to the table. Delia picked up a big white flour sack, folded it in two, and spread it carefully on the centre of the table.

Then they came in, Mossie and Sean and the servant boy, thumping their heavy boots on the big flagstone outside the half door and laughing and talking and chivvying each other. They gave no blessing as they entered, for they were the men of the house. They greeted the two women and pulled out the wooden súgán chairs. They took off their caps and hung them, each on the back of his own. They sat down and blessed themselves, and bent their heads for a short while.

'By the Lord God,' said Mossie looking round. 'Where is that Tadhg Doody, or has he fallen asleep on the spade out there in the orchard.' Mary went to the back door and called out to Tadhg, where he was turning side sods, below the apple trees, for a special garden for Delia and Mary to plant the sweet and floury Kerr's Pink potatoes. Tadhg came in shyly, and gave the greeting that a stranger gives. 'God Bless all here,' he said and took his place at the table.

There was not much talk, but getting down to work with big knives and forks, hooking up the big floury potatoes, and spearing and cutting the lumps of fat bacon, and the spread of white cabbage on the plates. Each had a full mug of new milk, and there was a cake of white flour and yellow meal bread at the side, to be cut and rubbed on the grease of the plate when they had eaten their fill of potatoes.

It was in that kitchen when I was three or four years old, and for years afterwards, that I saw and heard the many things that were the wonders of life.

Mossie was a tall man with broad shoulders and of big stature, with brown hair over a lean face. He was of a serious disposition, and much inclined to worry that things might go wrong. He always gave the impression that his black-haired handsome devil-may-care brother, Sean, was a kind of hardship on his mind. Sean was a dashing smiling knight who drew everybody to him with his brightness of countenance and lightness of heart. At times he appeared irresponsible and slow to get going, but then he could break out into a period of sustained work, so that no man in the parish could live with him, piking hay into the shed at harvest time or spreading turf with a three-prong pike in the bog.

Mossie was careful in everything he did and preserved everything about him. It was he who made sure that all gates into ryegrass or corn fields were shut, that horse tackling got a rub of oil and was hung up in the stable, that no sores came on the breasts or backs of animals from the rubbing of broken straddles or collars; he who checked cows' backs for warble flies and their udders for any sign of mastitis.

Early in the morning, his call through the kitchen not long after first light. 'Will ye get up out of that, the day is gone already, and no work done.' After the midday dinner, when others were dawdling with talk and laughing, he would suddenly get nervous, and jump up and say, 'Hey men, there's work to be done.' He'd pull on his cap and make for the door, the others following with various mutterings. Nobody would overload a horse or an ass in his presence.

He was the centre of a mystery that I could never solve at the time. It was he who took cows or calves or pigs to the fair in Abbeyfeale or Castleisland. It was he who spat on his hand, slapped it on the hand of the buyer, took the money and brought it home to his mother.

Woodbine cigarettes were the things that brought this mystery home to me. They were sold in small open packages of five cigarettes and they cost twopence a pack. Every evening, in the fine big kitchen, the same ritual would go on between Mossie and his mother. Mossie washed his face with water and Sunlight soap in an old enamel basin at the end of the kitchen table, combed his hair, changed his shirt, and then began circling his mother from a distance as if he were expecting something. His mother acted as if he was not there. Finally Mossie said, 'Have you got the tuppence, Ma?' Delia heard not a word, nor turned her head to one side or the other.

Mossie gave no appearance of being in any way disturbed by the lack of response. In the same tone of voice he repeated the question again and again, with the same result. Finally he stopped his casual meandering round the kitchen, and with ever so slight an edge in his voice, he asked the question again: 'Have you got the tuppence, Ma?' Delia said nothing. She put her hand into the pocket of her apron, withdrew two pennies, and placed them carefully on the edge of the table. Mossie just as carefully picked them up, put them in his trousers pocket, and departed the kitchen with every appearance of contentment.

I could never understand this. For I knew that Mossie had a purse, and I knew that in that purse was money, made up of notes and silver, and copper pennies. I had seen them often enough, when he was giving money to somebody or other to go to the shop for the three other packets of Woodbines that he smoked every day, away from his mother. It was much much later that I realized that Delia knew all about Mossie's secret purse as well.

It was Saturday night when there was great rivalry for the use of the old enamel basin and the Sunlight soap, but more particularly for the old bone-sided open razor. Many hot and indelicate words were exchanged from time to time, but no blows were struck. Delia's influence ensured that.

Mossie was mostly in for the first performance, whether because of seniority or cunning I was never sure. Performance it was for me as my own father never used the exciting cut-throat, but the boring safety one with the Mac's Smile blade.

Mossie took out the cut-throat and brought it to the window, in summer, or to the lamp in winter, in order to examine the blade. What he saw I never knew, but it invariably brought a comment from him such as 'That fellow must have hair on him like Murphy's boar,' or some such like. Mossie then took out the black strop, and hooked it over a bent nail at the end of the table. Then with long, slow, powerful strokes he plied the steel to the leather with great intensity of demeanour, back and forward, side and side. Several times he lifted the blade up and studied it anew. Then when everything appeared right he plucked a hair from his head with his left hand, hold it up to the light, and slowly drew the blade across it with his right. Mostly it worked on first experiment, and shaving was nearly ready to begin. But not yet.

The hot water and the steam sent the scent of Sunlight soap through the kitchen, as he applied the bar to the week-old growth of brown beard. Then minute after minute of rubbing and applications of more hot water and soap, until he was satisfied no more could be done to soften the tough short hairs.

Mossie then came to the small mirror securely embedded in the mortar of the wall beyond the table end, and polished it carefully with a clean cloth. In winter the oil lamp was moved to a nail alongside but slightly above the mirror. With delicate but firm touch his fingers moved the blade in slow rhythms of movement. At times his small and second fingers became elevated out of the way, like a lady raising a cup of coffee to her lips. The head to one side and then to the other, and the chin lifted high in the air, to attack the dangerous area of the neck round the jugular vein. Finally the upper lip was stretched and the small crevices under the nose dealt with. Then the last ritual of rubbing the hands caressingly over the whole FACE to prove without any doubt the final success.

There was an unspoken agreement in the house that during the application of the blade, not a sound would be made. Although occasional muffled imprecations from the table end was evidence that the agreement was sometimes broken, nothing that I ever saw round the farmhouse was deemed more worthy of respect than the blade of an open razor lying on the neck front of the man of the house.

The big farmhouse kitchen was the scene of much joy and also at times of lamentation and tears. A Saturday afternoon began to waft away on feelings of contentment and happiness. The work of the week was nearly over. Mary had cleared the table and washed the ware after the dinner. Everything was tidy and in its place, and the air was warm and heavily sweet-smelling, after the cooking. Before the men went back out to the work Delia asked Mossie to give us a song.

After a bit of twisting and turning he sat down again on his chair, took off his cap and leant forward thinking. After a moment or two he leant back hard and lifted up his head. The words came out hard and strong as he began the verse: 'Down by the Shannon the roar of the cannon.' He sang with great intensity, the high notes seeming to rebound from the rafters overhead. When he had finished there was a moment's silence and then Delia said, 'My soul to you, Mossie, you give a rise to my heart like you always do.' Mary said nothing but clapped her hands. Sean was standing by the door waiting for the end, smiling. 'Your soul to the devil,' he said. 'I was thinking you could have done with a small pinch of sugar before you started.' Then he went out smiling to himself with satisfaction.

When Mossie went through the half door we were left together, two women and a boy sitting round a turf fire. Delia sat at the left not far from the small window. Mary was on the right, on her own sugar chair, and I was on the floor, on the meal sack.

There was an ease about the place. Then Delia said: 'I think I'll have a pinch of snuff in honour of the day that's in it. Will you get my snuff box for me, child.' I knew what to do. I crossed the back of her chair to the left side of the hearth. I stood on a small butter box and opened the door of the tiny warm clevvy, where she kept the tea canister, and a few other things. There it was, the silver oval snuff box. I carried it like it was something precious. She took it gently, pulled off the cover, and with thumb and forefinger brought a small pinch to her nose and sniffed. It was not long before she was sneezing into a big brown handkerchief. And not too long after that Mary and I were sneezing too.

Delia took me by the arm and pulled me round to her, and looked at me. 'Yerra child,' she said, 'it'll do you no harm. They say it's good for keeping the colds away from a person. But on the fear of your life don't say a word to your mother.' She needn't have worried too much about it, for even at that age there were many secrets that a small boy had.

Delia's hair was pulled tight off her face and pinned into a ball at the back of her head. One by one she took out the pins until her hair rolled down to the centre of her back.

She shook her head from side to side until her hair blossomed out at each side into a dark fullness. She was in middle age but as yet there were few white ribs to be seen in the black hair. As I had done many times before I took the big black and brown comb and brushed and combed and brushed her hair for a long time until a small glow settled down on it. Then she took her hair again, and twisted it until she had rolled it back as it had been before.

Mary said: 'Do you know what, Mother, I'll bring down the gramophone.' She brought it down from the big bedroom, a square brown box and a big horn, with 'His Master's Voice' written across it, and a bunch of old records in faded brown covers.

What a time we had. Mary would begin with rousing songs like 'Kevin Barry':

> In Mountjoy Jail one Monday morning
> High upon the gallows tree,
> Kevin Barry gave his young life,
> For the cause of Liberty.

The song of Parnell, which ended:

> Sweet Avonmore, Proud Eagle.

'The Foggy Dew', which began:

> As down the glen, one Easter Morn,
> To a city fair rode I,
> There armed lines of marching men
> In squadrons passed me by,
> No pipes did hum nor battle drum
> Did sound its dread tattoo,
> But the Angelus bell o'er the Liffey swell
> Rang out in the Foggy Dew.

Soon we had romance in 'Love's Old Sweet Song':

> Just a song at twilight,
> When the lights are low,
> And the flickering shadows,
> Softly come and go,
> Though the heart be weary,
> Sad the voice and low,
> Then to us at twilight comes,
> Love's old song,
> Love's old sweet song.

Then sadness inevitably came in with:

> Oft in a stilly night,
> 'Ere slumber's chains had bound me,

Fond memory brings the light,
Of other days around me.

Delia's countenance visibly changed when Mary played, 'I'll take you home again Kathleen'. But the song that broke her heart with longing for her emigrant sons and daughter was 'Mother Macree'. The scraping of the old steel needle on the worn turning black record did not diminish the weight of sadness on her heart.

I love the dear silver that shines in her hair.
And the brow that's all furrowed, and wrinkled with care,
I kiss the dear fingers, so toil-worn for me,
Oh, God bless you, and keep you, Mother Macree.

Mother of my heart. The words that brought the tears of her heart unashamedly down. Delia held the big brown handkerchief to her eyes with both hands and Mary gathered up the gramophone and the records. She was silent with her own sadness in her dark eyes under her jet-black hair as she took the music box to its place in the big bedroom, then returned to the kitchen.

Delia looked up again and began to talk. 'God guard and save them over there, Mary, in these hard times. They say the bread-lines and soup-kitchens are everywhere still, although they say things are getting a bit better now with that new man in. They say he's throwing in government money to give a bit of work, all kinds of things, roads and buildings and the like, and special money for the farmers. Wouldn't you think it would not kill them to put a pen to paper and let us know how they are. Not a word from any of them since before Christmas, and all of them without a job. How could it happen to them over there? The biggest country of them all, and the wealth of the world at their feet. They say the Jews and the blacks have a lot to do with it, and bad cess to them if they have. Tisn't but when I was in New York nearly thirty years ago, the blacks had nothing, only everybody looking down on them and giving them the back of the hand. I used be sorry for them, although I didn't like the look of some of them. They are not beautiful like us, but are all God's creatures and they can't help it how they look. I have to say that any Jews that I came across had money. I worked for enough of them in their kitchens and their parlours.'

Delia looked down at me. 'Do you know, child, when you were combing my hair a while ago, I was thinking of all the things I used have to do for a rich Jewish widow that I worked for. You couldn't put a description on what the job was. I wasn't the cook, or a parlour maid or a kitchen maid, or a dressing maid, I was a bit of everything you could think of. She was a big fat woman, although not too tall, and of all the women I ever met, she spent more time looking at herself in mirrors. There were mirrors in every room and two in the hallway, and 'twas no small house, I'll tell you. 'Twas as if she thought that every time she looked into the mirror she might have got a bit better looking.

'I think she had it in her mind, by hook or by crook, to get herself another husband. The main trouble she had was to get down the fat, and before long that was my main trouble too.

''Twas a hard job she set herself, for by no manner or means could you describe her as being in any way good-looking. She was always trying new fads to slim herself down. This diet and that diet, this cream and that cream for morning, noon and night, but she might as well have been rubbing on the spit of a cuckoo. Maybe a pound here and a pound there, then back again as bad as ever. The trouble was she had a great wish for food, and at times it was mortifying the attempts she was making to keep away from it.

'She had wardrobes of all kinds of clothes and furs, satins and silks and seals and sables, and she had a small drawer in her bedroom filled with corsets and other garments that she used to pull herself together. My arms were often tired, nearly broken itself, from wrestling with those corsets and pulling in the lacing, before she'd go out on the town, for some occasion or other.'

Delia looked around at us from time to time to see were we understanding her. But Mary and I said not a thing, and she went on again:

'This day she rang the bell in her bedroom and called me in. "Delia, my girl," said she, "I've decided on a new plan of campaign. I got it from a magazine I had sent to me from California. We'll go at it three ways, diet, massage and bath beating."

'From that day on for up to two months I had no peace from her. Hours and hours massaging her arms and legs with this special oil, that was supposed to melt the fat. But the worst of all was the beatings in the bath. There was this gadget made of pink heavy rubber, with a handle on it. There she was sitting stark naked in the hot water, except for a small towel, and there was I leathering her with the pink rubber, round the thighs and bottom and shoulders, for all I was worth. When I think of it, I laugh at it. She never complained once of the pain, only sitting there with a spread on her, her head down, and her false teeth held tightly together.

'She lost a good bit of weight that time, but I think it was more the diet than anything else. I knew I couldn't stick it much longer, so I got a new job as housemaid for a nice lady a couple of streets away.'

'What happened to her,' asked Mary, 'did she get a new husband out of it in the end?'

'Upon my soul, Mary, I never found out. But I'd say a man would only marry her for her money, and if that happened, he'd like as not do her out of it, in the heel of the hunt.'

Delia said no more about that. The tears and the sorrow were gone with the story. Mary got up and put on the kettle and got out a caraway seed cake and a corner of currant bread. It wasn't long before the men would be coming in for the shaving, and dolling up to go to Knockbrack, or up the village, or wherever the girls they were thinking about were living.

- 5 -

'Can He Talk, Mama?'

IN THE MIDDLE thirties, when I was not yet six, I began to think that something very strange was happening to my mother. I noticed her face was pale and she moved languidly as if the energy was going from her. She was talking a lot to my father in a low voice, and whispering if I was too near, and throwing small nervous looks at me as if it was something important she didn't want me to know about.

I heard my father say: 'Why don't you go up and see the nurse, if you're worried.' I knew who the nurse was, Nurse Donoghue, who looked after the whole parish and everybody in it, no matter what was wrong with them. They said she was better than any doctor, which was just as well, as the doctor lived a good bit away, and cost maybe five shillings or more for a visit.

There was more as well. At breakfast in the morning before going to school, sometimes she stood up quickly and ran out through the scullery into the back garden, with her hand to her mouth. When she came back after a few minutes her blue eyes had darkened, as if with tears, and her face was white and strained. She smiled as best she could at us, at all the eyes that looked at her, so that we wouldn't be troubled, and wiped her face with a towel. 'I'm fine,' she said, 'I'm grand now, everything is all right now.'

She sat down again and took a little more of her toast, and a couple of sips of her tea. Then she stood up again as if revived, and raised her hands over us. 'Come on you lot,' she said, 'do you want to be late for school?' She moved around picking up coats and schoolbags, and the small dark cloud that was over us went away as quickly as it had come.

Then one evening after school she went off to the village to see the nurse. I was troubled as I saw her walk out by the empty flower beds through the white gate to the road. It was a grey-white evening in the beginning of the year. Twilight was settling down on a light fall of snow that had come the previous night.

Before she left, my father said: 'Be careful of your step, Annie, there's an odd slippery patch, after the frost.' I wondered why he did not go with her, if she had some kind of sickness. I thought he'd surely have put her into the car, if we had one. But the car was gone, for a few months back. I hoped we'd have another before long.

I watched the white gates until the darkness came and my father lit the oil lamp on the wall beside the hearth. Then I heard her steps and she came in. Her face was glowing and she was smiling.

'It's good news,' she said. 'It was just as you said, Jim, just as you said.' My father laughed. 'Didn't I tell you, didn't I tell you, it was that sickness that is better than health.' Then they both laughed out, and the happiness came again, and the oil lamp shone on all of us.

They told us nothing. Eileen was seven. My younger sister 'Baby' was only four. We called her Baby for many years afterwards, until one day she struck for freedom, and declared her name was Maura, which was her right. She had been named Mary when she was christened, and henceforth Maura was her name.

Eileen knew nothing, or if she did she kept it to herself. She was more concerned with her curls and her polka-dot dresses, like any child of her age. My mother encouraged her in all this. She appeared to agree fully with all the compliments that were strewn on her about her lovely curly brown hair and her beautiful face and complexion.

Making dresses for the girls, and adorning their hair with ribbons of red or green or yellow, was my mother's great delight. She sought out colourful cottons or satins, plain or striped or dotted, and brought the latest patterns from Tralee and Abbeyfeale. She was a gifted seamstress, and spent hours and hours cutting out the dresses and rough hand-stitching them in readiness for the fittings.

Eileen loved the attention that went with these many fittings, standing on a chair like a little model, full of compliance and sweetness, moving graciously this way and that as my mother inserted pin after pin after pin from a supply she held between her lips. At the end she coyly acknowledged her mother's care. 'I thing it's lovely, Mama,' she said, 'I thing it's lovely.'

Baby was as yet too young to be stricken like this, and in some curious way resisted my mother's attempts to beautify her as well. She dourly subjected herself to all the handling, setting herself rigidly and making it clear that all this was happening to her, under protest. When the finished dress was put on her for inspection and display, and she was expected to perform her pirouette, she looked down at it balefully. 'I don't like it, Mama,' she said, 'I don't like it. 'Twould fit Kate Ann.'

This was the most powerful disapproval that the small child could think up. Kate Ann was a particularly large and obese old woman who lived behind the village, whose name was called forth like this when the worst needed to be said.

As if by law of nature, Baby's period of revolt passed and she too became subject to the charm of her own endowments and the magic of beautiful dresses.

I still had some unease about my mother's condition. The sickness that came on her most mornings at breakfast time seemed to pass without too much notice. It went on for what seemed to be a number of months, and then it stopped abruptly.

Springtime came, and the days began to get warm and easy in themselves. My mother took out her bicycle again, and on Saturdays, every few weeks, she told my father she was going to Abbeyfeale to see somebody. Like everything else she couldn't keep a secret, and before too many months had passed I learned that the somebody she was seeing was the doctor. There was more thinking. But she appeared well in herself, better than I had seen her for a long time. She was walking with my father, and was strong on her bicycle, going anywhere she pleased.

The truth came to me simply enough. I had noticed my mother appeared to be getting fat, but put it down to the new appetite she had developed. Then I noticed the tittering among senior girls as she passed by, in the school yard at lunchtime, and the heads that were bent together, and the low talking that went on. I heard the words. 'The Missus is going to have a baby.'

I told her what I had heard, and she spoke to me about it then. She appeared to be shy and uneasy, but she said I was going to have a little baby brother, as I had two sisters already. She told me the baby was inside her, and she knew it was going to be a boy. A boy was different to a girl, she said, he was stronger and kicked around a lot more. 'Maybe he'll be a Kerry footballer,' she said, and she laughed as if it was a joke. When I thought about it, it was no joke to me. I had ambitions about this myself. I was going to be a Kerry footballer too, and I was not too sure if I wanted a rival in my own family.

*

The summer had gone by and the winter was approaching. My mother had gone into hospital in Limerick a week before to have her baby. It was a boy, just like she had said, and I wondered at the strangeness of this. We had a car again, the blue Baby Ford, and my father was gone to bring her home.

Nellie the 'girl' and child-minder was going mad around the house. She was a tall rangy young woman with black hair and dark eyes, and she was full of music and devilment. She was washing and scrubbing and dusting everywhere she could lay her hands on. There was a big turf fire down, with red flames dancing and throwing shapes on the black chimney, and there were white sheets and pillow cases spread across chairs, airing for my mother's bed.

Nellie was in the middle of something when she looked up as if startled, and danced to the scullery to read her daily task sheet, which my mother had pinned to the wall. 'What good will that do you, Nell,' I said to her. 'What matter does it make what day of the week it is? Today is the day my mother is coming home with the new baby. That's the day it is.' She looked down at me as if I were John the Baptist, who knew everything. Then she threw her arms around me and danced me round the kitchen too, and raised the roof with her own version of 'Down by the Tanyard Side'.

It was a November evening, with no moon, nor a star itself to be seen in the sky. The lamp was trimmed and lit, and everything was clean, and the faces were shining. The small blue Baby Ford brought the child home. We wanted to run out into the darkness to greet them, but Nellie held us there in the kitchen to wait, as if it was the right thing to do.

My mother came in with a small white basket held in front of her, close to her breast. She placed the little cot, lined with blue, on the kitchen table, and turned round smiling with her hands held out. For a little moment we held back, in shyness, as if we were looking at a new mother who had come in. Then the rush of love came on us, and she took us all in her arms together and covered us with her kisses and her tears.

I inspected the baby on the table, my mother and Eileen and Nellie by my side. We all looked down at the small miracle that had come in. Nellie's face softened in wonder, and my mother's face was pale and reverent. In a moment of confusion, I pulled my mother's dress and asked her, 'Can he talk, Mama, can he talk?' My mother placed her hand on my head, and smiled down at me with her eyes. She paused for a moment or two, as if seeking an answer, and I felt my foolishness creep over my face.

My father was watching from inside the kitchen door, a paper parcel in his hand. 'Can he talk, of course he can talk,' he said, 'and he can sing "The Soldier's Song", as well.' They laughed at his joke, and I laughed too. My sister Baby was whimpering at my mother's feet. She was too small to see. My father took the white basket and placed it on the floor. Then we all looked down together.

My father still held the paper parcel, with its mystery inside. It was too close to Christmas for any present for us, but from the way he held it, and the look on his face, I knew we were in for something to raise our hearts. With a flourish he ripped the brown paper off, revealing what looked like a small round bellows, with many sections closed together, each bound by circles of tin, and at both ends a number of white studs.

He called it a concertina, the like of which we never saw before. But Nellie had seen it before. 'I bought it for you, Nellie,' my father said. Which was just as well, as nobody else in the house could play it. Her eyes were bright as she took the concertina into her hands. She put her thumbs in the leather loops, and opened the music box out and squeezed it back again. A moan of sound came out, and then a stream of notes of every kind, as she moved her fingers quickly on the small white studs.

Just for a short time the baby on the floor was forgotten, and Nellie was the new hero. She launched into a rousing reel that might have sent us all prancing, but my mother firmly but gently shushed her into silence. The baby was awake and crying and he was the new master of the house. The name they gave him was Desmond.

I always felt it was the concertina that hastened the end of Nellie's sojourn in our household. A young woman who loved the music box, and a very small baby, lived uneasily together. The music was in Nellie's blood and she played her jigs, reels and horn-pipes whenever she could. A gradual breakdown in relationships was taking place and the strain was becoming too much for her. One day she took her possessions down the cement walk to the white gates, where a pony and car awaited her. We waved goodbye and she went back to her home in the mountains. The concertina lay for years on top of a wardrobe. We took it down sometimes and pummelled it with our eager wild fingers. An odd time the cobbler with the limp came in looking for books and brought it back to life with fierce playing. But mostly it had a lonely time, and it had a lonely end, like many other things and many other people about us.

– 6 –

Gander at the Gate

THE TRUTH of the matter is that I had never liked the look of the
fellow. When I looked at him I said to myself, 'There's a lad to keep
well away from.' He was as white as a small snowman and I'd see
him walking very boldly around Delia's farmyard at the head of his
harem, looking this way and that, his small white-blue eyes cold as
lumps of ice with frost on them. He'd slap his dirty yellow feet
around marshalling the females, sallying at them with his flat head
stretched out in front of him, giving the odd treacherous bite at
their flanks with hissing and screeching until they'd be doing what
he wanted, whatever that was. He was a sergeant-major if ever I
saw one, and when he'd be tired of tormenting his white slaves, driving them round and round and drilling them from one side of the
yard to the other, he'd make a whirl around, and with one high
screech lead them out through the gate onto the dirty, hoof-marked
boreen down towards the river to eat the grasses in the wet fields
there.

I knew in my heart and soul that one day I'd have to take him on. Like the men in the books of the Wild West, the good and the bad, no matter what manouevering they went on with or how much ground they'd cover, the day would come when they'd have to meet up to settle it once and for all.

I'd think about it a lot when I'd be on my own, because that gander was the worst badman I'd ever come across. I'd think of how I'd finish him, at noon some day, like the two men walking slowly down that sunny street in Tombstone for the final draw. I'd have two guns on, and the holsters would be hanging low on either thigh, strapped down with leather thongs. One gun might be all right for an ordinary occasion, flapping around on one leg or the other. Or for any occasion if you were only an ordinary cowboy, with a forty-five to shoot the odd rattle snake or coyote, or to fire off into the air when you were riding point to turn a herd that had begun to stampede after getting some fright or other. I'd bring it about so that I'd come into the yard with the sun behind me, because it was well known to me that it was a thing of the most aggravating and deadly nature to go into a fight with the sun in your eyes, and the result could be such that you'd never clear leather again to the end of your days, that is if you had any days left at all.

It would be all over very quickly. I'd give him no chance. Before he'd have time to go for me round the shins, I'd plant one between his little wicked eyes, right in the centre of his little icepack head. He would not utter a single screech, but fall over on to his back with his yellow legs up in the air for all the world to see.

But things hardly ever work out the way you think they might. At least that's the way I often found it. I remember it was a beautiful sunny morning. It was not yet eight o'clock because there was no stir from my mother and father getting up to get ready before we all went down the road and over the ditch on to the path across the bogs and over the footbridge, to be at Knockbrack school by half past nine. I was as happy as Larry lying snug in my small bed in the corner of the big room. I could hear the birds going at it hammer and tongs in the orchard outside the back window and in the big and small trees that seemed to be everywhere around the half acre on which the house was built.

The sounds were different now from what they had been when I had wakened up for a short while as dawn was breaking. Then they had sounded like a magic choir of small sweet singing, thrilling and piping and fluting like they were all trying to outdo each other in some heavenly competition. But that was nearly over now, except for the odd fellow that still fancied himself. Many of the others were making a different kind of racket, making short flights between the branches, fighting and pulling and falling over each other. And dominating were the hard screeches of the thieving magpies, flashing around and threshing as if their lives depended on it.

I had plenty of things to be going on with. Looking across the room to the big bed Eileen and Baby were still asleep, lying on their backs with their two little noses stuck up in the air. Examining the shaft of low sunlight that was lying across Eileen's head and lighting in gold the tossed curls of her fair hair and spilling along the white candlewick bedspread. It was going to be another scorcher of a day. I knew it by the brightness of the room, and by the clearness of the sounds coming through the open front window from Delia's farmyard back the road a bit and down the front boreen. The cows were milked. I knew it from the clanging of the milk churns, and the loudness of Mossie's voice, shouting in temper at the donkey as he backed her between the shafts of the small red and blue cart before going to the creamery, across the Oweveg river and back the tar road to Headley's Bridge. I studied the ceiling boards over my head, with their patterns of small animals and birds' heads and the big horrible face of my terrible giant that was manufactured from grey black lines and smudges and timber knots over in the corner. And the black division that Uncle Jack had forgotten to paint over, when he and Danny Boy the handyman had pulled down the whole gable of the house because my mother had wanted the big bedroom, and the sitting room downstairs, to be six foot wider for her new three-piece suite.

Mama was up at last. I could hear the familiar patter of her feet on the landing and down the stairs, shortly followed by Dada's heavier clumping. Sounds of a fire being lit, followed by banging of the water basin from the scullery as washing took place. There was as yet no bathroom, and water was drawn in bucketfuls from the well down the road, or from Delia's trough outside the farmhouse door, until it ran dry in the later summer.

'Get up out of that, we'll be late for school.' Dada's voice sounded throughout the house, and the two sleepy girls emerged from under the bedclothes onto the floor. Dressing at speed and then helter-skelter down into the scullery to be first to the water basin and towel. Squabbling and squealing, pulling and tugging, cries and complaints of horrors enacted. Dada's exasperated intervention. 'Rory, there's a drubbing coming to you and I might have time to give it to you now.'

Mama standing by the table looking heavenly with her golden hair and white skin, and around her the sweet smell of Ponds Cold Cream, and the small hands setting the table and slicing the brown and soda bread that she had baked herself the night before in the covered oven hanging from the crane over the open fire, with the red turf coals piled on top. The kettle coming to the boil, the oat-meal porridge bubbling in a small saucepan on a bed of red embers, and the eggs murmuring against each other in another saucepan alongside.

This was the innocent if fateful setting that impelled me along the pathway of confrontation with my, as yet, only farmyard enemy.

'Good God Annie, there's no salt,' my father said, looking at her, as if she were after breaking his fishing rod. His mischievous blue eyes behind the large brown spectacles turned on me. 'Off with you Rory, down to Delia's for a pinch of salt, and don't be long, run, run.'

I was off like a bullet, down the cement path, between the beds of flowers, and out through the big white wrought-iron gate that Coffey, the blacksmith, had made in his forge at the top of the village. I rounded the outer pier at speed, until the thick beech hedge in front covered me from vision, and then I halted to consider the situation.

How was it that I was always the victim when there was anything to be done? Not my sister Eileen, who was two years older than I. Always Rory this, Rory that. 'Run here Rory, run there Rory. Go for cigarettes, Rory, go for a razor-blade, Rory.'

Aggrieved and under pressure though I was, I suddenly became aware of the wonder of the place I was in. It was an old country road, brilliant in sunshine and greenery. Glistening green trees and shrubs of all kinds pushed out over the road on both sides. Alders, ash and beech, blackthorn and whitethorn, green briars and fairy-thimble plants, jostling with each other for space everywhere. Both roadsides were covered with wide green carpets, speckled and marbled and beautified with summer flowers of many colours. Primroses, cowslips, buttercups, violets and bluebells called on me to look at them as they moved in the light morning breeze. The sun was warm on my bare feet, and the golden-brown dust of the road crept into the small spaces between my toes.

My bird came into my head, my golden thrush with its white speckled breast pressing on its five china-blue eggs, in its mud-lined nest in the thicket nearby. The thrush flew out as I approached but I gave the nest and the eggs a quick inspection. The bright blue orbs with their black specks gave no sign of breaking yet.

Salt, salt. I pulled myself together and hurried on to the black iron gate that guarded the boreen that went down to the farmhouse. There inside the closed gate he was, my thundering blackguard of a gander. His head and neck were stretched out with his breast close to the ground, and an evil look in his cold eyes, as he hissed at me in full warning. Where was my forty-five now that was to make me a hero forever? I looked down at my blue gansey and short trousers. No twin holsters did I see but bare knees blackened and dirty from many a recent campaign through ditches and fields and riverbanks since my mother washed me the previous Saturday night, and scrapes and cuts from briars and blackthorns criss-crossing each other. I had never been so close before, and I could feel no courage in me like a gunfighter might have as he walked down that street at noon.

I could only feel a weakness at the back of my knees and a complete conviction that I would not get through those gates, that I was beaten to the ground, never to rise up again. Through the fear, an anger began to rise in me, and I began to search my mind for curses that I could bring down about his head, and the fate that I would wish on him if it was within my power to bring it about.

If I had a bit of an ashplant with a good round head on it that had been toughened after a few weeks in the chimney, I'd lay about him to such a degree that his head would split open, his eyes would leave their sockets, and his brains would be spilled around the boreen, for the thrush on the nest and all other birds to be feeding on for days to come, like they fed on the flesh of the men hanging off the trees after the mine at Ballyseedy.

Or if I had a big knife the like of which Charlie O'Donoghue had when he stuck Delia's pig, I'd sweep it across his throat in such a way that the blood would spurt out of him into the bushes, and his head would be so addled that he wouldn't know whether he was coming or going, and he'd reel around the place from here to there, until the last ounce would go out of him, and he'd fall over on his back with his legs kicking the air until the last hiss was gone.

I was now trembling with two fears, fear of the gander and fear of my father. The gander won and there was nothing for me to do but to slink back home to the kitchen after my first great humiliation. I told the story as best I could, and I could see anger gathering on my father's face. 'Fear,' he said. 'You should never be afraid. Fear is a man's greatest enemy.'

I couldn't understand what he meant, and I stood there expecting the worst. Then I saw his face softening, and the old humorous twinkle came back to his eyes. 'You'll be all right,' he said. 'You'll grow out of it. I was afraid myself, and I tried to put it out of my mind. It's not an easy thing to do, but you'll have to keep trying.'

Then we all marched down the road to school, across the bog over the footbridge that my father had built, which was used by half the parish as a short cut to the village for messages, and by the people going to Mass on Sundays from the townlands of Knockbrack and Kilmanihan and others south of the river.

There were many other fears in my childhood life, fears of all kinds and classes, and I kept thinking for a long time how my father said he was afraid himself. Which I found very strange, after all he had been through.

– 7 –

Luke Comes Home

AS IT TURNED OUT, only one of Delia's three exiles was finally driven back home by the American crash. When the letter arrived announcing the news, the whole house and the people in it seemed to become affected by a new emotion. It was Luke, the second youngest boy, who was coming back. It was early summer and the happiness was there among them every day.

The house was turned upside down. Every room and every corner was washed and painted. The big storeroom at the south end of the building was cleared out, and the contents of bags of corn and other farmyard bric-à-brac were stored in a dry room on the north side of the cowhouses.

The big room was turned into a comfortable bedroom. Mossie went to Castleisland town in a horse and cart and brought home a new bed and a small shining bedside table. Delia and Mary went in the horse and trap and came back with a variety of household things to adorn the kitchen. A new paraffin oil lamp, a small white shelf for the wall, and new white curtains for the small windows.

Buckets of white burnt limestone dust were brought from the kiln and made into a smooth whitewash for the house inside and out. The walls of the cowhouses and other outside sheds and the walls that enclosed the farmyard were whitewashed into new brilliance, reflecting all day the sun in the sky. White light shone out everywhere, dazzling the eyes of man and beast. It was as if a fairy, from the land of the little people, had waved its wand and brought about a heavenly transformation. In this way the Keane home changed into a place fit for the homecoming of even a new bride, coming to spend a life of joy in this place.

Luke's coming was a month away and I thought the time would never pass. But as I found out then, and many times later to my regret, the day always comes, and Mossie and Sean and Mary went to Cobh in a big black Ford car to meet the ship from America.

He came in like a prince, his face handsome and smiling. His hair was black and curly, his eyes a dark brown, and his suit of a pale grey colour, the like of which I had never seen before.

The joy in Delia's face and the long tearful embracing touched me in a manner, and with a memory, that time never erased from by mind. There was special meal and special drinks and endless hours of talking out the story of the five years that had gone past, the story in America and the story at home. A long vigil at the fire that night, and the next and the next. After a few days a seamless slipping back into the family life as it had always been, and as if he had never been away at all.

That was a spring and summer that I could never forget. As much as was possible for me I attached myself to Luke, and like a small dog at his heels I followed him everywhere. At the beginning little was expected of him, by way of work. We roamed every acre of the farm together, through gaps and over ditches, and down the long twisted boreen to the river, and he recalled the stories of the places and fields to me.

'This boreen was known as the priest's road,' he said. 'In the old days, and up to the time I was a small child, Brosna and Knocknagoshel were the one parish, and the parish priest in Brosna, or maybe the curate, would come over the hill on horseback, cross the river at Lyre, and come up this very boreen to say Sunday Mass in the church above.'

On we went up by the river over wet land and through briar ditches until we came to a small wood in a corner where two small rivers met. It was close and dense with clusters and tangles of sally and hazel and blackthorn and whitethorn, just then turning to green in the spring of the year.

'This was the place where we rambled and played when we were garsoons,' he said. 'The whole place was alive with wild birds of all kinds. Snipe rising out of the boggy land, and woodcock calling from the bushes. There were blue tits hanging upside down on the sallies, and over there on the river, coot and waterhens paddling everywhere. And in the dark of an evening you'd hear the curlews wailing in the sky.'

We looked over the rising ground to the south and over the small fields to a small farmhouse.

'That's Herlihy's house,' he said, 'right beside Knockane graveyard. All my people are buried there. My father is there, he died very young.'

He laughed. 'I don't like that place myself, very much. But there's one thing sure anyway. Paddy Herlihy has plenty of company. I don't know how he passes that graveyard on a dark night. You'd want to be half drunk, and maybe that's how he does it.' He laughed again.

We went on up to the right, away from the river, till we came to a big field.

'This is the biggest field in the farm,' he said. 'Do you know what they call it, the Ploughmatch. Before I was born, my father held a ploughing match there, before the end of the century. There were thirty pairs of horses in that field, they say. 'Twas a good enough way to have somebody else do the work for you.' Luke threw back his head and laughed again.

We were now looking west, up the sloping ground to Knocknagoshel village. A cluster of houses in the distance, a few gable-ends and chimneys, and rising above them the belltower and the wet black roof of the parish chapel glistening in the sunlight.

He talked a bit about the chapel and about a couple of parish priests he remembered. He did not know, nor did I, the story of that chapel, a story that might be told of any other chapel in the country.

Luke remained at home through the passing of that year. He moved into the work each day with Mossie and Sean. He cleared dykes with shovel and spade and pick. He went into the small wood with a crosscut saw, and hewed out the thickest branches of felled ash trees into short lengths for stacking and drying for the following winter. But I knew he was restless, with incessant smoking of Afton and Gold Flake cigarettes, at sixpence for ten, while Mossie and Sean smoked away at Woodbines at tuppence for five. It was if his five years in America had raised him up above Woodbines and he couldn't allow himself to come down to them again. Mossie mocked him gently, smiling.

'So the Yank can't smoke Woodbines anymore. Maybe if I was after putting down five years of high life in America, I wouldn't smoke them either.' Luke took the chivvying well.

He was constantly running out of cigarettes, and was always glad to see me coming. He hailed me from a distance.

'Hi there, buddy, hurry on down here.' As I approached he said, with his American twang, 'You know something buddy, we're bursting for a smoke. Will you run to the Mall for a pack or two?'

I knew he had little money, but he searched his pockets carefully. He looked at me.

'You know buddy, I seem to be short.' He looked at Mossie.

Mossie grumbled, but he took out his purse from an inside pocket. In a few minutes I was doing the thing I hated most. Running messages for somebody to the village.

We went ploughing together, with the strong black mare and the well-made bay gelding. Mossie planned it like a small military operation. Collars, hames, cruppers and girthstraps checked. The four traces examined along with the main swingle-tree crossbar for the plough, and the crossbars for the horses. Mossie checked the ploughshare and mould board, for direction and firmness, and ran his thumb along the edge of the soil-cutting coulter. A squeeze of oil from the can on the small landwheel and the bigger furrow wheel and all was ready.

Luke was eager to open the first furrow. But either he had forgotten or he never knew how to handle a pair of horses behind a plough. The share went too deep into the ground, the horses backed onto the plough head, and the big wheel wouldn't stay where it was supposed to go. Luke gave up after a number of fruitless high-pitched directions from Mossie.

Luke took his failure well. He had a small smile on his face, and he looked at me.

'Say, buddy, why don't we sit here on the headland, and shoot the breeze for a bit.' He took an Afton from the pack, flicked a red sulphur match with his thumbnail, and lay there smoking calmly, breathing his small grey smoke into the quiet air about us.

He said nothing, and as I took it he wanted to think for a while, I said nothing either. I was thinking too, and I was saying to myself that ploughing was not much fun, not like going to the bog to cut a bank or two of turf for the long winter nights that I knew would be coming before long.

It was a good year. A warm west wind for much of the time brought moist air and rain for most of the spring. A warm June with showers in the night made the land kindly and fertile. The good earth had blossomed everywhere with blessings of green leaves, and the colours of wild flowers, and abundance of good sweet grass. The barley and oats and wheat were coming too, pushing up through the soil, urgent and strong, springing clean and broad and green in the first half of a good harvest year.

Mossie or the others rarely spoke of the profusion of beauty that surrounded them. They never remarked on the primroses or violets or hawthorn blossoms. A stretch of countryside or roadsides covered in a sea of yellow whin blossoms never seemed to touch their hearts. I often wondered at that, and thought that perhaps these had always been so much part of their lives that they had ceased to wonder.

But they did not cease to wonder at the grasses of the good earth, and the potato stalks rising clear above the drills.

Mossie met Tadhg Doody on the road. 'God be with you Tadhg,' Mossie said. 'Did you ever see the like of it for growth? It'll beat everything we met yet, if the man above throws a kind eye on us for the harvesting.'

'The big meadow is right,' Tadhg said. 'Are you going in there tomorrow or the day after?'

'I'll do it tomorrow if this weather holds, and I'm thinking it will. I'll need you on Thursday for the first shake out, and we'll have it in cocks by Saturday.'

It happened as he planned it. By eight o'clock that evening the mowing machine was ready, with oil in every metal hole and crevice that would take it. The long cutting knives were taken down and every blade was honed sharp with the grey edging stones. Mossie and Sean sat hunched outside the front door in the yard, each with a stone in his hand and a pan of water on the ground, and the long knives between their knees. Dip and rub, rub, rub. Dip and rub,

rub, rub, until the blades shone like grey silver and the edge would nearly cut green grass in the hand.

By eight o'clock the following morning the machine was singing like a giant metallic bird, the singing of iron and tempered steel. The song echoed the country round as other machines in other fields answered the sounds, as other farmers sat in their high steel seats urging their pairs of horses on under the warm morning sun.

I was with him before long, sitting on the headland waiting. The team came towards me, breathing deeply, with a slight sweat on their skins. The tall green leaves and the meadow flowers fell before the knives like a host of soldiers in a great battle. I thought of some poor hare or rabbit or nesting birds that might fall before the flashing knives. I thought of the corncrake I had heard through the summer night as I lay awake, wondering where he came from and what he looked like; I prayed he had chosen another place to build his nest and that I would hear him again, in his full life and strength, coming through the open window of my little room, riding on the pale moonbeams that came to me from the sky.

The cutting went on hour after hour. The long knife left row after row of fallen grass on the right-hand side. From time to time the horses were pulled up for a short rest, and Mossie smoked a Woodbine. Some time later he stopped the horses at the top headland and called to Sean, lounging on the grass with his cap over his eyes against the hot sun.

'Hey, wake up for a bit and take over here,' he said.

''Tisn't tired you are already,' said Sean, jeering.

'None of your smartness,' Mossie said, 'I'm going for water.' He went off along the headland, kicking out his heavy boots through the grass to get the tiredness out of his legs, out through the iron gate and on to the boreen. Before long he was back with two buckets of water. The horses drank deeply, but Mossie jerked up their heads before the buckets were empty.

'Why don't you let them finish it?' Sean said, criticizing.

'I'll tell you why. Because it's dangerous giving working horses too much cold water on a day like this. That's the why,' he said, looking at Sean in small irritation. 'Here, I'll take over again.' He climbed again onto the seat and away he went.

It wasn't too long at all before the job was done. He got off the seat and looked down the field, wide swathes of grass stretching down for a long way. The bright green was gone, with the grass stems turned up, grey and white brown, with only flashes of silver green showing here and there and the long corridors of grass root stubble in between.

'We'll shake it out tomorrow,' he said, and we all went back to the house.

The next day was important for the household. It was the first time the new mechanical swathe turner would be used. The old way was four or five men, in the big field, shaking out each dense grass swathe with two or three prong pikes, raising the heavy meadow grass and shaking it into the air in ordered rows. The new machine was to end all that, the swirling short iron spikes, drawn by a horse, throwing up two swathes at a time.

The new turner appeared to work well, but its work was viewed with some suspicion, and Tadhg Doody and Sean were sent down each row with their long pikes to shake out any lumps that the blind machine had not seen.

They turned it again later that day, and by evening the grass was turning a light golden brown, and only the last vestiges of green could be seen here and there in the loose and swollen hay rows.

Mossie looked at the sky and held up his hand in the still warm air.

'The weather will hold,' he said. ''Tisn't right yet. We'll make it up tomorrow.'

The next day came bright and promising with no cloud except for a few small mare's tails passing slowly across the blue sky. We were all in high spirits as we waited for the sun to burn off the dew that had fallen during the night. We were waiting on the top headland beside the gate, the men in their shirts, and Delia and Mary in their loose black skirts and dark blouses, and the two- and three-prong pikes resting against the gate pier. I became aware of Mossie getting restless and looking at the sky. He held up his hand.

'The devil in hell,' he said, 'do you see what I see?' He was looking west, where just over the horizon a small black cloud had appeared. He had anxiety on his face and he looked over at me.

'Bad luck to that man on your father's wireless. He said the weather was settled. Not a blessed word about showers, and it's going to be a heavy one. We might have just enough time to save it if we go at it now, there's hardly any wind.'

They all knew what to do, Mossie and Sean, and Luke and Tadhg Doody, and the two women. Swiftly they set about making the hay into small haycocks about a foot high, building them dense and hard in the middle and smoothing down the top and sides. They called them crowers.

Mossie shouted at me, 'Go for the Kates, they have no hay down.'

I was off like a greyhound for the Kates farm house, about four hundred yards away up near the village. They were first cousins of the Keanes, and before fifteen minutes had passed Sean and Simon and Kate were making crowers in the big meadow as if their lives depended on it.

We beat the rain, and before the heavy shower came down the crowers were ready. The big drops bounced off the tops and sides with little soaking.

It was only a slight setback in the life of a farm. The next day came brilliant again and by midday the tops of the crowers were shaken out and dried, and the mechanical raker had scooped the hay into big high rows for cocking. It was Sunday and the women went to Mass but the men absolved themselves and kept to the work. By early afternoon the cocks began to go up, two people to each cock, one in the middle trampling down, and the other piking and shaping into a neat oval top to throw off the rain. The women piked and trampled as good as the men. I was in my heaven, standing like the best of them, taking and laying out the hay like an old hand. It was I, too, who twisted the wire crookeen that made the long hay ropes to tie down the cocks against the wind.

At four o'clock or so Delia and Mary went to the house for the tea. They came laden with a basket of bread and cold bacon, and a sweetgallon full of sweet strong tea. The nectar of the Gods could not have tasted better in that day when we made up the big meadow and saved it from that heavy shower, that had come upon us.

The summer was passing and Luke was getting more restless. He was coming more and more to our house to listen to the news on the wireless, and to read the *Irish Press*, de Valera's new paper, that was only out a year or two. He was looking for news from America, to find out if Roosevelt was making anything out of the country. As the weeks went by he was getting into better humour. I knew it would not be long before we'd lose him.

Meanwhile, we carried on. On the fine days we'd go swimming in the river, off the limestone rocks near the waterfall. On adventurous days we'd go downriver to Lyre, the big black hole that would put shivers on you it was so deep. I could not swim, and dangerously Luke carried me on his back across the deep water. I knew my mother would die of fear if she knew about it, so I left her with other things to be afraid about.

He had a fascination with guns, and he borrowed my father's double-barrelled shotgun and a pocketful of cartridges and fired away about the place as the fancy took him. Sean said he couldn't hit a white horse, and I believed him in the end. He rarely shot anything, although he had every crow and magpie in the place, not to mention blackbirds, thrushes, and even robins, scared out of their wits. A rising snipe would be gone before he had the gun raised, and Sean said the pigeons were so friendly with him that they saluted him as they flew past.

But the fun and the joking had to end, and the day came when Luke returned to America. Another American wake was held and new tears were shed. Delia was crying every chance she got when the others weren't looking, and I cried too. The day he walked out that last morning was the last time I saw him. He lived on in America without returning, and many years later he died fairly young, of a heart attack, before he was sixty years of age.

*

In the early few years I thought none of us would ever die. My mother and father and my sisters, Delia and all the rest, would always be there, mostly tranquil and happy with life. I saw dead bodies many times – the fish and birds and rabbits that my father killed, the corpse of a cat on the roadside, or a cow that died in a field. Even the stabbing to death of a fat pig for the barrel appeared as a passing event of life, like the coming of spring or a fall of winter rain. The sensitivity of the mind and the tenderness of the heart was still in hibernation, like a small animal still in its winter bed waiting to awaken.

Pity came with the years. Small pity at first for a sick animal or the face of a weeping child. Pity for an overloaded donkey beaten with a stick or goaded with a nail. Pity for the wounds on the back of an animal, from the chafing of a worn saddle, pity for the raw hairless back of a dog drenched with boiling water by an angry farmer's wife in defence of her farmyard fowl.

The first overwhelming surge of pity, pity unto tears, came from the death cry of a dying calf. The cry came to me through a clump of trees, and filled the air with terror and suffering. The death bawling went on and on, and I searched until I came upon him. It was a little red and white animal, a few days old. It hung by its hind legs from a branch of an ash tree, its front legs moving slowly as if seeking something. Its throat was cut straight across, and the first gushing of its blood had ceased. It now came in small stream onto the blood-drenched ground. From its nostrils came a dripping of brown mucous. Its eyes were open, unseeing and unknowing, and the death stare had not yet set in. Its death cries came less often, and with failing sound, until the last gasping stopped and it was still. I was still too, my heart was breaking and tears were falling.

It was the hand of man that tied this small animal to the tree branch, and drew a knife across its throat. It was done because it was a worthless thing. It was worth the price of its skin, half crown to five shillings, and he died like this, that the blood would leave its flesh, so that parts of it might be eaten. It happened during the time they called the 'Economic War'.

This was the first full emergence of my store of pity, but death of a human was still not known to me.

It was Delia who first brought me into the rite of human death.

'We've a journey to go on,' she said to me one day as I went into the kitchen. 'Tackle the donkey, there's a woman dead back in Boola and I have to go to the wake.'

We went back the road to the bogs until we came to her own mountainy meadow and turned right up a long stony boreen, until we came to a small thatched farmhouse.

The small kitchen was full of women with shawls and men with caps, sitting on sugar chairs and wooden forms. The wake was well under way, and nearly everybody had something in their hand, a glass of whiskey, or port wine, or porter, or a sandwich and a cup of tea. The day was young and there was an air of reverence and quiet talk. A door was open into a room off the kitchen, and people were going in and out of the room every few minutes.

We were welcomed in and greeted all round. Delia said 'The Lord have mercy on her soul', and began to cry. A glass of lemonade was put into my hand, and Delia went up into the room. I was sitting in a corner, and couldn't see much of the other room through the door. I could see the bottom part of a bed covered with a white sheet that had a small pointed hill on it.

'I declare to God,' I said to myself, 'they're the toes of the dead woman.'

Delia came out looking wan and sat down beside me in the corner. Before long she had a glass of sherry in her fist and was taking small discreet sips out of it, as if she didn't like it that much.

The talk went on all round about the dead woman, saying how good she was and full of charity to everybody.

'She never missed Mass in her life, and was always up to the altar on first Fridays,' said one.

''Tis the truth you're telling, and what's more she had a screed of rosary beads, including a mother-of-pearl she got at a mission ages and ages ago,' said another.

'Rosary beads?' said a third, 'she had more than them. Did you know she had holy water, from a sight of places the Blessed Virgin appeared, Lourdes, and that other place, is it Fatima they call it, and other places abroad.'

'Ah, she was a great woman entirely, her family never wanted for anything, and she worked herself to the bone from the time they arrived.'

I had a good look to see if there were any keening women around. A few of the women with shawls and white hair, had the cut of a keener about them, but none of them raised a wail or a lament of any kind. I knew that special keening women travelled round the country from wake to wake, crying out and wailing and reciting the good points of the dead person.

This brought the thought of the banshee, the fairy woman, to my mind. She might be seen under a tree, on top of a house, combing her long white hair, with a long black cloak on her. Once she wailed at all around the place, the sick person was for the high road.

I whispered to Delia was the banshee around the night the woman died. 'My poor boy,' said Delia, 'the banshee never cries for the ordinary people, only those of the blood, with an O or a Mac before their name.'

I was trying to tell Delia that this didn't appear fair to me when she told me be quiet, that the people were looking at me. I kept quiet for a bit, although I still thought it was highway snobbery.

Something was biting me and I gave Delia a poke in the side. 'I want to see the corpse,' I said.

Delia looked at me and said nothing as if thinking. Then she said, 'I didn't mean for you to see her, it might do you harm.'

Then all of a sudden she stood up. 'Come on,' she said, 'I'll bring you up.'

Up we went to the room, and there it was all in front of me. The corpse was lying on the bed, her face as white as the pillow. Her grey hair was brushed back from her face, and her lips were pulled together tight and sunk in as if she had no teeth. Her eyes were closed and her nose was pointed up thin, as if there was no flesh on it. For all the queerness about her, her countenance was calm, as if she was sleeping without pain. She was dressed in a brown shroud, and her small white hands were locked together, below her bosom. A mother-of-pearl rosary beads was entwined in her fingers. The white sheet was smoothed on the bed from her waist down, and on her body were two white saucers with brown snuff in them.

There were a few in the room and all of us kneeling by the bed, our heads down praying for her soul. Then we got up and all took a pinch of snuff, and when we sneezed we said Dia Linn (God with Us) to each other.

We were not long back out in the kitchen when somebody called for the rosary, and we were all down on our knees again. I was praying they wouldn't go the full five Mysteries, that would be fifty Hail Marys and five Glory be to the Fathers. But lucky enough they only said one decade, ten Hail Marys, which I counted out on my fingers, and one Glory be to the Father. This suited me fine, as I was not much good at praying at the time.

This first sight of the dead didn't penetrate too deep into me, and did not do me much harm for a good while. But in the months that followed, I began to think more about dying, and particularly about my father and mother. The more I thought about it the more it bore down on me, and the more it drove me to the point of despair. It did not bear thinking of, it couldn't happen, it wouldn't happen, and if it did happen, I'd close my eyes and die away myself. But time, the great healer, brought its soothing balm to my spirit, and the more I paddled by boat on the river of death, the easier the passage became.

When my Uncle Simon died of a burst ulcer at the age of thirty-nine, I was able to look down at his corpse, still wearing the long white surgical stockings of his failed operation, with only a faintly troubled mind. I was sad for the sadness of my father, Simon's brother, and I remembered with fondness the times I had with this lovable and eccentric man.

The next corpse I saw belonged to a comrade of my father, who had fought with him in the time of the Troubles. We were in Ballybunion, and with great reluctance I left the summer beach to go with my father to the deadhouse in Tralee. The dead man, not yet old, lay on the wooden table. My father pulled down the white sheet and looked at his face for a long time. Then he spoke words that I thought strange at the time: 'You poor old hoor you, better you then me.' Then he gently covered the face again, straightened his shoulders, and blew out his breath. 'Come on,' he said, 'we'll go back to Ballybunion.'

It was back near Lyrecrompane near the joining of two converging rivers that I went to my best waking. Another old comrade had died, and it was late in the evening when we got to the house. We paid our respects to the corpse, bent our knees and said a prayer. Back in the kitchen it was soon obvious that nearly everybody was in some state of intoxication. Porter was moving everywhere. One man, drunk as might be, was staggering dangerously, carrying a white enamel bucket full of porter. With expansive and lavish gesturing of his dispensing jug, he forced the black velvet liquid on anyone with a vessel in his hand.

'By Jasus,' said a man, 'you're doing yourself a great wrong.' 'How's that?' said the great dispenser.

'What do you mane, how's that?', said the man. 'I'll tell you how's that. You're going around filling every man with porter, and filling not a drop for yourself.'

'By Jasus you're right,' said the great dispenser. He dipped the jug deep into the porter, dropped the bucket on the floor, and fell back into a deep chair with the jug clasped tightly to his face, as if he'd never let it go.

A select few guests, including my father, were soon brought up to the parlour. From there we could see though the throbbing hell's kitchen, into the room where the corpse lay on the bed.

In our company was the brother of the dead man, well drunk, and it soon became clear he had become enamoured of a buxom visiting Yankee woman, a distant relative. He made several unsuccessful advances towards her person, amid great hilarity, until at last he laid his hands on both sides of her ample breast. He was hauled off amid some commotion. But she took no great offence, and he took no offence, and things settled down to an acceptable degree of bedlam again.

To take the harm off it, and to bring the evening to an appropriate end, he gave as fine a rendering as you could wish to hear of 'Cool Water, Cool Water'.

– 8 –

Goboys on the Loose

SATURDAY of a summer's day with the sap well risen all round, including into our own limbs and heads, and the devil pinching furiously everywhere, was a special day for us 'goboys', small restless knights of the countryside. There were three us, my cousins Jimmy and Johnny, and myself, and too often an unwelcome attachment to the party, the boys' younger sister Moll, a small black-haired girl with brown eyes who always travelled about thirty yards behind us for her own safety. If dire threats of her imminent departure from this world, and a few well-aimed small stones in front of her, failed to dislodge her, which usually happened, we made the best of it and let her tag along. We had nothing against her personally. For a girl she was fine, very active and tough, with a stoical quality about her. The trouble was we figured our image and esteem of ourselves would be seriously damaged if we were observed too often foraging around the country in the company of girls.

The Cud Kits lived across the valley, in a small thatched cottage, beside the tar road, on the other side of the Oweveg. Later, they built a nice modern cottage. We were about second cousins, I'd say, because we never discussed the matter too closely. We had an unspoken feeling that too close an inspection might throw up a thing or two that we would find hard to understand, and that we'd have to go over a ground that we'd rather not travel.

That being so we knew we were cousins, and we had a great pride in the fact that we were all O'Connors. The name called up in our minds the images of the last High King of Ireland, who had tried to put paid to the Normans after all their marauding that time long ago. And we had a vague idea in our heads too, of the O'Connors of Carrigafoyle Castle, north a bit on the river Shannon, who were Kings of Kerry for a sight of generations back.

Jimmy was particularly preoccupied at times about his forebears, those that went back a good while. It was a matter I couldn't help him much with, for I didn't know. So I'd always answer him with a good deal of vagueness and circumspection, calling up images of ancient warriors and knights in armour on fine steeds, jousting down the centuries with the invaders, rescuing the occasional defenceless maiden, and suggest that maybe we had come down the line from some of them.

That went down fairly well at the time. But this day he looked me in the eye with new intent and said: 'Your soul to the devil, Rory, I want to ask you something. I asked you times before and all you did was fill me up with fine stories that were all right for a while maybe. Now the question is where did our O'Connors come from, the Knocknagoshel O'Connors, the Garraha O'Connors.' He looked as always with an expression of hope and expectation on his innocent brown face, and a shine coming out of his two black eyes.

At that moment the devil started pinching me very hard, and I did something that I was sorry for when I thought of it later. I raised my head up and put a furrow on my brow, then I put my hand to the side of my head, as if I was thinking hard. Then I said to him: 'Musha Jimmy, I couldn't be as sure of it in my head as I might be about other things, but to the best of my belief the O'Connors were tinkers from behind Tralee.'

Sadness passed over Jimmy's face like the shadow of a cloud crossing a sunny hillside, and tears filled his eyes. 'Oh Jaysus, Rory,' he said, 'that couldn't be true. Don't, oh don't say that.' He looked at me as if he wanted me to put him out of his pain. But I'm afraid I was cruel enough at the time to say no more, except to jump up and down with Johnny, laughing to our hearts' content. And after a while, a good while, Jimmy joined us in the laughing too.

This Saturday, I was slouching around the road in front of our house, scheming up in my head the kind of things I might do for the day. 'I'll call the Cud Kits,' said I to myself. Soon I was up on the ditch, looking down across the valley and blowing long blasts of whistles through my teeth, with two fingers from each hand holding down my tongue for greater effect. A good few blasts and there they were, the two small figures scuttling out of the small white house onto the tar road and down, making for the river. And then came Moll behind them, her small legs flying, determined as ever not to be kept out of whatever escapades the day might bring.

Within a few minutes they were there before me, the two heroes panting like hunting dogs, and small Moll, floundering her way through a muddy gap, a good field behind.

'Your soul to the devil,' said Jimmy, 'is it how the house is on fire, with all your whistling, or what are you up to at all?' I did not answer for I was looking at Johnny, the younger but the bigger of the two, who had gone into one of his fighting antics, looking for notice. He was in a half crouch, his legs wide apart, with his tongue clenched between his teeth, and a wild look in his eye, the bunched fist of his left hand thrust out in front of him, and his clenched right hand drawn back behind his right hip, as if he was about to deliver a mortal blow to a terrible enemy. And then he swung a haymaker that turned him around nearly off his feet.

'Did I get him?' shouted Johnny, 'Is he out for the count?'

'The devil take you,' said Jimmy, 'you wouldn't knock the thistles off a whitehead flower on the mountain, and they ready to go in the first puff of wind.'

'I'll tell you what,' said Jimmy, ''tis a great day for a fire. We'll set a blaze to Cotter's furze field. 'Tis on boggy land and it'll burn for a week.'

'Upon my oath,' said Johnny, 'what kind of a fool are you at all. Didn't you see him shovelling in a dyke in the top field this morning. He'd see us as sure as the birds are singing, and we'd never bring our legs out of it. And what would your father, the Master, say then?'

We were beginning to sweat by dint of thinking and considering in the hot sun.

'I'll tell you what,' said I, after an idea struck me. 'Delia Keane has a bull that they tell me is as wicked as a bag full of cut Kilkenny cats. He's back in the ploughmatch field, I saw him there every day this week, stamping and rooting the ground, with his head thrown up in the air, snorting and roaring.'

'Had he his upper lip in a curl and stretched across his bare teeth,' demanded Jimmy. 'I know it for a pure fact, that a bull that doesn't curl his lip across his teeth is no good at all for wickedness.'

This was a serious counter, and I had to think fast. 'You mightn't know as much about bulls as you think you know, Jimmy,' I said. 'You don't know much about the new bulls they are using now, brought in from Arabia. They don't have to curl their lips at all, and they're the wickedest bulls that were ever put on the face of this earth. You didn't know that, did you?' Jimmy said nothing.

'Who'll do the whistling and who'll go to the centre of the field?' said Johnny. 'I know the whistle well.' He gave an immediate demonstration, beginning with a high piercing note, and then coming down the scale in tantalizing puffs, until the last slow seductive sound.

We had to admit that Johnny had got inside us in the matter of whistling, and no one challenged him. But who took up the all-important and dangerous post in the centre of the field was yet to be decided.

'Jimmy is the fastest runner,' I ventured. 'He'd have the best chance of getting out when the run is made. I'll go along inside the ditch, making short runs to draw him off, if things get too hot.'

I could see that Jimmy was thinking hard. If he denied he was the fastest runner, he'd lose caste, and he wanted to avoid that if possible. But on the other hand the only time any one of us wanted to go into the centre for the run was when we were talking about it. We knew enough of the danger of bulls, and we'd heard enough of too many farmers horned on the ground and into the grave.

Jimmy's face brightened and he looked up. 'We can't do it anyway,' he said.

'You knighted amadán,' said Johnny, 'what are you talking about?'

'Upon my oath, I'm talking pure truth,' said Jimmy. 'Tell me this so, who has a red rag, or a red jumper itself, to wave at the bull? Doesn't every Christian know you can't go drawing a bull after you without a good screed of something red, to haggle him with.' With this we decided to look elsewhere for diversion.

We were contented enough for a while saying nothing, kicking up our bare feet in the air and looking at everything. We were in a fine spot, lying on thick grass on the headland of Kate Donohue's big field below our house, with a grand view out across the valley of the small river, with the rising ground of Knockbrack, the speckled hill, spread out a good mile from south to north in front of us, and facing always into a setting sun. Way back on the right, the grey concrete creamery building beside Headley's Bridge, called after Lord Headley, an old landlord who had sucked the country dry for many years a long time before.

The hot sun was high in the sky for it was approaching the midday hour, and the rays knocked sheenings and flashes off patches of the river at points where low ground made it visible. Shimmers and spangles of gold and silver light came back to us from places where rocks broke the water. Halfway to the right we could see part of Lyre Hole, deadly for all but the best of swimmers, where white trout and brown trout, and eels and salmon itself, were always nosing about there among the reeds and nudging the water into small circles, inquisitive about the world above. It was at this spot that the Oweveg, after its six-mile journey from Lyre Mountain in Castleisland parish, joined with the Tullaleague tributary from its rising in Hill of the Flagstones, a thousand feet up in the Glanaruddery mountains near the Meadow of the Grass.

Back from there, past the roadside houses on the tar road from Castleisland to Abbeyfeale, and past the dull grey house of Jim Thompson, the man with the cure that all Munster knew about; and still down the Oweveg, going north, past the riverside thickets of blackthorn and whitethorn and willow trees where the woodcock hid, past the boggy wetland where the snipe and curlew fed, and down to the Knockbrack National School, where my father and mother taught. And down again past the water thickets, where coot and waterhen raced across the water with their young behind them, and the coverts where wild duck rose up in flashes of blue and green and black at human intrusion. Further down again, between small flat riverbank fields to the Metal Bridge, where the Oweveg was joined by the Glenna stream, from its rising in the west in Cloughboula and its flow north of Knocknagoshel village to this place, to turn the big mill wheel of O'Shaughnessy's Woollen Mills for one hundred and fifty years. Here the Oweveg was nearly home.

For home was the broad waters of the Feale river, at a place where the counties of Kerry, Limerick and Cork met.

Young eyes travelled along the Speckled Hill farther up, the pattern of small farms, squares of green and black and gold, each with its own small house of thatch and slate, and the cattle, small figures of white and dun and black against the green hillside.

'Upon my soul,' said Jimmy, 'this is a fine place we are in. It must be the grandest place in the whole wide world.'

'You put your hand on top of it,' I said, 'for a truer word never came out of your mouth. And the best of all is that we are as free as the air, with nobody to put a halter on us. My father is gone to Tralee in the Baby Ford to a meeting, and my mother is gone to Abbeyfeale, on her bicycle to visit Grandma. Delia Keane's yard is like Knockane, they must be gone to town in the trap, and I saw Mossie making west in the horserail, he must be gone for turf. And your crowd don't put too tight a rope on you.'

'Your soul to the devil,' said Johnny, 'what are you going on about? My mother has us torn and tormented about going about the country with you, at all hours of the day and night. She said the other day we were all goboys, and you the worst goboy of the lot of us. And she's always going on about going on the river, and Jimmy's weak chest, and how one of these days you'll be the death of him.'

'The devil take her,' said I, 'she must be a right old harridan. That's the worst I ever heard. If she's so worried about Jimmy why doesn't she put a pair of Cud Kits wellingtons on him to keep out the water? But I suppose they are so full of holes that the cure would be worse than the disease, anyway.'

'What will we do so, I'll tell you what,' said Jimmy. 'We'll cross the river, and shell Kate Walshe's carhouse. They say she's half a witch, but she won't be able to recognize us, she's as blind as a bat.'

'You stump of a fool,' said Johnny, 'that might be the worst we ever did. I heard my father saying that blind people have a second sense. They'd know who your were by the smallest step of your foot, or the smallest whisper you could give. And anyway this very morning I saw Jimmy Joe, that son of hers, he must be home from America again. They say he's as cross as a puck goat, and as thorny as a long briar.'

'What about that?' said Jimmy, 'I have it as a fact that he's nearly as blind as his mother. He goes about with a pair of silvery glasses perched up on his nose. And there's devil the damn he could do about it if we showed him the back of our heels.'

'Hold on, my boy,' said Johnny, 'there's another thing. Did you know he learned to swim? Over in America they couldn't teach him, 'til one day a man got an idea. He took Jimmy Joe up to the top of a bridge, they call it Brooklyn Bridge, I think, and pitched him into the river. Now he was in a pickle. He told the story himself to my father. Jaysus Christ, says he, 'twas sink or swim, and I swam, and from that day to this, I'm like an otter in the water.'

'And what has that to do with it?' asked Jimmy. 'The Oweveg river is not the Atlantic Ocean.'

'Hold your whist for a minute, and don't let your blather run away with you. They say that fellow is as clever as a pet fox. And what if he manoeuvred us over towards Lyre Hole, and came after us? We'd be foundered in a hole of ten foot of water, and he slashing around us like a walrus. We'd be done for entirely.'

Jimmy and I were not entirely convinced by Johnny's story, and I think we reckoned there were better things to do than watching Kate Walshe dancing and screaming round the tar road and raining witches' curses down on our heads. That would do for another day. Maybe after school some evening.

Jimmy was thinking hard again. 'I'll tell you what,' he said, 'I see a way out of my mother and the river. On our way up I saw a sight of the biggest dock leaves I ever saw in my life. They were nearly a foot long and nearly as much across. We'll make stockings for my legs and tie them on with hemp. They'd keep out a sight of the water, I'd say.'

The decision was made and we began to make the preparations. Jimmy and Moll went off to gather the dock leaves, and Johnny and I reconnoitred round Delia's stable, looking for a good rope. We found one, a good twenty feet of new rope on a new horse's winkers, and we went off looking for the black mare we knew was grazing in a field near the river. Long black hair from the mare's tail was what we were after, to make súilíns or loops to tie on sally sticks to whip the fish out of the water.

It took us a good hour to catch the mare. She was in no way inclined to keep still for two suspicious-looking young marauders approaching her with a big loop of rope. Johnny roped her at last in the corner of a field, with a throw of the loop that would have outdone the cowboy in Duffy's Circus. Twenty strong black hairs a foot long, four hairs to the plait, and we had súilíns on sticks before you could say Jack Robinson. Then on to the river, the fairly shallow pools, among the rocks below Lyre Hole, where the smaller fish disported themselves. Moll and Jimmy were left to manufacture the dock-leaf stockings that were going to protect his weak chest. It wasn't long at all before they came along whooping and laughing, with arms full of dock leaves and about thirty feet of light hemp rope they took off hay cocks on a field on the way down. In no time we were all in the river doing our work, Jimmy up to his knees in green shrubbery.

The fish we were taking were not up to much, a few inches long, and none that a decent fisherman would not have thrown back again to live for another day. We did not know if they were brown trout sprats, or white trout fry, or salmon parr. Nor did we care a deal. The sport was the thing. The miracle was that we caught anything at all with the shouting and laughing and fighting that went on.

*

The summer day went by smooth and sweet, like the taste of wild honey in the mouth. We were well spread out along the river, each at his own favourite waterhole, heads down, examining the light and shade on the riverbed, watching for the small outlines of the little fishes, silver and grey and green and blue, resting beside the rocks with their noses pointing upstream against the flowing water. Moll as usual was working with her brother Jimmy, as close as she dare come, for he was of fairly benign character and least likely to explode against her for throwing her shadow on the water and frightening the fish. Unexpected movement or shadow disturbed the sprats and sent them flashing to another lay-by at another rock. The small loops on the sally rods crept quietly up past the fishes' tails, up past the smooth bodies until the gills were reached, and then the sudden whip upwards, and the little fish fighting out the last seconds of their young lives.

The small sounds of water, flowing and lapping, and the light humming of insects among the sally clumps and ferns and wild grasses of the river bank, and a feeling of peace, and time passing, that would go on for ever.

But the solitude and the tranquillity was rudely broken. Jimmy, as ever likely to do something different, fell into the flowing river, and his howling brought us quickly to his side, with Moll faithfully holding on to the back of his blue jumper.

He was well soaked all over when we dragged him out and flung him on the bank with many imprecations, the tattered remains of his dock-leaf leggings shedding water like weeping willows.

'God of all the Mercies,' said Johnny, looking down at him,

'what are we going to do now? Nell Browne' – his mother – 'will have our lives, as sure as God made little apples.'

Jimmy was lying there as if the spirit had nearly gone out of him. He had not swallowed too much water, but his face had a white look about it, and his black hair was matted close to his skull, like the wings of a drowned crow. He was saying nothing except for an occasional grunt, and Moll was sitting beside his head crying away to herself. I knew we'd have to do a good bit of considering and I looked up to the sky. It was blue all round, without a cloud in sight, and the heat of the sun was still strong. I was about to come in with some kind of suggestion when I saw a brightness coming into Johnny's face.

'Your soul to the devil, and all that came before him,' he said, 'I'll tell ye what we'll do. We'll go back up the river to the Rocks for a swim and we'll spread Jimmy's clothes on the stones to dry.' So we dragged a reluctant Jimmy upriver, through a few thorned hedges and muddy dykes, until we came to the Rocks.

We slid down an earthen chute from the high bank and we were there. To us the Rocks was a heaven-like place, hewn out of a big limestone placement by the centuries. Our river dell was nearly surrounded by large green river trees, abundant in foliage, and leaning deeply and heavily out over the water on all sides, making room only for the big deposit of flat rocks in the centre. From the south the river came from a large black pool, through a break in the rocks, and filled a beautiful swimming pool three feet deep. From this the water flowed out through two big shoulders of rock in a big white waterfall four feet below. And all around were big dry spaces of limestone, honed smooth by ages of winter floods, to lay your body on in the sun.

There we placed Jimmy, and stripped him of his few sodden garments, and him as naked as the day God made Adam in the Garden of Eden. It was no time for false modesty, but in deference to whatever it was, he sat with his back to us, with his hands in a protective position between his thighs. It was clear he was not accepting his situation with too much grace. He sat for a time looking balefully over his shoulder, and glowering at Johnny and me, and at his clothes spread out on the rocks.

Before long hope had come back to him and he laughed up at us. 'By the Lord God and his Blessed Mother,' he said, 'I have this to tell you. 'Twas the luck of the devil ye came up to me so fast. If I had swallowed much more water, there would be nothing more for me than to be stretched with all the rest, over there in the graveyard of Knockane.'

'In the name of the saints in heaven,' said Johnny, 'what brought you to the edge of that hole? Did you think you were Jim the Master, with a long fishing rod in your hand?'

'Your soul to the devil, I did not, nor anything like it,' replied Jimmy. ''Twas the shadow of a salmon that I thought I saw, and I went a bit up the river to see could I place him in the darkness of the bank.'

'You're a stump of a fool, the likes of which it would hard to find from here back to Dingle,' said Johnny. 'But howsome ever, you failed to drown yourself, and 'twas the luck of all the devils in hell that saved you in the end.'

Jimmy accepted the situation and made no further attempts to argue. And soon the three of us were in the pool, splashing and frolicking and tumbling in the water like young otters.

When she saw our nakedness Moll withdrew to the south end of the rocks, and kept her eyes fixed on the sky over the green river shrubbery, as if she expected some vision or other to appear to her at any moment. It wasn't too long before some new excitement confronted us. 'I declare to God,' said Johnny, 'but do you know what I'm after seeing, but a swarm of young eels trying to climb up the waterfall. Look, look at them now, I tell you.'

And sure enough there they were, cluster after cluster of small brown eels, four or five inches long, flinging their bodies like demons up the white cascade of water. Time after time they threw themselves up to be beaten back, and then, in a kind of desperation, they hurled themselves sideways onto the slippery surface at the side of the falling water, and some of them made it over the top and into the pool. For moments of time we could see their black eyes, and their thin brown bodies struggling in a way we had never seen before.

'Good God Almighty,' said Johnny, 'what is driving them on like this, like the demons of hell were on their tail?'

'It's a mystery entirely,' said Jimmy, 'and nobody on earth can understand it. That's what my father told me once.'

'Faith,' said I, 'you never said a truer word. Kerryboy told me even he does not understand it. You can know about the salmon, in some small way. They come to the rivers where they were born to lay their eggs and spawn, all the way from under the icebergs in the Artic Ocean, where they feed and grow. But when the urge comes on them these fellows will drive like demons, from whatever pond or stream they are in, to get into the Atlantic Ocean. And if there is no other way of doing it they will go over the ground, along the dew of the grass. And they'll go out into the Atlantic to a place called the Sargasso Sea, according to Kerryboy, and there they'll breed and die, and their young will come back again. But what I can't understand is, what brought their fathers and mothers up the Oweveg river in the first place.'

There was nobody to explain it to us so we let it lie. We lay there for a considerable time cogitating, until the chill of the evening began to come down upon us. The sun was sinking in the west behind the Glanaruddry mountains and the shadows of the coming night were gathering around us. The swallows were beginning to come down, with their small black bodies and forked tails swooping over the river, their mouths open to catch the insects that were dappling the surface of the water.

We dressed, and the surface of our skins was cold. Jimmy's wet garments were only half dry, and we swung along the river bank, our small fish trophies on our shoulders, threaded through their gills on fern shoots. I turned left into Delia's boreen, called 'The Road of the Priests', for it was up there the priests came on horseback from the parish of Brosna to say Mass in Knocknagoshel, before the two parishes were joined in 1916. And Jimmy and Johnny and Moll Cud Kit went their own way, across the car passage by Lyre Hole and up on the tar road north to the thatched cottage to face the ire of their mother, Nell Browne.

*

'Twas a good while before we spent another day like that campaigning on the river. It was not long before I found out that the very thing that we had all been dreading had come to pass. Jimmy got a cold in his chest and I didn't see him for two weeks or more. The worst of all was that the contamination went from his chest to his ears, and Johnny told me 'twas like all the woes of the world, listening to him coughing and groaning, and the shrieks coming out of him when the pain in his ears got bad. And Nell Browne rampaging round the house calling down all kinds of imprecations and curses on the goboys of this world, especially that Rory the Master, for leading Jimmy astray.

And Cud Kit himself would be sitting at the fire, his two black eyes following her round wherever she went, his teeth and his lips clamped on the stem of his pipe and saying nothing. When I thought of it afterwards, I was saying to myself it was no wonder at all that old Nell was so fractious, for the next time I met Jimmy he was deaf in both ears. It was a condition that stayed with him, more or less, for the rest of the time I knew him, although I heard years later that there had been some improvement.

Jimmy's deafness caused us a good deal of trouble in almost everything we were doing after that. Quietness was the one thing we wanted in nearly all occasions when we were on a mission. Whether it was coming up on the blind side of a half-wild ass or a skittish young horse for a gallop, the last thing we wanted was Jimmy breaking twigs under his feet, or knocking stones on a wall, or rustling whitethorn or elder bushes as we came over a ditch, without a notion in the world of the destruction he was causing us. The result was that he was banished to the back of the line in any kind of a delicate operation, and Moll was promoted to travel in third position. Jimmy did not like that at all, but there was nothing he could do about it, except a bit of low muttering to himself from time to time.

The worst trouble he made for us was when we were out after young rabbits. We'd go over by Knockane graveyard, and do a good deal of manoeuvring and peeping over the dry stone walls, wondering whether we might see a ghost or two. Of course we never saw anything, although Jimmy said once he thought he saw a woman in a black shawl flitting behind headstones at the far end, and then floating straight through the limestone flag door of a brown vault. We never knew if there was any truth in it, although we brought our legs out of the place fast enough, and down across the river and up to the Woodline road, and up a steep round hill to the fields on top.

It was called the Woodline because hundreds of years before the whole side of the escarpment was covered by big stands of all kinds of trees, particularly giant oaks. Until, of course, the landlord got his hands on them and cut them down and shipped them to England to make planks for their man-of-war ships and put a roof on St Paul's Cathedral and maybe Buckingham Palace itself. But now the whole ridge from Talbot's Bridge to Headley's Bridge was left to a few small farmers, and to a couple of people from the village to graze their single cows, but above all to the finest crop of fat rabbits that you ever saw.

Early in the morning of a summer's day, or late in the evening in the golden light of a sinking sun, the fields teemed with the small bodies of every age and size, so that you'd almost think there was a brown blanket spread over the land. This was our magic place, where we invoked the spirits of the chase and used our childish skills to try to outwit these small wild creatures before they got back to the safety of their burrows.

The strategy was to get between them and the burrows unheard and unseen. In the stillness of our wait we'd watch them, their small heads down, eating the sweet grass, and everywhere from time to time pairs of little ears rising up for furtive looks around their wild paradise. For us it was a kind of heaven too, dreaming of the small round bodies of the young that we'd take home with us and tame with care and soothing words, until they'd come up to you of their own free will and take the offerings of green food from your own hands. We had no thoughts of strangulation or death, or of fat graziers for the pot, as in the minds of hunting men. For us it was enough that we might own and tame the wild young things, to live freely in small hutches, to choose to stay with us, happy in the small gardens round our homes.

A quick clapping of hands and the scurry would be on. All heads up and the streaking of brown bodies and the white flashing of tails in all directions, but with the impelling instinct all round to make for the burrows. We caught the very young often enough, and held them in our hands, and saw the cowering fear in their wide brown eyes, and felt the tiny quick beating of their hearts. And our own hearts beat too and softened towards them, and all our dreams departed, and we laid them gently on the grass and sent them home to their mothers.

And yet in a curious way we felt we had failed, failed the wild instinct of the hunter that was in us all, and the hardness that should have been be in us, like it was in the men we knew. And we looked at each other saying nothing for a while, wondering why we were as we were. And Jimmy would throw back his head and laugh and say: 'Faith, the deaf man did not do anything wrong today, for all the good it did us in the end.' Then we'd laugh too and say nothing. And we'd pick up our small brown sack that should have been filled with the glory of our hunting day, and we'd pick up our ash-plant hunting sticks, go down the round hill, across the river, up by the graveyard, and home to our mothers too.

– 9 –

Bridie Comes Back

DELIA'S HEART raised again when word came through that her eldest daughter, Bridie, was coming home on a visit, along with her one-year-old son, Georgie. Bridie had married a man from Brosna village, six miles in the Cork direction, and he was well fixed in the New York police.

All the scouring and painting and whitewashing went on all over again. In deference to the fact that Bridie was a woman with a new baby, Delia and Mary vacated their big bright bedroom on the north side of the house, and installed there Luke's new bed in preparation for the homecoming. They crossed the kitchen and took over Luke's room, the old cleared-out storeroom, big enough of itself, but fairly dark and gloomy.

I walked into the kitchen the morning after they arrived, and the women were all flitting around to a degree I had never seen before. Bridie was a tall, dark-haired woman, and after a half-hearted handshake and a word with me, she carried on with her activity.

The focus of all the movement appeared to be a small basket with high sides, lined in a beautiful satin-like blue material, sitting in the middle of the kitchen table. At one end was a hood, also lined in blue, like you'd see on a child's pram. It was not long before I saw him lying on his back with his legs and hands flying around him, and the smile of an angel on his round pink face, under a blue silk bonnet. It was Georgie, born in America, at the other end of the world.

The cause of the extreme fussiness was apparently Georgie's breakfast and the carrying out of Bridie's precise instructions on how it should be prepared.

Mary was at one end of the table squeezing out fresh orange juice, anxiously glancing every few seconds at the baby and at Bridie's face. On the other end of the table was an array of small tins of baby food, and Delia and Bridie were discussing which tin should be opened. It was clear that some tin had been opened, as a small saucepan, pulled back from the coals, contained some kind of porridge or other.

The various misunderstandings were quickly ironed out, and Georgie sat up in his basket and was fed, to his great delight, a three- or four-course baby breakfast, the like of which I had never seen before.

Shortly after the baby was fed he began to show drowsiness. The three of them laid him down in his blue basket and he was soon fast asleep. Then the three of them took him up to the big bedroom, where he could sleep in peace until he got hungry again.

They all came back with smiles of satisfaction on their faces. I was not at all pleased at the lack of interest they all had shown in me. It was beginning to dawn on me that here was a rival who might be difficult to overcome for the affections of the house. I knew even then that I was only a neighbour's child, while he was Delia's grandson, all the way from America, the like of which she might never see again.

It turned out as I thought it would. My reign as Delia's child prince was over. The strange thing was I didn't mind too much. I loved Delia like a second mother but I had for some time become impatient with all the affection she put on me, like trying to kiss and hug me, and washing my knees and combing my hair. In fact the more I looked at the way that poor American child was being treated, the more I pitied him. He appeared always to have a spoon in his mouth. Hardly an hour went by but there was somebody washing his face or his bottom, rubbing on powder or cream, billing and cooing at him, tickling his belly or straightening his clothes, and tying his blue bonnet. He loved thumping around the floor on his hands and knees, but not a yard could he go but he'd have a minder beside him, worrying him and harassing him with calls of danger.

He appeared fascinated with the big open fire, and was driving towards it every chance he got. I have never seen such despair on the face of a child as he went for the red coals and was baffled every time by a woman hanging out of him. He was without sense of danger of any kind and roared his anger when they dragged him back.

*

I was a big boy now, eight years old, and my freedom was almost unrestricted. My dirty face and torn trousers no longer brought comment or repairs. I ran round the country as I wished, despising easy passage to any place, tearing in a straight line through dykes and ditches and hawthorn shrubbery. With shoes on, I went through the river without pause, and let the air dry them on my feet. My mother said she had given up on me. But I knew she understood the need for freedom that boys have, for a short period of their lives.

She was pleased that I sought the paper every evening when my father had finished, and listened to the wireless for news of the world. It was here I heard of great heavyweight boxers like Joe Louis, and the great Irish wrestlers Danno Mahony and Steve Casey.

Mahony came from Ballydehob in County Cork. He was in America at this time and had beaten everybody he could find to go against him. They said he was the greatest heavyweight of the day. But the man for me was Casey, from a family of wrestlers, boxers, and oarsmen from Sneem, County Kerry. In the early thirties they won everything that was going at regattas at Kenmare, Bantry and Castletownbere. Many of the brothers went to London and from there to America.

I read later that the *Boston Globe* newspaper put out a challenge to any team of four in America to take on four Casey brothers in a rowing contest. Russel Codman, the American champion, took up the challenge but insisted on a race for singles sculls.

The Caseys accepted, and Codman undertook to pay ten thousand dollars if he was defeated. It was a big occasion, with newspapers from all over America covering the race. Jim Casey finished first, Steve was second, and Tom came third. The American champion was fourth.

But it was Steve Casey that I was following in the summer of 1936. Danno Mahony and himself had beaten all the heavyweights in America, and a match was set between the two for a Sunday, at Mallow Racecourse in County Cork. For some reason or other the fight caught my father's interest as well, and we all set off early on a sunny afternoon for the greatest occasion of my life. In the blue Baby Ford was my father, my mother and myself, and as a special treat for the returned Yank we brought Bridie Keane along as well. I heard them talking of the bishop of Cork, preaching against holding a wrestling match on a Sunday.

'I declare to God,' my mother said, 'don't you think the bishop could find something better to do than banning the fight. I hope there's no trouble.'

My father laughed. 'Yerra,' he said, 'don't mind him. I'm sure the people watching won't be in any danger of losing their souls, looking at a couple of wrestlers. There's no reasoning with these fellows, as they've shown often enough. The people of Cork won't take a bit of notice of him, they've seen it all before.'

We rolled down past Fealesbridge on through Newmarket and approached the outskirts of Mallow town. My father was right. The roads were black with people, as if they were going to hear a speech by de Valera. There was a fair sprinkling of motor cars, with many hundreds more walking, and hundreds more still in every kind of conveyance, bicycles, horses and traps, and plain cars with ponies and donkeys.

'By God,' said my father, 'this is biggest turn-out for a Sunday mission the bishop of Cork will ever see.'

My mother laughed. 'You'd better be careful now, Jim. You know what they say, mocking is catching, and you'd never know when you might be in need of his service.'

'You might be right, Annie,' my father said, laughing as well.

I had never seen anything like it. The big square ring was set up in front of what appeared to be the racecourse stand. It was raised a few feet off the ground with double ropes all round. The floor was made of wood and covered with some kind of canvas.

Some of the people were up in the stand, but crowds were milling round the ring, men, women and children. It was like being in the middle of a fair, but with no animals for sale. There were no bookies like you'd see at the races, but betting was going on here and there, with heads together and money changing hands. There were thimble-riggers and three-card-trick men, with their minders looking around for any guard that might be in the vicinity.

'Find the lady,' said a thin man with a red shirt. He was shuffling three cards in his hands and spreading them on a small square folding table with rickety legs.

'Find the pea,' said a small round man with foxy hair, from another position. He had his table too, and was switching a small pea around under three thimble-shaped cups, with a speed that no eye could follow.

The dress of the people was of great variety. It was a sunny day and many of the men were in shirtsleeves. Nearly all had a cap or a hat of one kind or another. Some of the women were in light summer dresses, others with skirts and white blouses, and here and there were women with shawls. Children were flying around everywhere, some with sandals and shoes, some barefoot.

Small stalls were set up at one side, displaying apples and oranges, bars of chocolate and sweets. Big silver-coloured cans of ice-cream were open here and there, with women dispensing scoops of it into yellow cones as fast as they could take in the money.

My father drew my attention to a tall, strongly built old woman standing on her own to one side. She had grey-black hair tied in a bun. She wore a dark dress and had a large black shawl around her shoulders.

'That's Steve Casey's mother,' he said. 'She comes from a Sullivan family. They were known as the Mountain Sullivans because of their great size and strength.'

I thought about her for a while. An old woman in a shawl, coming all the way from Sneem, to see her son fighting the great Danno Mahony for the heavyweight championship of the world. I wondered at her courage, and she not knowing what the day might bring to her son. Broken limbs, maybe, or other bad injuries, or maybe a broken back itself.

It was much later I learned of the Mountain Sullivans, Dan and Patsy, two huge men who rowed for the Vanderbilt family at regattas in the United States. So impressed were the Vanderbilts that they sent to Sneem for more men like them to crew their boats. Theirs was the blood that fortified the Casey brothers in their rough lives.

The Master of Ceremonies got into the ring with a megaphone and announced the programme. There were two preliminary bouts between big rough men. Two names come to my memory, Charley Strack and the Russian Bear. I forget who won. It was of little interest to me. My man was Steve 'Crusher' Casey.

Danno and Steve came into the ring at last, Danno in a light-coloured robe and Steve all in black. When they stripped the robes there were murmurs from the crowd, who were now pushed well back from the around the ring. From the programme I learned that Danno was six foot two, and weighed over seventeen stones. He had a very large frame, with a round face, and big soft muscles on his arms and shoulders. He was dressed in light-coloured shorts and a light-green vest, cut away at the shoulders and armpits.

Steve Casey was six foot three, and was a stone lighter. When he took off his robe there was a gasp at his strange outfit. He was dressed completely in black, with a tight-fitting top, and his lower gear, a black trousers from waist to ankles, hugging his thighs and calves all the way down. He looked lighter that Danno, and his muscles looked lean and hard. His face too, was lean and brown, under dark hair.

The fight began tamely enough, with both men circling and testing each other out, feinting down to the leg of the opponent then stepping back, reaching out quickly and patting each other's head, waiting for reaction. Then a quick movement, a leg taken out quickly and both men on the floor, seeking leg or head holds until a rope was touched and the fighters were up again.

For a good deal of the time Danno appeared to have the advantage, forcing Steve to floor with sheer strength in finger locks, and locking and twisting Steve's head. A great cheer went up from the Cork crowd when Danno took Steve by the wrist, dragged him forward quickly, turned his back and threw him over his shoulder on to the canvas. Was this Danno's Irish Whip that I had heard so much about? Danno did this time and time again, and I feared for the Kerry wrestler.

But Steve did not appear to be perturbed by Danno's successes. Occasionally he gave as good as he got, dumping Danno to the canvas with various holds. As the fight went on he appeared more and more confident, and seemed to be lasting out better, through better fitness or training. Occasionally too, he reached for one of Danno's ankles and swung him round and round his body, letting him go along the floor in a mighty slide.

The fight went on and on, with both men getting more and more exhausted, and yet there was no end in sight. Danno tried everything he knew, but he failed to hold Steve's shoulders on the floor for the three count, or stranglehold into submission.

It must end, I said to myself, or else they'll have to declare it a draw. But neither man was in a mood for a draw. The heavyweight championship of the world was at stake, and it would have to be fought to a finish.

Yet it would not end. Both men's faces were covered in black dust and sweat, with streaks of red from bloody noses. Human beings cannot stand this, I thought, one of them will die.

But they did not die. They fought on again. Over an hour had gone by and still no finish.

The end came at last. It was Steve's swinging ankle hold that finally brought it to an end. This time it was different. Steve got his hands to both ankles and began the swing. But this time he did not let go until the body was raised above the top rope. A last mighty turn and the body arced over the ropes, and onto the gravel of Mallow racecourse. Danno's back and shoulders took the brunt of the great throw, and bloody damage was caused. Danno got to his feet and bent forward. He straightened up again and raised his right hand into the air, a weary gesture of dismissal and defeat. He did not return to the ring, and Steve was declared the undisputed heavyweight wrestling champion of the world.

Later that evening we had tea in a hotel, and I saw Bridie the Yank slip a colourful ashtray into her handbag, as a souvenir, she said. I got angry with her, inside me, without saying anything. How could she do this; how could she steal an ashtray in a town where a Kerry man had just been crowned a champion of the world?

*

The taking of the ashtray, in its own small way affected my relationship with Bridie. It was never very warm, the way it was with all the rest, and with Luke when he was home. Now I looked upon her with a new feeling of aloofness in my mind. I did not know then that ashtrays, and other small things, were regarded by American visitors as legitimate trophies, to be displayed on their return.

There were other things. She made me uncomfortable with her constant talking, in a way that did not interest me, about the way things were in New York, and her showing to others of her hats and coloured dresses and necklaces and earrings. I felt there were other things to talk about, other than what she had and what other people had.

I had a constant feeling of pity for poor Georgie. He never had a moment to himself, with people talking about him, caressing him and poking at him, pulling at his clothes, and straightening his bonnet. Nothing was ever right, it was either too cold for him or too hot. If he got a smudge on his dress, it was carefully rubbed away. He daren't go into the yard, except in somebody's arms. And if, as sometimes happened, he broke for freedom, and ended up sitting in a brown puddle, splashing and laughing, and throwing lumps of clay in the air, it was as if some tragedy had come down, such was the caterwauling that went on when he was discovered.

Delia's preoccupation with the child was more and more evident as the days went by. It was if she had never borne, and reared, children of her own.

But she knew, and we all knew, that the day was coming when Georgie and Bridie would have to go back to their home in New York. At times, with Georgie close to her breast, she would look out the window and her eyes would shadow with tears.

The morning they had to leave, and the scenes that took place, were the most harrowing that I had ever seen or even imagined. During all the bustle of packing and getting ready, Delia had Georgie in her arms, weeping without cease, and crying aloud her endearments, and attesting, between sobs, to the end of her life if he should be taken from her.

'What will I do, my heart, I cannot go on without you,' she cried out, again and again, in a way that filled me with anxiety and brought looks of concern and unease to the faces of the others around.

The final parting was the most terrible. Delia seemed to lose all reason, and refused to give over the child. She sat on the bottom step of the small stairs leading up to the south loft. She wrapped her two arms around the main stairpost, with the child in the centre, imprisoned by her body, upper arms and thighs. No speaking or pleading would move her.

In the end, Mary and Bridie came around her, and with persistent force, and as gently as they could, pulled open her arms and took the child. Delia lay there for a while wailing. But whatever strength was inside her, she took it in her hands, and raised herself up. She now held herself with dignity, and said her final goodbyes at the doorway, with flowing tears, but no sounds of sorrow. It was as if she had contemplated the final act, and had at last composed her mind to face it, whatever it might be, and whatever the future had in store for her.

– 10 –

Mayne Speaks Out

IT WAS a midsummer day, and the warmth of the sun touched me all round as I moved through the corridor of green, along the country road. There was a small movement of air from the west bringing with it the faint sweet scent of wild roses. I knew where it came from, a little white house hiding in shrubbery back the road. It was Mayne's cottage, and out in front the entangled foliage of the hedge, entwined all round with long fronds of her own sweet briar, covered with her own small red roses, giving off this essence of sweet life and all its promise.

Mayne was a toothless old woman whose face showed too many years of hardship. Deep lines channelled across a face almost as pale as the crinkly white hair round her head and face. For all that, bright eyes, blue as spring violets, shone with mischief and humour, and her smile and laughter were never far away.

She came along soon, as I knew she would, paddling along barefoot, as she always was in summer, her poor misshapen feet making strange indentations in the dry dust along the edge of the road. She carried a small bucket in one hand and a tin sweetgallon in the other.

She stopped to bid the time of day. 'Mary Mother of God, my beautiful sweet boy, but amn't I the lucky woman to come across you this day. I am on my way to Kate's well, for a sup of water to make a drop of tay. 'Tis my third trip today, and there's a tyrant of a stray dog, in a field below the well, that has the heart crossways in me. I'd swear by the Lord, he's a mongrel the tinkers dropped when they were nesting down there a few days ago. Wherever he came from, you're my little man now to guard me against all the world.'

I was proud to guard her with my ashplant of a stick as I marched beside her like a civic guard.

'Do you know, my fair little boy, my heart is scalded with dragging water from this well. I make five trips a day and the rheumatism is burning up my knees and shoulders. Look at my hands, they're like bunches of old dried onions.'

She held out her hands for me to see, and then she smiled and laughed out, her blue eyes crinkling.

'Yerra, what would the likes of me be complaining about. I'll tell you nothing but the truth, but it's a great thing, and a mercy from God, to be alive on a day like this.' She laughed out again and looked at me.

'But that's not to say I haven't a thing to say for myself. That Jack, my man, has a lot to answer for. He's rampaging round the place like a donkey stallion, with nothing to satisfy him. It's Mayne this and Mayne that. He's the wan that does for most of the spring water. Every half an hour, it's "Mayne are you making a drop of tay?" as if he were parched from a booze of porter. Between spring water and tay, you'd think he was living at the priest's house.'

We passed down past our own house, three hundred yards further, and I took her vessels and climbed down to the well, deep inside the ditch of the roadside. I brushed some swimming spiders and insects aside and plunged the vessels into the sparkling water. It was good water, cold and pleasant tasting.

As we started back, I was carrying the bucket and Mayne the tin gallon. I could see she was up to something. She was laughing and chuckling to herself.

'Your soul from the devil, child, do you know what we'll do. We go for Delia's, on the way back, and ambush her in her own kitchen. We'll see how the world is buttering her parsnips these days.'

We left the water vessels at the top of the boreen, marched down through the sunlit yard, and in through the open half door.

'God Bless all here,' said Mayne, moving silently over the stone floor, on her bare feet, to a súgán chair beside the fire.

Delia rose quickly from her own chair at the side of the hearth and held out her arms.

'A hundred thousand welcomes to you, Mayne,' said Delia, 'I haven't laid an eye on you for an age, and you living on my doorstep. How are you, and Jack, and the boys Tadhg and Dan?'

'Wisha, how would they be but as always,' said Mayne, laughing, 'breaking the heart and soul of an old woman. Streeling around the small kitchen that I have with their hands hanging. Falling over each other, and looking for tay ever minute of the day. Wouldn't you think that they could find something to do for themselves, thinning a few turnips or rising to a drill of spuds, instead of depending on the few shillings of the dole. They used to get a few days here, I suppose there'd be nothing to do now at all at all?'

Delia said nothing for a bit. There was a small fire burning, even though it was the middle of summer. She kicked a sod of turf a few times, and then looked up at Mayne as if she was thinking.

'The way it is, Mayne, 'tis a bad time for work. All the crops are down, and my own two lads are half idle, themselves. The only thing now is the turf and that'll take only a few days.'

Mayne shrugged her shoulders in resignation.

'Wouldn't you think that my fellows would put an eye on a woman somewhere, and go out from my skirt. The young have no spunk anymore to take a lep out into the world. Their father was a lazy old hoor that wouldn't go for a bucket of water, but he married me when we had nothing but the clothes on our backs. There was a mad go in him for a woman. 'Twas many a dread and a heartache that same Jack caused me with his leching.

'He was a rale martyr to it. Did I ever tell you, Delia, what the doctor said to me? I was feeling that bad that I thought I'd never see the spring. "Woman," he said to me, "You must have no more children. If you do, it'll be the death of you. You won't come out of it. Your region is worn out from overuse. Go home and tell your husband. Tell him from this out you'll have to sleep in separate beds."

'I went home and I moved a settle bed up into the loft, up a small ladder from the kitchen. By God, said I to myself, I'll be safe now, anyway. And so I was for a period of time.

'I think it was the Pattern Day, a fifteenth of August, and the seven parishes were up the village drinking. I was dead asleep late into the night, when I heard the noise at the ladder. I opened my eyes and there was Jack's cap coming up over the loft floor. I blessed myself and asked the Lord what to do. He gave me no sign or word, and whether he did or not, what could I do anyway. I blessed myself again, and faced the death. 'Twas a funny thing, Delia, but after that it wasn't so bad. And every time it happened, I blessed myself, looked up to heaven and said: Bless me Lord, for I'm facing the death again.'

'The Lord between us and all harm,' said Delia, 'I'm very surprised at what you've just told me. For a long man that was a bit on the scrawny side, you'd never think he'd be such a little stallion.'

'Stallion,' said Mayne. 'May the Good God forgive me my sins. But I'll tell you the truth, Delia, and may the Good Lord be praised. But if it weren't for the weight of the years that are on me, I'd be facing the death many's the time still.'

Delia was silent for a moment or two reflecting on something. Then she said:

'Yerra, Mayne, it wasn't the worst thing entirely that could have happened to you, at least he wasn't gone from you for ever, and it didn't do for you like the doctor said. My own man died at forty-five, before the children were grown, and many's the cold night I spent alone in my bed. It's a hard thing being lonely like that, and often the time I cried myself to morning. Only for Mary my daughter moving into the bed to keep me company, 'tis a hard comfort my life would have been.' Delia picked up the tongs, and straightened a sod in the fire.

'Your soul from the devil, Mayne, enough of this. Have you anything to tell me to raise my heart?'

'Wisha, I have indeed, and plenty. You know the girl Jeannie, that's with the farmer and his wife Mamie, west of Nolan's bog. You know her well, a fine big girl, fair hair and a good roomy look about her. She ran into a bit of trouble the winter before last, in a hayshed down the road from her father's cottage. You remember, out of the goodness of her heart, Mamie took her in and the child was born in the house.'

Delia nodded her head and there was an expectant look on her face.

'Well, Delia, the devil in hell away from us and all belonging to us, about a week or so ago, Jeannie went to the well for water, and Mamie was watching her coming down the yard, with the sun on her side. It's as true as God, she told me this herself. When Jeannie came in she took another close look at her, and I'm blessed to God and His Holy Mother, there it was to be seen. 'Jeannie,' she said, 'tell me that it couldn't be so, that I can't believe the sight of my eyes. Tell me that you're not on the way again.'

'Jeannie answered her bold as you like. "I'm on the way all right, Ma'am, these four months past."

'Jeannie told her the story. She was coming down the cutting, away from the house, a morning in early spring, when this strop of a man came out on top of her, and had his way with her. She said she did not know him from Adam, and had never laid an eye on him before.

''Twas too much. Mamie gave a roar at her. "In the name of all the saints," she said, "Why didn't you screech, and we'd have heard you in the house."

'"Screech," said Jeannie, "why didn't I screech? Tell me this, ma'am, why didn't he screech? Could you tell me that?"'

Mayne screeched out laughing herself, her face wreathed in lines, her blue eyes shining. Delia didn't laugh out. There was an uncomfortable smile on her face, and she kept glancing at me. She needn't have worried too much. I was ten years old, but I was living and observing amidst a considerable variety of moving life, and couldn't but see, with great interest, the ongoing compulsion of all kinds to reproduce themselves, again and again.

Mayne didn't seem to give too much thought to these kinds of sensitivities. Her mind was on her stories and the riddles of life she was telling of.

''Tis the devil entirely, Delia, to understand the ways of people. But it could be that when girls like that get a taste of it, they can't get it out of their heads.'

'Wisha,' said Delia, ''tis a hard life women do have in a place like this. One slip and the whole world is against them, and no place to hide their heads.'

''Tis the truth you are telling, Delia asthore. What are they supposed to do, the young slips of girls, with the long days, and the long nights stretching out ahead of them. Who's to blame them too much if they look for a bit of joy in an old hayshed, or at the side of a dry ditch. But all the same, there's a sight of them at it these times. There's no let up at all. In too many houses, back towards

Boola, and Lyrecrompane, and down on the back road to Listowel, and in the village itself, in too many houses there's a bundle on the way.'

Delia shook her head sadly. ''Tis a wonder the religion and the priests couldn't put a halter on them, and put them on the right road,' she ventured.

'Put them on the right road, is it?' asked Mayne with a laugh of derision. 'Sure the priests have their jaws worn out with their sermonizings about the occasions of sin and the sins of the flesh. But they might as well be singing the Rose of Tralee. That new priest that came in to us from back country, thinks of nothing else. He has the legs worn out of that fox terrier dog that he has, searching in the lanes, and the ditches, with his storm lantern, and thumping the bushes with his blackthorn stick. The parish priest himself said from the altar a couple of Sundays back, that Sodom and Gomorrah couldn't hold a candle to us. He said things were gone that bad that the only thing left was to bring in the Missioners, to put the fear of God into the hearts of all the heathens in the parish. Do you heed me, Delia? He said he'd bring in the Missioners, with their black cloaks and long black dresses.'

'Yerra,' said Delia with a dismissive gesture, 'sure it's about time they paid us a visit. 'Tis six years ago come Easter since they were here last. One wouldn't know whether they do much good although God knows they frightened the daylights out of us at the time. I knew a few of them around the place and they went around with pale faces for a week after they had gone. Some of them, Mayne, were not much good, too full of milk and water. Give them their due, the best of all were the Redemptorists. They were the lads to put the heart crossways on you. They gave the best description of the Wrath of God that you'd hear anywhere, and the picture they gave of hell with the yellow flames, and the brimstone crackling and burning, and the smell of sulphur, and the red-eyed horned devils poking in at you with white hot bars, 'twas enough to keep you awake at night for a week. I give it to them, fellows like them might do some good all right. Although, Mayne, I'd lay my warrant there are ones in this parish, and nothing in hell or anywhere else would turn them.'

'And another thing', said Mayne, 'that I don't too much agree with myself are those scapulars, that they do be selling from the stalls outside the church during the Mission. Everywhere you'd go they'd have them hanging round their necks, inside their shirts. They might be all right for keeping out an evil spirit or two, but they are a fright for collecting nits and young fleas. I declare to God they'd fill the beds and nobody would think of taking them off at night, and nobody would think of washing them, I tell you, and nobody would think of washing them.'

Delia made a little shrug of her shoulders to Mayne's remarks about the scapulars, as if she did not want to talk about it any more. She took up the tongs and nudged a sod of turf in the fire. Mayne was sitting still thinking, and then she brightened again.

''Pon your soul, Delia,' she said, 'I have another bit of news for you. Did you hear what happened back on Johnny Sean John's farm? The sow sickened and the whole litter were gone in two days. Then the sow herself went. 'Twas only a month ago he found a rotten egg, buried on the boundary of his farm. They blame a certain neighbour for the curse, there's a spleen going on there for a long time, 'twas over some right of way, a few feet of boggy land, but you can't say a word. 'Tis best to keep out of it.'

Delia blessed herself. 'You're right, Mayne, these things are better kept far away from you. Although I heard of a small farmer, I won't mention a name, he found a parcel of rotten mate in a dyke beside a boundary ditch, and his whole herd slung. He hadn't a calf that year. I heard of another man, and not a crop would grow one year after he found a clutch of rotten duck-eggs.'

'They say', said Mayne, 'if you were to find the eggs or the mate before they were completely rotten, and you brought the priest in time to say the right prayers, the spell could be turned and nothing would happen.'

'What is it at all,' said Delia, 'and where does the power come from? Some say it's from the devil, and more say it's the fairies.'

'The devil is one thing,' said Mayne, 'but they say the fairies can be very wicked if you get on the wrong side of them. There is one story that long long ago, they came from an enchanted people who vanished into the hills and the ocean after they were attacked from marauders from across the sea. I can't remember the name they had. But there is another story that they come from the country of the dead. They were fallen angels, some of those who took the side of Lucifer when he rebelled against God, and were cast out of heaven for all time. 'Tis said they were on their way to hell when they changed their mind, and they tried to get back into heaven, but the gates were closed against them. Now they are wandering through the underworld, lost souls, trying everything they can to get back again.

'I said they can be wicked. There was a priest out on a sick call one night near midnight, when they came around him and begged him to use his powers for them. When he told them there was no hope, they raised such wailing and lamentation that they could be heard over the whole countryside. Then to punish him, they lamed his horse, and only for the fact that he was carrying the holy oils for anointing the dying in his pocket, they'd have done for him entirely.'

'You can get on the right side of them too,' said Delia, 'by putting unsalted food on the doorstep at certain times of the year, like November's Eve. Or if somebody sneezed, if you said "God Bless Us," like we always do, and threw a scrap on the ground, or spilling a drop of new milk from a cow after calving, 'twould keep bad health away from man or beast.'

'I heard it told', said Mayne, 'of a girl the fairies stole on the night before her wedding. Although someone else said they met her years later in America and she married to a rich man. She was supposed to have run away with a crowd of travelling actors passing through the village. It might have been a made marriage and she was not satisfied. But, that aside, the worst of all is when they steal a baby and leave a changeling in its place. There might be not be much difference except that a quiet baby might suddenly get cross or peevish, for no reason. There was an old man who brought his fiddle to a house. He was looking after his grandchild while the mother was away at a fair. He began to fiddle a tune, when the child lept from the cradle and screamed, 'That's the wrong music.' Then shortly afterwards he took up a red coal on the tongs, to light his pipe, and the child ran screeching out the house. He knew at once it was a fairy child who could only listen to fairy music, and couldn't stand the sight of iron or fire. He shouted after it, "Send back the stolen child," and shortly afterwards, the real child toddled in through the door.'

'The Lord between us and all harm,' Delia said, and after a moment or two of contemplation she got up from the chair. It had gone on long enough. The two old women were tired of the talking. Delia made the tea, and took down the currant cake. I brought Mayne home, back to the cottage, with her spring water, and left her at her little gateway and her sweet-smelling bowers of wild red roses.

I thought of Delia, as I came home the road, as I always thought of her down through the years. Above all the people I knew outside my own family, Delia remained my most special friend, to the end of a very long life.

She died at the home of her daughter Mary, surrounded by her grandchildren, who had come to her to be loved by her, in her own special way.

Mayne lived a long life too, until she passed away in her little cottage, surrounded by her wild roses.

– II –

The 'Girls'

THE 'GIRLS' came and went from the house, with the years. Some stayed only one year, others two years or more. Mostly they came from the foothills of the mountains back west, some from labourers' cottages, some from small farms. All had passed through the national schools and could read and write. They went to Mass and said their prayers, and knew they should be good. They were sent out in their late teens by their struggling mothers and fathers to be housed and fed, and to earn a small stipend by their work in service. Their wage was one pound a month.

Going into service in the house of a doctor, or a publican, or a teacher, or some such like, was a valued achievement. They were sheltered from the rain and wind, and there was a snugness in their lives. Service with a farmer could often be hard and hurtful to their bodies and souls. They struggled outside in the bitter weather, caring for the animals of the farm. They were sometimes treated with disrespect, sometimes cruelty. Other farmers' wives brought them into their families and nurtured them like their own.

Wherever they were, they raised up their eyes and looked long-ingly into the future. They saw visions of a home and a husband and their own children. But in our house, for the time being, they seemed to look little further than the coming Saturday, and mused about boys they had become enamoured of, and the local dance hall that might bring them opportunity.

I saw them at their dreaming. A girl standing by the fire in reverie, the fork, which she had used to probe the boiling turnips, raised to her lips in contemplation. A girl by the big kitchen window, still as a bird on a tree branch, her eyes misty with fanci-ful thought, her hand clasped over her breast, looking out over the flowers at the white gates and the empty road.

Some of them were beautiful and I was in love with them. It was a love that was in the mind and not the body. I loved the beauty of their eyes and their faces, and the curving of their breasts. Sometimes I longed to lay my head on their white breasts, and take their nipples in my lips. Sometimes, by accident, I saw their breasts uncovered. This stirred something small within me. Sometimes I saw their dark secret places. This stirred me too. When this hap-pened there was no guilt on my mind. The stirring was not strong but weak, like the flutter of a wing.

The girls loved me too, and took me in their arms, and kissed my face, in a way that was innocent, without intimacy. At times they examined me when naked in a bath or bathing by the river. These were cursory touches without tarrying, as if to confirm some-thing in their minds, and they passed on to other things.

They never spoke to me about their love troubles, and I was badly tutored in these things around the age of ten. But I knew enough to be aware that after the dances were over, the local hay sheds were their parlours of delight.

Lizzie was the latest girl to come to us. She was small and dark with a pale pensive face and a great desire for the fun of life. My mother said all she thought about was boys. She said to my father: 'It's all hours when she comes in. She's in that hay shed back the road every Saturday night with that fellow from the mountain, and some Sunday nights as well. She's in danger, I'm afraid, she's going for a fall.'

My father passed it off, but there was worry on his face. I knew they spoke to Lizzie about it, as she was in bad humour for a couple of days. But soon she was back to her full self, and shaking the rafters with her singing of love ballads from the ages, when we had the house to ourselves. She sang out:

> Let him go or let him tarry,
> Let him sink or let him swim,
> He does not care for me,
> Nor I don't care for him,
> Let him go and get another,
> That I hope he will enjoy,
> For I'm going to marry a far nicer boy.

Then her song of defiance:

> For I won't be a nun, for I can't be a nun,
> For I am too fond of pleasure and I won't be a nun
> There's an officer on guard, and it's with him I will run,
> I'll get married and be happy, and I won't be a nun.

For Lizzie it was back to the hay shed. She was blossoming like a flower and full of good humour. It was the morning sickness that showed the first signs. Before long my mother spoke to her about it and asked her if she was on the way. At first she denied it with great fervour. 'Honest to God, Missus, honest to God, it's a bad stomach I have, it's a weakness my mother had before me.' But it was all to no avail. A visit to the nurse in the village, and then another to the doctor, and there came confirmation of the awful news. Mary cried all the time and said her mother would have her life. My mother was distraught too, as if she blamed herself.

There were more tears when her mother arrived, and there were secret conferences and much whispering in our small garage, by the house. The cure was marriage, but after long negotiations this could not be arranged. She couldn't go back to her mother's home. The scandal was too great to be endured in public. She and her unborn baby were taken to the Union in Killarney, where Mary joined many other miserable ones until their time came. The Union was the haven that preserved the pretence of respectability, even though the whole parish knew about it before many days had passed.

The father of the child was another poor unfortunate, without too much of life's goods. I heard later that he went to visit her in the Union after the baby was born, and when he saw them there his heart got courage, and he took her away with him to try to make a life together in whatever way they were able.

It was not too long after that the cruel arrow of love smote us again. She was a new girl in the house, beautiful with long red hair, but poor like all the rest. A tall handsome figure of a man, the son of a farmer, brought her down, and although my father visited him more than once, he scoffed at the idea of marriage. More tears were shed and new tragic figures moved around our house. The victim fled the parish, and the baby was born in England where nobody knew of her so-called shame or that of her mother.

The dismissive stance of the errant father, in his failure of paternal obligation, brought quiet anger among the people. They spoke in lowered voices about that thing called fate, and the long reach it had. Some called it the hand of God. After the passage of time, it stretched out and touched the family of the man who had despoiled her. One Christmas Eve a brother of the wayward lover, in a different feud, brought a shotgun to the window of a neighbour's home, and in a fit of wild anger shot the son of the house dead in his chair beside the fire. The people, in their own perverse way, nodded wisely, and blessed themselves. The man who fired the shot was found guilty but insane. After a couple of years he recovered his sanity and walked the roads again like any other man. The people grumbled again, and wondered how this could be so.

*

One lovely girl brought more than one or two young men to our door. They arrived when they knew my mother and father were out, after a good deal of peeping outside. Some came seeking a drink of water, or to redden a Woodbine cigarette with a cinder from the fire. They looked, and made conversation and laughed, and hung around awkwardly. The faces of the shy and inexperienced ones blushed red when their tongues tied up and the words wouldn't come.

The girl knew the purpose of their coming and was uneasy. She knew that the Master's kitchen was no proper place for them to be playing their games. The lovelorn got little reward from their visiting. Those with the mettle to make movements of graceless advance were routed with language of disdain and stinging dismissal. Those who were too bold were stopped with a final threat.

'Clear off out of here with you, or I'll tell the Master. He'll cool the heat in you with his two guns there behind the press.' The bold ones wrinkled their faces and departed.

The shy ones were treated more kindly, and with gentler discouragement. They sank deeper into their discomfort, and gradually moved to the door. After quick words of departure, they sought the coolness of the air outside, and the shelter of the open sky.

One evening, after she had urged a suitor into the night, the lovely girl sighed and looked at me.

'I have my own boy, you know. What would he think if he knew these amadans were coming in and cavorting round like in a dancing parlour, looking for something? I declare to God I've a good mind to tell the Missus. She'd snap their heels for them. But in the end I'd get the blame for enticing them. That's how it always is, I'd get the blame when the day was done.'

There was a day when the lovely girl came to me with her finger pressed to her lips in conspiracy. 'Do you know what's happening?' she said, and there was a look of fear in her eyes.

'Do you know that there is a peeper out the back during the day watching me through the bushes. I seen him three days this week with only his cap and his eyes showing over the briars on the back ditch. I don't know in the world who he is, and he has the fear of God put into me. He might be another Jack the Ripper like that fellow in England long ago.'

Sworn to secrecy, the ten-year-old sleuth got down to work. I found a suitable branch halfway up a well-shrouded pine in the tall trees that surrounded our half acre. There was a good view of the nearby terrain, and there I set up my watch from time to time.

It was a warm Saturday afternoon with a light breeze, a day of great perfection for drying clothes. It was wash day in the house, and the lovely girl was out the back, on the cement pathway, with her bath of hot water and timber washing board.

Her arms were bare to the shoulders and her red hair was bunched high in ribbons at the back of her neck. Her waist was pulled tight with a coloured apron. She was singing to herself, and she moved her body to the melody as she drew the clothes up and down over the corrugations of the timber board. I was in my perch observing, and it struck my mind that here was a scene that might bewitch the heart of man or boy.

I heard the footsteps a good way off, making their way on the long boreen that came down from the village. He came around the last bend walking slowly, a countryman enjoying his place in the greenery and the warm air.

I knew him, and restrained from shouting a greeting. He was a tall lean man with big bones and a fine pale countenance, dressed in worn rough trousers and jacket, and strong boots. An old brown cap was pulled forward on his head, and his face was unshaven.

He came without pausing to the place he was making for, a break in the dense bush foliage at the back of our house, fashioned into a stile with stone steps, to lead into our back garden. Then he threw his body on the small bushes, his elbows on the ditch top, and his hands to the sides of his face shading his eyes. He was well hidden from the house and he remained there looking, looking down the open garden, over the pathway that led to the back of the house. He was very still.

I was very still too on my tree branch. There was a kind of fear inside me at this strange situation. I knew him well. To me he was an old man, although he was not much over forty years of age. He lived in a small farm, with his old mother, and brother and sister, about half a mile away.

They lived in a crumbling thatched house, and had cows and calves and horses. They were good people, but were always struggling with life. The walls of the thatched house were leaking, and the outhouses needed repair. Sick calves were brought into the kitchen, from draughty cabins, to try to preserve their lives. They went through the motions of harvesting their crops, but were always the last to cut their hay. Inevitably the rain caught them, and the hay was of poor quality, from being open to the elements, even after the cocks were made. Their large potato field, diligently planted and sprayed against blight, was still undug into early winter, and part of it was lost. From time to time a malaise set in which prevented them moving forward. They were a kindly people trying to do their best, but then suddenly losing the energy to do any more.

It was as if hope was moving away from them, and they had to try to rouse themselves again and again. The enigma of their lives was such that from time to time I wondered at it, and in my own childish way tried to analyze it.

I had called to their house, on my way to the village for messages. The old woman sat on a súgán chair by the fire, like the figure of an angry statue. Her hair was combed back tight against her head, and her face had many wrinkles and an expression of discontent. Her hands were placed firmly on the lap of her large black apron that reached to the ground as she sat. Every so often she smoothed the black apron with angry hands.

She was civil enough with me and did not seem to resent me as much as other people. After a while she softened a bit and took from her pocket a packet of white lozenges. 'There's a sweet for the Master's son,' she said and held one out in her palm. Then she took up the tongs and poked the fire with great vigour, smiting the sods into flame.

Life had treated the old woman badly. Her husband had died of pneumonia at an early age, leaving her with four teenage children. When they grew up the eldest son went to America. The devils of life were rarely far from her door. Her only daughter bore a child out of wedlock, and her son went a similar road with a girl from back country. There was no marriage, and no children of the house, and this hurt her into anger.

The news of an impending marriage sent her body into motion, beating her hands on her apron, and shrugging her shoulders in disapproval. Small, almost soundless, disparagements came from her lips. She spoke out:

'They don't know the road they're going,' she said, 'but they'll know soon enough. Wait until the heat leaves them, and the weight of life comes down on them, then they'll know. I tell you, then they'll know.' She smote the fire again and sent the sparks about.

The thin figure of her daughter moved round the kitchen table, noisily putting down plates and mugs in preparation for the dinner, and throwing up her hands, and raising her black eyes to heaven for patience.

The tall son with the fine face, who later became enamoured, from a distance, of our lovely girl, sat inside a small window, the *Kerryman* paper raised up in front of him to catch the light, his tin coloured glasses on the end of his nose. He was smirking and rustling the pages. He liked other people, and knew of things that were happening. But he got some small satisfaction by asking me questions that I could not answer, and laughed at my discomfiture.

This was the gentle and eccentric man whose peeping had put the heart crossways in our lovely girl. Life had passed him by without all the comforts of a wife in his bed and children about the house. I knew in my heart he was harmless, and half understood how he might seek some consolation by looking from a distance at a beautiful girl going about her work.

I told her the story and she scoffed. 'That old fool,' she said, 'who'd be afraid of that old fool?' She went to her tasks and her singing.

We told nobody about it, and both of us returned to making our own way through the days, as best we could.

– 12 –

Kerryboy

TOM 'KERRYBOY' was a man I always loved to see coming into Delia's farmyard, when I'd be mooching around there looking for things of a winters evening, with the dark of the night closing in and the light from the fire flickering and jumping through the small panes of the farmhouse window. To me he was a man of learning who could tell you many things, whether it was concerning the proper place and time of year to see the fairies, or an odd ghost, or the kind of name you'd have to have so that a banshee might visit you and ólagon and wail for hours round your house when somebody was going to die.

He also had a sight of knowledge about Santa Claus and the place he had above near the North Pole, and the kind of arrangement he had for stabling his reindeers during the year between Christmases, and the kind of aggravation and tormenting he got on the way down, trying to manoeuvre his way over cracks in the ice and over snowdrifts as high as houses, with maybe a maverick reindeer, as skittish as a young mare ass, pulling this way and that. And the danger all the time that the sleigh would be turned upside down, and all the purtys spilled into the Arctic Ocean, never to be seen again. He also had considerable tutoring on the subject of heavy-weight boxing, and while the fairies and the ghosts were all right for the odd time, it was the stories of the heavyweights that I'd listen to for ever.

He'd come squaring into the farmyard like a small gate, thump-ing his heavy boots on the boreen that came down from the new Board of Works road, like a soldier marching, with his eyes the colour of dark bog deal and his big face smiling under his black hair. I'd have usually carried out one of my many tours of inspec-tion before he arrived.

It was a farmyard of wonder about sixty feet square, with the long low house, whitewashed and slated on one side, and across from it an equally long, low white building, slated as well, where the animals were kept. On each side was a low white wall, and near the dwelling house a large platform of old flagstones, with a trough at one end, filled from a spout of old pipe with water that came down all the way along narrow dykes, over three farms, from a spring well in James Mary Leahy's land below the village.

It was a place of enchantment for me, especially in the gloaming of a winter's evening, with the dark and mysterious shadows deep-ening everywhere and even the crows gone silent in their roost on the stand of big ash trees beside the house; and high up on the perches their dark bodies looking like small black smudges against the darkening sky, and their heads buried under their tight wrapped wings for warmth against the cold of the coming night.

Despite the direst of warnings from Delia about falling over machinery or into holes in the dark, and a slight tightening of fear on my neck and face, I'd go my way. Down by the side of the ever mounting dunghill outside the cabins, along the dirty and wet flagstone walkway, my first visit to the fat pig in the stye at the far end of the building. Into the rising smell as I approached and the quiet grunting, then through the opened door the dim large body in the darkness stretched out on straw on the only dry place at the far end of the wet and dirty floor.

I salute him quietly. 'Ah, so there you are. As sure as God I think you'll be ready by Christmas, although you don't know it, you poor crathur. You don't know it either but Charlie O'Donoghue will come down from behind the village with his long knife, and sit over there by the trough, edging it on a stone, for half an hour. And Mossie and Sean and Tadhg Doody will bring along ropes and stretch you on the high flagstones with your legs in the air. And they'll tie your legs at the four corners and bring them together in one big knot. And Tadhg Doody will look at Charlie and say, "Have you got the edge?" And Charlie will eye Tadhg for a minute and swish the long knife under his nose. And Mossie will look up with crossness on his face and say, "Keep your minds on the job, men." And Delia and Mary will come with their big silver pan, and settle themselves beside your head, with their skirts pulled up so they can spread their legs under them. Then Charlie will hold up his knife like a doctor and make a nice shallow cut from your chest to your jaw. And then the knife will go in and Tadhg Doody will shout, "Have you got the heart?" And they'll turn your head and the blood will flow like a river into the pan with not a drop on the ground. And your screeching will be heard in the next townland. And after that there'll be puddings and pork steak for half the parish.'

Next, the cow cabins and the air warm from the bodies and the breathing of the twenty cows, each with its head secured in kindly timber stalls, and the sweet smell of the part-eaten hay pervading everywhere. And such happiness and ease and gentle sounds that I would wish to lie down beside them and drift into sleep for that night, and for ever after.

Beside the cow cabins the stables where my two great giants of horses lived. One brown and one black with the coats grown thick to protect the great muscled bodies and limbs from the winter cold. A turning of two heads and a gentle snicker of recognition and contentment, and a return to their nuzzling of warm hay in their half-filled feeding manger. I salute them too. 'You, my black beauty of a mare with strength that no horse can match, in bringing hinds of hay over boggy ground from the meadows, or in pulling a ton or more of black turf up Mall Hill. And you, my glistening roan with your long clean limbs that could outrun a fleet deer in the hunt, or a greyhound itself in full chase of a March hare.'

On an evening such as this I had just left the stable, and was proceeding on my round to the duckhouse, the henhouse, and the sow with the litter of bonhams, when Tom 'Kerryboy' came stamping into the yard in his usual high humour. For some time past my head had been filled with the thoughts of the great heavyweights, and Kerryboy had promised to tell me some stories about them. It was the mid-thirties and I was about seven years old, and Joe Louis was just coming on the scene in America. I had heard a bit about John L. Sullivan, from the bare-knuckle days, and Gentleman Jim Corbett; Jack Johnson, the black fighter; the giant Jess Williard; Jack Dempsey, the 'Manassa Mauler'; Georges Carpentier, the 'Orchid Kid' from France; Luis Firpo, 'The Wild Bull of the Pampas'; Gene Tunney of New York; the big Italian, Primo Carnera; Jack Sharkey, Max Baer, and the German, Max Schmeling, and a few others.

'Tonight's the night,' said Kerryboy with a good thump on my back. 'There's a bit of frost, is it cold enough for you, is there a good fire, and are the lads in? Don't answer, for tonight, come hell or high water, I'm going to tell you the story of John L. Sullivan, the best fighter that was ever put on the face of this earth.'

He pulled the half door open and we faced into the kitchen. It was a very large room, with a big dresser on the right-hand side, filled with plates and cups and crockery of all kinds. On the left a long wide table, and directly across the room from the dresser the whole side of the room, from wall to wall, was filled by a huge fireplace, surrounded now along both corners and out across the front, by up to a dozen súgán chairs, on which Mossie and Sean, Delia and Mary, and the usual ramblers were seated. There was not a sign of a paraffin lamp, or a candle either, and the only light came from the burning turf sods and the blazing end of a big ash branch stretching about nine feet out into the room. As the flames leaped, the shadows leaped with them round the walls. On the wide black iron crane at the back of the fireplace hung the big black kettle, pulled well up from the fire, until the time came round to make the tea. The kitchen was cosy enough, and it was a good place and a good night for a story.

'God Bless all here,' said Kerryboy as we went in. 'A hundred thousand welcomes to you,' said Delia, the woman of the house, in Irish. 'You brought a bit of the frost with you I see, and you brought the rambler in as well,' said she, looking at me. 'I did,' said Kerryboy, 'but I must say, musha, you're a hard woman to please. If 'twas rain I brought, you might have some cause of complaint. Howsome ever, I'm here now and tonight is the night of John L. Sullivan.' He settled himself in and was contemplating for a bit, like a man taking a pinch of sugar to clear his throat, before singing a song.

'Before you start,' said Paddy Murphy, Delia's brother, 'I have a conundrum for you. Who was the first English heavyweight boxing champion?'

'Conundrum, my arse, in pardon to you,' said Kerryboy. 'I wouldn't waste my time talking about British heavyweights. As a matter of fact, I never knew of one of them who could knock snow off a rope, even with a thaw setting in. In fact, the only British heavyweights who were ever any good were Irishmen, if you know what I mean. The only Englishman who gave anything to boxing was Lord Queensberry, who brought in the Queensberry rules. And what did he go and do then but bring down our own poor Oscar Wilde, and he at the height of his fame, over some trouble he had with a son of his called Boozie, or something like that.'

Interruptions stifled, Kerryboy continued. 'Of course you know John L. was "Kerryman",' and he paused for effect.

'Pon my sowl,' said Tadhg Doody, a noted workman with farmers, 'I never knew that.'

'Yes indeed,' said Kerryboy, 'his father's name was Michael O'Sullivan, and he came from behind there in Tralee. He was a small man and they say he was as agile as a young goat. He was always looking for fight, and they say when he was aroused, he was as savage as a wild cat. He had a big heart, and would never give in. He worked for a building man, carrying a hod, and there was not a man in Tralee, that was any good, that he didn't bate. His mother was a woman from Athlone. I don't know what brought her down to this part of the country, but it was a good day she came anyway.

'It was in the breeding, of course. His grandfather, another Kerry O'Sullivan, was a noted wrestler. He whipped many a man in the county, and it was said there was not a man in Kerry that would face him with a shillelagh, at a fair or any other place.

'John L. himself was like his father and grandfather. You wouldn't believe how small and light he was for a heavyweight fighter. He stood at five feet ten and a half inches tall, and fighting fit, he weighed no more than thirteen and a half stone. How could a man, so small and light, destroy the giants of the world over so many years? Nobody could understand it.

'They said it was the fury that was in him. They said the speed and ferocity of his attack amazed the American spectators, bringing down good fighters of fifteen, sixteen and seventeen stones. He was a savage the likes of whom they had never seen before. Outside the ring he was as touchy as a young bull at mating time. But they loved him with a love never given to a fighter before or since.

'You might have heard of a fellow called Nat Fleischer who was supposed to have known everything about boxers. He said that no boxer, not Dempsey or anybody else, had thrown such a spell on the followers of boxing around the world. They thought he was a kind of god, the greatest fighter in the world, whether with bare knuckles, or later, with padded gloves.'

Kerryboy paused for a bit and looked around. There was silence with everybody thinking. Jim Dennis, a first cousin of my father, had his head down. Tadhg Doody's big jaw had dropped a little and there was a slight mist in his eyes. Murphy drew a kick at the end of the big ash branch and sent sparks flying round the fire.

'Jaysus Krisht,' said Doody, shaking himself. 'How could a small man do that.'

Kerryboy got himself ready and began again. 'John L. was born near Boston in the year of 1858. That was eleven years after the Famine here at home, and nine years before the '67 Fenian Rising. I do not know was it in the month of October or November, I'll look it up again, but howsome ever, let it pass. By the by, Lawrence was his second name. The L stood for Lawrence. By the time he was twenty-one there was not a man in Boston that could stand up to him. It was a man who called himself a Professor, Professor Mike Donovan, another Irishman, who really found him. Donovan was world middleweight champion, and they said he was one of the most scientific boxers you could find then. He came to Boston to give an exhibition like. John L. was put in against him and drove Donovan all over the place and nearly knocked him out.

'But like then as now, New York was the place to be. They brought John L. to New York and his first important fight was held on a barge, anchored in the Hudson River, against a man called John Flood, nicknamed 'The Bull's Head Terrier'. They fought with skin-tight gloves that they sometimes used at the time, 750 dollars to the winner, 250 dollars to the loser. The fight lasted sixteen minutes. Flood's sponge was thrown in in the ninth round. John L. was twenty-three, and after that things moved fast.

'There was a boxer at that time called Jim Ryan, who was born in Thurles, County Tipperary, and emigrated to America. He won the American heavyweight title in his first professional fight, against a man called Joe Goss. After eighty-six rounds Goss couldn't come out of his corner.

'Be that as it may, they decided to give John L. his chance against him for the championship, in Mississippi City, with bare knuckles, for a purse of 2500 dollars a side. The year was 1882, and John L. was twenty-four years old.

'The fight was under what they called London Prize Rules, before Queensberry came in. You could muscle a man all over the ring, wrestle him and throw him to the ground as well as throwing punches. There was fierce excitement and things happened that had never happened before. Newspapers hired writers of books and dramas and even clergymen to tell what they saw. Even Oscar Wilde, that I was telling you about, was hired to write about it for an English paper, he was giving lectures in America at the time.

'It all ended up in a bottle of smoke. Ryan was no match for him. John L. went after him like a tiger, smashing him and throwing him around. After eight rounds Ryan could hardly move. But brave enough he came out for the ninth round, John L. battered him and knocked him out.

'The next few years was the biggest circus that American boxing had ever seen. John L. went on a tour of America and offered 1000 dollars to anyone who could stay four rounds with him. He bate them all.

'I won't trouble you with too much more about him, except for a few things that must be said. I told you what I thought of the

English heavyweights, but there was one of them I must mention, as he gave John L. a bit of trouble. It was like the gunfighting in the Wild West. Everybody who had an opinion of himself was out to bring down the top gunslinger. This Englishman was called Charlie Mitchell, the best they could produce, and he came to America, as he said, "to knock out Mr Sullivan". He got his first chance in 1883 in New York and John L. knocked him out in the third round. It was now 1888 and John L. was after a great campaign of six years, with no defeats. Mitchell got his second chance, and of all places they fixed the fight for a place called Chantilly in France, even though prizefighting was illegal there at the time.

'There was a hoor of weather round before the fight. The ring was set up at the back of a stable, and they had to fight with mud up to their ankles, after a full day and a half of heavy rain. 'Twas the greatest mishmash of a fight that was ever seen, slipping and falling all over the place. After thirty-nine rounds the seconds decided to halt the fight and call it a draw. Which was maybe as well, for the police moved in just afterwards, and John L. spent the night in a cell with a bandage round his head. Mitchell was put in a cell as well. He was the worst of the two of them, and had to be given a sight of care from a doctor. The French jailer took away their silk handkerchiefs, for fear they might hang themselves. Both of them were crying, from vexation.'

Kerryboy stopped talking and began feeling around in his pockets until he produced a piece of dirty cloth that acted as a handkerchief, and he blew his nose, and then gave a bit of a rub to his face. It was clear the others were not tired of it yet, and it was clear too that the last scene had affected them somewhat. They looked around at each other and made a few comments. Doody stood up and took a big white mug from the dresser, and got a drink of spring water from a white enamel bucket, on the table just inside the door. Paddy Murphy used his foot again to move the big ash branch a bit farther into the fire, and threw on a few sods of black turf from an old basket at the side of the hearth. After a while they all settled themselves again in the súgán chairs. There was no move as yet to light the paraffin oil lamp, although Delia had it hanging on the wall on a nail behind her, full to the brim, and with the two wicks trimmed.

Kerryboy was ready again and began to talk. 'There are only three more things I'll tell you about John L. One other fight, and then the last one, and a bit in between. John L. was furious about the draw with Mitchell. I think he felt it demeaned him or something, as if word might get out that he was not up to it any more, although he was still only thirty-one years of age, after seven years on the go at the top. There was a heavyweight called Jake Kilrain, who had put a lot of good men down, and who had fought the Champion of England, a man called Jem Smith, for 106 rounds in 1887. The fight had to be stopped because the darkness came down on them, and they called it a draw. John L. had been refusing to fight him for some time. He was like that if he got a thing into his head, and another thing about him he would never fight a black man, whatever the reason was. After France they were taunting him about Kilrain, and he had to agree to a match. It was 1889, and the fight was fixed for a place in Mississippi, bare knuckles, for a purse of 10,000 dollars, under the London Prize Ring rules.

'It was a blazing hot day, and the twenty-four-foot ring was pitched in the open, on green turf, beside a stand of trees. The spectators crowded in on all sides round the ring, many of them holding the top of the two strands of ropes in their hands. Further out around the ringside were a party of twenty Mississippi Rangers, armed with Winchester rifles. John L. objected, but was told they were necessary to keep the peace. Kilrain gave as good as he got for the first half of the fight, showing great spirit and gall, but John L. eventually bested him, and Kilrain's seconds had to throw in the sponge in the seventy-fifth round, and lifting him off the ground took him away to recover. It was now that John L. claimed the heavyweight championship of the world, as Kilrain had already drawn with Jem Smith, the English champion. And ever after that it was the Queensberry rules, with gloves on, that were used in the heavyweight championships.

'And now comes the hard bit for me to tell, a story that would sadden your heart. John L. spent the next three years strolling up and down America, and even Australia. He even took up acting on the stage, and spent his time carousing long into the nights, with stage people and hangers on. He never put on a pair of gloves except to take part in four-round, or so, exhibition bouts, and the strength sapped out of his lungs and heart, and his body thickened with the stones of weight he put on. The end of his great ten-year reign was coming near. He signed up to meet a young, good-looking Californian boy, called Jim Corbett, nicknamed the "Californian Dandy", or "Gentleman Jim". The fight was fixed for the autumn of 1892 at New Orleans, with five-ounce gloves, for a purse of 25,000 dollars and a stake of 20,000 dollars.'

Kerryboy dropped his head as though in meditation. The others sat quite still, a look of anxiety and expectation on their faces. Kerryboy straightened his back, and raised his head, and in quiet and dejected tones slowly continued the story. 'John L. wouldn't do any proper class of training, of course. He went through the motions of daily exercises, but no proper road work, or hard sparring, no nothing. He acted as if he was going in for an exhibition bout. He had no respect for Corbett, he thought he was going to take him like all the others. But he wasn't.

'John L. went in rushing around like a bull in a china shop, swinging himself around with missed punches, and falling over the ropes. He thought he could land the big right, like always. But Corbett danced around him, and after twenty rounds had him nearly cut to pieces. In the twenty-first, Corbett went in and knocked him out. It said in the book that the John L. defeat rocked the sporting kingdom to its foundations.

'The book said men of his generation did not regard it as a mere misfortune. It was a catastrophe. The Battle of New Orleans was to them what Waterloo was to the people of France. And he was only thirty-four years old. He had thirty-five fights, won sixteen by knockouts, drew three times, won fifteen others, and was only beaten and knocked out once, by Gentleman Jim Corbett. Why, oh why, did it have to happen then? you well might ask. He had so much more to offer if he held himself right.'

Kerryboy stopped talking and bowed his head as if in contemplation, or prayer. The others moved restlessly, a look of sorrow on their faces. Paddy Murphy and Tadhg Doody turned their heads away. They were both crying.

Kerryboy raised his head suddenly and said in a voice of renewed energy. 'Listen to me I'll finish it. John L. had nothing to do except go on with his playacting and stage work. He was still very popular with the people. Wherever he appeared, the theatre was full. They say he had earned nearly a million dollars in this kind of work, by the time he retired from it in 1915, twenty-three years after the Corbett fight.

'There was one thing I could never understand. In his last years, what did he do? He became a teetotaller, and went round the country giving lectures against alcohol. John L. Sullivan, who'd ever believe it? He died in his own state, Massachusetts, in 1918, the year the Great War ended. He was sixty years of age, too young for a great man to die. The Lord have mercy on this soul.'

After a short time, Delia jumped up to break the sadness. She made for the oil lamp. 'Enough of this gloom,' she said. 'I'll light the lamp, and we'll all have a drop of tay, before ye go home.'

- 13 -

Uncle Jack

MY UNCLE JACK gave me a fair share of tormenting in my young life, but he was also my great protector. He was my mother's brother, the youngest child in a family of three boys and four girls, born in a small cottage at the edge of the town of Abbeyfeale on the road to Limerick city. Their father, my grandfather, was a small man called Maurice, a gardener who spent his whole life tending the flowers and the trees and cutting the grass at the local Convent of Mercy about four hundred yards down the road. I never knew him as a child except to see him in a small old photograph, standing up with what looked like a fair bit of pride beside an ass's car with a small donkey between the shafts. He was wearing a cap, with a good moustache and a fine pipe with a nice curled stem in his mouth. He looked very old to me, and as he fell out of the same car not too long afterwards and died from his injuries, I never knew too much about him one way or the other. He was no more than seventy years of age.

Jack, being by far the youngest, was reared a pet and was a reluctant scholar. His big sisters dragged him down the road to infants class in the convent school winter and summer, until he grew out of his childish ways. He was then sentenced to about ten years, to complete his education in the local national school in Church Street. It was shortly after the start of the First World War at the time, and Jack carried out his own small wars with the teachers who were trying to make a man of him. It was said he could have done well at the lessons if he set his mind to it, and he had a great attachment to simple lyric poetry, and balladry, which he carried with him to the end of his days.

The trouble was he had a mind of his own, with a kind of a pride in himself, and he disputed this, that and everything with great adroitness and dexterity, with anybody who was unfortunate enough to become entangled with him. This was not an endearing quality with hard-pressed teachers, especially as Jack was not so much interested in the subject at hand, but in winning the argument. The result of this was that, as they said, he never succeeded in making anything of himself, unlike his sister, my mother. She, with the help of the nuns, went on to become a Junior Assistant Mistress, a kind of national school teacher, and taught for all her working life at Knockbrack school, a mile across the valley below Knocknagoshel village.

He became, as he said himself, a jack of all trades, and became adept enough at fairly skilful work, such as painting, fixing roofs, fixing gates, or even at times doing small extensions to cowhouses or pigs' cabins. These things he spent his life doing, around the town of Abbeyfeale and places farther out.

One of the most endearing and successful things of his life was the way he looked after his mother, my grandmother Máire. She came of farming stock, a mile or two up the hills from Abbeyfeale.

There is little doubt that for a long time he harboured the idea that one day he would get married. After many unsuccessful attempts, he finally found somebody whom he described as a lovely girl, and courted her for a year or two or more.

He was a person of great liveliness, always making fun and telling stories, putting conundrums and questions to me that he knew well I could not work out or give any kind of an answer to. Then he'd throw back his head and cackle and wheeze at my discomfiture. Then all this changed, and I knew there was something wrong. Something changed all right: his lovely girl, after a lot of thinking and heartache, had decided she could not marry him, and would become a nun. I don't think he ever blamed her, for despite the kind of fecklessness that was in him, he had faith in the ultimate wisdom of the Almighty.

After this he devoted himself more and more to his mother. She was a small round woman with a round cheerful face, friendly dark eyes and a slightly mottled pink complexion. She had small red veins appearing close to the surface of the skin, caused by weathering of sun and rain. Her air of friendliness and good cheer made her loved by all. Not that she had anything particularly pressing to be thankful about, after a life of struggle and deprivation, doing her best with very little, trying to look after the needs of a large family. Many of them had to sail for America before they reached the age of twenty, hardly ever to be seen again. But like her son Jack, for her, everything was in the hands of God.

I visited her a good few times, although I never slept in the small cottage, set back a little from the road, with the edges of its small windows entwined with brambles of wild red roses. To me it was a fairy house, with a blazing fire on the hearth and a kettle always singing, and the walls covered with holy pictures and icons, and the tiny red lamp winking at me from over the fireplace under a picture of the Sacred Heart. The pleasing sounds of funmaking, and Jack outdoing himself, with riddles, songs and cantations. Then out into the long grass at the back of the house, small legs dragging and stumbling over clusters of dock leaves and wild shrubbery. Down the long narrow half acre towards the small river, and the well with the sweet water that never ran dry. The neighbours with their buckets and gallons and kettles, collecting the pipe overflow onto the small side road because it was the best to be found anywhere. There was the pride of Grandma, showing me her grey white goat, shimmying in small jumps at our approach and threatening our lives, with sloped horns held down, pretending to be ready for the attack.

'Don't mind her,' Grandma said. 'She's putting on a show for you. Look at the eye of her looking for attention. That's what she's doing now. But never mind, she's a great milker. Always drink goat's milk if you can get it. They say it's great for the chest, and for clearing the blood.'

Then back into the house, with the kettle boiled, and the small table with its white cloth, and the sweet cakes, and the brown scones, and the yellow butter, and the red red apples. In that small house, with its fairytale grandma, was the sweetest of sweet life, full of wonder and heart-warming love, soon to be gone forever.

It was on a Saturday morning in the summertime that she came to visit our house. She came in a kindly lift, in the motor car of Tom the Post, bringing the mail from Abbeyfeale to Knocknagoshel. It was early, around eight o'clock, when I awakened in my small bed to the sound of a pebble clinking off the front window. A few seconds' wait, and then it came again. A mad dash to the window and a look down on the broad shining face.

A shriek about to break out. 'Shush, you'll wake the Master.' For she knew as well as I did that Jim the Master was a bad sleeper who might have been awake for half the night, and woe betide anybody who wakened him without good reason. Three pairs of feet tiptoeing down the stairs, the big white door eased open, and Grandma, with her big bag of sweets, smuggled into the parlour that was well away from the parents' bedroom, at the other side of the house.

For an hour or more, the whispering and giggling and munching, with varying degrees of guilt and fear. We all knew it was close to being a mortal sin to eat sweets before breakfast. Then all the house roused up, and all the inmates were set free to roll and rollick and chatter as they pleased. The fire blazed, the pan sizzled, and the lime water was dished out from the big gallon in the scullery to make our bones strong and our teeth white and healthy. The time passed in happiness, until Tom the Post's car was hailed down again, at three o'clock, outside the big white gate, and Grandma was wheeled back to her small rose cottage four miles down the road.

The day came at last when Jack's love for his mother was put to its greatest test. Grandma took a stroke which left her impaired and lacking in strength. They said it was high blood pressure, and her heart was weak. Day after day, week after week, Jack tended her as a nurse would, in the small room, inside the door at the front of the house. Cups of tea, and spooning the soup into her mouth, and rushing for the capsule to put under her tongue when the attacks came. One day the capsule did not work and Grandma died, the only Grandma I ever knew.

*

I knew of Jack first when I was about three years old, and he was twenty. Jack made our house his second home. In his own simple way, and in tune with the culture and thinking of the time, he was very proud of my mother. Lack of money and opportunity had meant that she was the only member of the family who had got anything near to a profession, through her own cleverness and cultivation of the nuns. She had tried hard to put him on the road to further education, suggesting this way and that way, that course and this, but to no avail. Sometimes he'd promise or even start something, but his heart was not in it, and it faded away.

Jack travelled from his mother's cottage, on the outskirts of Abbeyfeale town, to our house, a half mile east of Knocknagoshel, on a fine Raleigh bicycle. It had its own pump, spring-held on one of the frame uprights, and a strong steel carrier over the back wheel, on which Jack ferried his box of tools. But the thing that fascinated me more than any other was the bicycle lamp, which he carried on a bracket between the handlebars over the front wheel.

Now Jack, perhaps because he was not over-endowed with the trappings of wealth, had a special regard for all of his own possessions. Whether it was his saw, or his hammer, or his wood plane, or his screwdrivers, or his Raleigh bicycle, all were treated with great care and respect, and were regularly cleaned and serviced. Woe betide anybody who took any of his things without his permission. He said everybody had a special way of handling his own tools, and anybody else using them put a kind of turn, or mark, on them that he did not like at all.

I knew this well, but for a long time I had my eye on his bicycle lamp, the like of which I had never seen before. I could understand a lighted candle, inside the big protected lamps of a horse and trap, or a storm lamp, with a wick, fuelled by paraffin oil, but I couldn't make out a lamp made to light with a handful of small grey pellets and a half cup of water.

He called it his carbide lamp, made to work only for special people, like himself. But it wasn't too long before I saw him unscrewing the top, putting a handful of the pellets inside, and then with great care pouring in the water. A few minutes and he opened the round glass front, loosened a control screw at the side, cracked a red safety match, and a small hissing light appeared as if by magic.

'It's my magic,' he said, 'and don't the devil pinch you to put your hand next or near it.'

But the devil did pinch me, and it wasn't very long before I had it in my hands, and away with it down the fields. How it worked was what concerned me, so I sat in the shade of a ditch a couple of fields away and took it apart. I surmised that the most important part was probably a small nozzle inside the lamp, from which the light came. A few rocks from side to side, and a few twists, and the nozzle broke off in my hands.

He caught me, of course, sneaking back, and my bottom was sore for a full hour afterwards. I swore to myself that if ever I did anything on him like that again, I'd put myself in a position that he couldn't get his hands on me. I carried out that promise more or less successfully. I remember that I also had the effrontery to tell him, from a safe distance, that when I grew up I'd be a boxer, and I'd give him the greatest whaling he ever got in his whole life. It was a threat, that, fortunately, fate never decided should be carried out.

Jack was forever doing odd jobs around the house, mostly in the area of painting and decorating. Jack had most positive ideas as to how particular tasks should be carried out, like any self-respecting tradesman should. This was more or less respected by my mother, who reserved her decisive opinions for the more artistic side of the operation. Like the paint that should be used, whether it was to be a light blue, or a deeper blue, or green, or any other colour that took her fancy; whether it should have a silk or matt finish; or whether the wallpaper should be a light biscuit, with a red rose pattern, or pale gold with scattered violets. Unfortunately, Jack too had some fairly strong convictions in the field of art, which he argued with his usual passion.

The preparations for each particular job would go on for a considerable time, often for a full day. Jack would be dispatched on his bicycle to Abbeyfeale for samples, which he would duly deliver, rather ungraciously, some hours later. It was then that the real warfare began, when the samples were displayed, held up for inspection, and debated, with increasing heat. Both sides stuck firmly to their guns, until my mother, in final exasperation, played her trump card.

'Jack,' she would say with emphatic fury, 'I'll tell you what you'll do now. You get up on your bicycle, and go down home to Abbeyfeale, and tomorrow, and the day after, and the day after that again, and next week, and the week after, in fact never again let me see light nor sight of you in this house. Now, what have you to say to that?'

The end was predictable. Jack, from his position of weakness, inevitably had to retreat, but always in a smokescreen of mutterings of the future recrimination and sorrow that would result, from her very bad taste. My father rarely got involved in these disagreements. He held himself detached from unimportant matters of this kind. He had other things on his mind, as he, perhaps, tracked, in his imagination the shoals of salmon and white trout making their way up the river Feale, from the mouth of Cashen, at Ballybunion, or counted the days to the opening of the grouse or pheasant shooting.

The skirmishing between Jack and my mother would continue to the end of whatever was being done. Jack's final product was fairly acceptable, but he had little patience with the finer aspects of his work. He had little taste for the drawing of fine lines with small brushes, and he rarely made little more than a genuflection towards the careful spreading of newspapers, or old sheets, to protect floor coverings or the surfaces of my mother's precious furniture.

The recriminations that Jack had predicted usually came to pass, but they had more to do with his own slapdash approach to his work than with my mother's original choices. Yet I can never remember a time when peace was not finally restored, and diplomatic relations resumed, at least, for a period.

*

Jack was closely involved in the biggest and most discommoding, and, for me, the most dramatic event, that ever occurred in our household. The house was built in the late twenties when I was about six months old, from plans my father got from the English newspaper the *Daily Mail*. A competition had been held in the paper, and the plans that won second prize caught my father's eye, and he wrote away for them. After six years or so, mother eventually persuaded my father that, prize-winning or not, the room we called the parlour, and the bedroom above it, were too small, and a decision was taken to set it right.

This involved taking down the whole gable wall at the right side of the house, along with a garage built up against it. One fine summer, Jack and a small builder called Dannyboy, from outside Abbeyfeale, were chosen to undertake this fairly formidable job. Whether my father was in full possession of his senses at the time I do not know; but in any case the venture provided us all with a stimulating mixture of apprehension, and fun, at times to the point of hilarity, for several months of that year.

This was something my father had to get strongly involved in, if we were to have a house over our heads at all for the coming winter. He appointed himself captain of the gang of three, with Dannyboy a kind of corporal, and Jack a disgruntled private. My father had a good head on his shoulders, and had been closely involved in the building of the original house. He thought it prudent to write down demolition instructions on paper, and the sequence in which they were to proceed.

The trouble was that a good captain should always be on the job, but my father had to be absent at his schoolteaching each day, from roughly nine in the morning to after three in the afternoon – a long time for imaginative and daring demolition men to work without supervision. They began as planned, at the peak of the right-hand gable, taking out the first stones and then proceeding to row and row of the heavy-hewn stone, until a yawning gap was made from front to back wall. I'll never forget the look of consternation on my father's face when we came home from school that day and he had made his first inspection of the work.

'Jesus Christ, Jack, that bedroom floor will come down,' my father cried. 'Get off that bloody wall, and get some propping for the parlour ceiling, or you'll have none of it left.'

The trouble was that the two adventurers, too lazy or otherwise to bring down the heavy stones as they took them out, had thought of another plan. As soon as the hole was big enough they lowered the stones, on ropes, on to the floor of bedroom, hundredweight after hundredweight of stone, with no propping underneath.

The red-faced knights propped the ceiling, and disaster was avoided. They took down the stones. My father laughed wryly. 'Well that beats Banagher,' he said, 'and Banagher beats the devil.'

For those several weeks my mind was never too close to what was happening in the classroom of Knockbrack school. It was with Dannyboy and Jack, diligently pulling down the only home I knew, in the hope that when all was done the house would be six feet longer. At three o'clock, when the school day was over, I was away with my sack of books down Kate Walshe's boreen, across the wooden footbridge over Oweveg, up the sloping bogland, and across the fields to the house, to see what new wonders the handymen had wrought. I was first on the scene by a good quarter hour, and gave it close inspection, with plenty of comment, and criticisms, and predictions on what my father would say when he arrived. The workmen, particularly my Uncle Jack, got little pleasure from my dissertation.

'Run on now, my small man,' Jack would say, from his high position, 'and put your head in a book, where you might learn something that might be of some use to you, instead of giving under us with your smartness. By God, you must think you're a little schoolmaster in the making. We must get a pair of glasses for you, to perch up on your nose, and you'll look the part for sure, and your father might get a job for you over in Knockbrack.'

Then he cackled with delight at the point he had scored, for I recognized it was fairly close to the bone. But I took it without rancour, for I was fond of Jack and I knew, in my heart and soul, that he'd swim the hole of Lyre for me if the need ever arose.

Anyway, verbal setbacks of this nature never deterred me from my mission of derision, in Jack's case. I knew he would always rise to the bait. Experience had taught me the need of placing myself in a strategic position, close to an escape route, when I engaged in activity of this kind. This I usually did.

It wasn't too long before a new opportunity arose for me to practice my odious art. Everybody had left the house for some reason or other, and Dannyboy had gone with my father for supplies. Jack was working from a vantage point, very high up, on some sort of makeshift scaffolding, and I was hovering around, as usual, looking for sport. My attention was drawn to a scraping sound, and then a fairly hefty crash. I came upon a scene to raise the heart of any goboy. The long ladder was stretched, nice and neatly, on the ground, and Jack was marooned, in a most satisfactory way, on his high perch, like a jackdaw on top of a chimney, but without the benefit of wings.

He began to give me fairly precise instructions, about throwing up a rope, and tying one end to the last rung of the ladder, for hauling up. The devil was at me again, and try as I might I could do nothing. I could say nothing either, but just stood there, looking up at him, with a smile on my face.

He pleaded with me, cajoled, promised me a sixpence, a ride on his bicycle, and various other enticements, but the devil said no, he would not relent.

Jack decided to resort to another gambit. He threatened me with every evil he could call down on me. The wrath of my father and mother, the drubbing he himself would administer to me, and when all these failed, the sin that would be on my soul if he fell down and got killed. He finally resorted to an assault on my fore-bears.

'Do you know what you are? You are the greatest little caffler that I ever came across. You must have a bad drop in you, from somewhere. One thing I can tell you, it didn't come from my side of the family, wherever it came from.'

'Caffler' was a word I hadn't heard before, and I gave some thought to what aspects of evil character it denoted. Then I saw my chance.

'I have you now, Jackeen Keane. I'll tell my father what you said about the bad blood in his family. He'll be right and pleased about that, I tell you.'

Jack was now really incensed. He roared at me: 'I'm coming down to get you.'

Throwing caution away, he eased himself over the edge of the scaffolding and began to make his way down a long pole, towards the ground.

There was no option but retreat, at high speed. The next hour was spent lying in a drill in a garden of early potatoes, where the thick leaves provided me with good cover. Jack's search for me was fruitless. I could hear his muttered imprecations about me for a good while, until he gave up and returned to his work. I knew what I did was wrong but there was nothing I could do about it now except blame the devil, who was always hanging around, every-where.

But none of this skirmishing took away from the joy I felt in the company of Dannyboy and Jack, particularly in evenings, when they came in to wash up after the day. They stripped to the waists in the scullery, with pans of water and sunlight soap, they rubbed themselves clean. The smell of washed cement was new to me. They delighted my heart with their singing of songs of all kinds. The images they raised in my mind with 'Bantry Bay':

As I'm sitting all alone in the gloaming,
The shadows of the past draw near,
And I see the loving faces around me,
That used to glad the old brown pier,
Some are gone upon the last loved homing,
Some are left, but they are old and grey,
And they're waiting for the tide in the gloaming,
To take them on the great highway,
To that land of rest unending,
All peacefully from Bantry Bay.

I could see them as clearly as if they were out in front of me, the fisher girls with baskets swinging, running down the old stone way, the piper with his sweet notes tuning, all to gladden the heart of a boy.

A big canvas had to be found to wrap around the gable of the house, which was now an empty space with exposed floorboards of the parlour and bedroom. Protection had to be provided from rain and any cold winds that might be blowing from the north. We still had to sleep in that room, myself and Eileen and Mary. There was a bed there also for Jack, if he could be enticed to stay the night, so that he could be at work early, and not make Dannyboy wait an hour or more in the morning for his bicycle to appear at the front gate.

Jack had a deep suspicion of any place that had the possibility of being a little damp, or of any draughts that might give him cramps or muscle pains. He'd accept no assurances about the airing of sheets or blankets, and would have to make a thorough inspection before he'd be satisfied. Even with that, 'twas many the night I woke up at midnight to find Jack dressing himself, declaring that the bed was damp, and he'd depart on his bicycle to his warmer home in Abbeyfeale. Knowledge, next morning, of his leaving would bring the cryptic, and unvaried, remark from my father: 'That Jack is a great blackguard.'

The work on the house went ahead and by mid-summer the extension was completed, after many and varied minor disputes involving matters such as the ratios of sand and cement, the nailing of slates, and the boarding of floors and ceilings.

Much of the reason that Jack got himself into trouble was that he rarely gave sufficient thought to something to be done, before he did it. He'd yank a nail out of a wall, bringing plaster with him, when what was required was gentle easing. Anything he went near, whether pottery, jars, flowerpots, or even mirrors, were in constant danger of fracture from impulsive belts of his hammer. He was a great practitioner of the hammer, seeming to believe that if he hit anything often enough and hard enough, he could solve any problem or remove any obstacle. He was invariably right, apart from involving a number of nearby innocent objects as well, which also went flying.

Years before the house episodes, Jack was left at home one Saturday, minding the children, while my mother and father went to town. Eileen, my elder sister, was about four, and was well enough behaved. I spent a lot of my time strapped to a dual-purpose vehicle, to protect me from the results of fearsome sallies I was liable to make in all directions. The vehicle, when let down, ran on four wheels like a small motor car, with me inside. When raised, it became a kind of two-storey structure, with me seated on a kind of chair on top, and an attached feeding tray in place in front. Long and fearsome was the howling that came from that chair, and fierce and menacing was the smashing on the table with any object I might have in my hand, spoon or otherwise.

These manifestations of ferocity came, perhaps a little surprisingly, from a two-year-old round-faced boy with blue eyes and a head of golden curls. Knowledge of events I describe came from later intelligence reports, as my memory cells had not begun to operate with any degree of effectiveness at that stage. Reports have it that these golden curls were as precious to my mother as her own flaxen hair. Perhaps even more so, as it was unlikely that wherever she went, other women would gather round oohing and aahing at her crown of glory. And in any case, being my mother, she could take almost as much merit from my hair as she could from her own.

What drove Jack to the unpardonable crime he committed that day will, perhaps, never be known. It is possible he had some prescience of the misery I would inflict on him in later years, and decided to make one pre-emptive strike for justice. Perhaps it was an impulsive reaction to the baleful presence, and tornado of sound, that issued on him from my direction. Whatever the reason, he took my mother's scissors from its hook on the side of the bookpress and removed every single golden curl from my head.

For what ensued, when my mother returned, I have to depend on perhaps somewhat unreliable family tradition. Suffice to say that Jack suffered the greatest laceration ever inflicted with the power of the tongue by a sister on a brother. He was then banned from the house for life, a sentence which, I was told, lasted a full month.

- 14 -

Uncle Jack Takes Up the Gun

JACK, despite his lack of success with formal book learning, had a fairly good knowledge of Irish history and kept a close eye on the political events of the day. Like most of the people round Knocknagoshel and Abbeyfeale, he had a deep suspicion of anything English, and inevitably saw the Republican side in the Civil War as the one that had fought for the greatest good of the country. In other words he was a de Valera man, and was as gleeful as the majority of others around when Dev came to power in the early thirties. He had little time for General Eoin O'Duffy and his political force the 'Blueshirts'. The name itself was uttered with distaste in people's conversations and brought fierce angry looks to their faces.

They didn't believe that the Blueshirts were seeking to protect freedom of speech for the pro-Treaty party, and were fearful they might stage a sudden coup. As well as that there was a strong venom in their hearts over what they saw as giving over the North of Ireland to Britain. So when de Valera set up the 'Volunteers', as a sort of counter force to both the Blueshirts and the IRA, Jack and a few other young men around the place, including Delia's son Sean, hit for the recruiting office and joined up.

When Jack come home on his first leave, he paraded himself around with pride, displaying his tidy green uniform and beret, and his shining brown shoes and long gaiters. Although he was below medium height, he looked a good enough soldier, with his narrow waist and broad proud shoulders. He also had a short brown cane, with a silver tip, which he swung with great dexterity when walking out.

My father had some doubts about Jack's willingness to operate under discipline, as he was well aware of his slightly anarchic tendencies and his inclination to take a bit too much pride in his own thinking.

'Remember Jack, the main thing you have to do is obey orders. Don't argue with the corporals, or the sergeants, or anybody above you, even if you know you are right. Disobeying orders in tight situations can put lives in danger, including your own. Remember this, and remember it well, one bad officer is better than two good ones.'

Whether Jack took any notice of my father's lecturing, I do not know. But I wasn't aware, anyway, of any trouble arising. My mother said he was clever enough, and might be promoted up to sergeant if he carried himself right. I even heard her talking to my father of trying to get him into an officer's course, but nothing ever came of it.

Jack was in the Volunteers for a couple of years, and then one day he came home, bag and baggage, and never went back. He kept away from our house for a good while, but as always happens, things ironed out, and he was back in our lives again. Nobody told me, at the time, what had happened, but I knew there was some sort of cloud in the sky. It was years later, when we were talking one day, that he decided it was time to tell me the story.

'The Army was nothing as bad as I thought it might be. It was hard at times, but I got used to it. The first three months were the worst. At first, there was only drilling in the square, you know, left turn, right turn, about turn, and things like that. Then we went on to arms drill, how to handle a rifle, learning the movements of sloping arms, presenting arms and ordering arms, things like standing at ease, and standing easy.

'I liked going on the firing range. A thing called Application, to see if you could get five bullets into a twelve-inch square, or an eight-inch, or a four-inch. Some of them could put the five into an area as big as half a crown, some of them went through the same hole. I was a fairly good shot, and could do an eight-inch group, no bother. Then we went on to hand grenades, bombing they called it. Pulling the pin, counting to four, and then throwing them overhand at a target, from behind cover.

'There was a lot of physical exercise, body exercises in the square, short and long runs, and marching nearly every day with full kit, a couple of stone or more in weight, with your rifle as well. Some of them couldn't take it and had to go sick. When the weather was hot, there was hardly a day but someone would keel over in a faint. I had no trouble like that, I was very fit, I did a lot of running. Some of the fat fellows lost a stone weight in the first month, and another stone the second month.

'The forced marches sorted them out. Up to twenty miles, in full kit, at nearly four miles an hour, on a hot day. If they didn't keep their boots and socks right, the leather would cut through at the heels, and blood would flow from the blisters at times.

'I met all sorts in my time, small and big. There were some great men, strong men as well. I met men that could lift you up by the belt and hold you over their heads in their two hands. Then they'd take down one hand, and you'd still be up there. I met some very nice men, and others who were great blackguards. I learned one thing early. When the blackguards start, say nothing, but go for them. They might be twice as big as you, but go for them anyway, and keep at it, no matter what. 'Twas a funny thing, but once they knew you'd go for them every time, they kept away from you after that.

'You'd want to watch out for the stripes. If you hit a private, they'd cover it up. But if you hit a man with stripes, you'd likely be in trouble. I got a week in the glasshouse once for downing a sergeant. He was a real bastard, and the officers knew it. I could have got more, I could have got my walking papers then, but I didn't.

'This time I'm telling you about, we were up in the Midlands on some kind of manoeuvres. The commanding officer and his staff had taken over a big house, as headquarters. 'Twas a house, like, of the landed gentry, with a big avenue of tall trees leading up to it. I had done all kinds of stints, and this night, I was on sentry duty.

'I remember things were very edgy at that time. Some time before that, the IRA had got away with every bullet and bomb the Army had in the Magazine Fort in the Phoenix Park in Dublin. They made a raid one night, disarmed the guards, and took the whole shebang, in four or five lorries. They got it all back in a couple of days, but there was great shame among the top boys and we were all warned to keep our eyes skinned, and watch out for everything.

'I was well used to sentry work, and knew all the rules well. Anyone coming, you gave him the command to halt, and after that told him to advance to be recognized, and so on. If he disobeyed your order three times, you were authorized to open fire, if you thought you should.

'I was no more nervous than anybody else. There were three other sentries at points round the camp. I remember it was a lovely moonlit night, and the moon was throwing shadows from trees that were growing around. I'd say I might have been a bit uneasy, as there was cover everywhere for any attackers. I was walking up and down to keep warm, ten or twelve paces one way, and then back again, and watching everything.

'The top of the long avenue of trees was no more than fifty yards away from me. Whatever look I gave down the avenue, I saw this shadow making its way up towards me, under the shade of one side. It looked like a man, going very slow, and stopping now and then, and looking around. This could be it, I said to myself, and took a half cover, and presented my rifle.

'"Halt," I called to him, but he took no notice. "Halt," I called again, but he ignored it again. "Halt," I called a third time, but he kept coming. I raised my rifle and opened fire, and down he dropped. Then I heard the sound of running feet behind me, and I saw men coming at me. They were on top of me in a couple of seconds, but I kept pulling the trigger, as they had me on the ground, until they disarmed me. How was I to know they were the six men from the guardhouse, turning out? I thought they were the IRA. How was I to know that the man on the avenue was the butler from the big house coming home drunk from the local pub? He was all right, anyway. The bullet just creased his skull, and knocked him out.

'They arrested me and put me under guard for the night, and the next day I was taken under escort to St Bricin's Military Hospital, in Dublin. Do you know where they put me? In the Psychiatric Section. The Psychiatric Section, I ask you, and I as sane as any one of them. And for what, I ask you? For carrying out faithfully the orders they had given me.'

Jack was still angry at this injustice after all the years. Then he laughed and said: 'There's one thing I'll have to admit, although I didn't admit it at the time. Things might have worked out better if I hadn't opened fire on the guardhouse men.'

There, at last, was the full story, as told by the man himself, on why he was discharged from the Volunteers, on the grounds of medical unfitness. I often wondered if he was really medically unfit, or just a bit too quick on the trigger, as he had been, in many other ways, throughout his life. In fact, I'd bet more than a penny that there were few people I knew who were as sound in the head as my Uncle Jack was, in his own way.

Jack went on reminiscing about army life, and then looked at me with a half smiling, half cunning look in his eyes.

'I'll tell you another story, that's a bit dangerous. It's a story I told to only one other man, and you'll know why, as I go along. 'Twas only a couple of months before they threw me out, and not far from the place I was talking about just now. We were all out under canvas, bivvies we called the tents. The weather was good, and this Saturday the whole battalion were given pass-outs for the day, to the local town. This fellow and I decided we would not go, and called in sick. We had something else on our minds.

'Thing were nice and quiet, and very slack around the place, by way of guard. We manoeuvred around until we saw our chance, and we broke into the armoury and stole two fine Webley revolvers, and about fifty rounds of ammunition. We wrapped the guns in oil-cloths and put the whole lot into a biscuit box and secured it well. We went out the road a couple of miles, in civvies, until we found a grand dry bridge. We took out plenty of stones, under the arch, and put the box nice and deep inside. We sealed it all up again, and camouflaged it well, with mud and old mortar, until you wouldn't know it had ever been touched. We took the spare stones well down river and dumped them there.

'Why I did it, I do not know. I always had this interest in guns, and as for the other fellow, he never cared if he never saw a gun. But we did it, that's the kind we were.

'Many's the time I thought about those two Webleys, and wondered what had befallen them. This Sunday, it must have been ten years later, after twelve o'clock Mass, I was coming up the street to the cottage when a thought struck me. I turned on my heel and walked down to the house of a certain man, called Tom. I knew he had a car for hire, and I might do a deal.

'He was in, and after a few minutes whispering, the deal was done. If the guns were still there, I'd give him a Webley and twenty-five rounds as payment for the drive. 'Twas most of a hundred miles, but we found the bridge, and there was the biscuit tin, and the two guns and ammunition inside it, dry as pepper.

'That Webley was the bane of my life for many years after that. My heart was scalded looking for safe places to hide it, up in the loft, under the floorboards, and in dry ditches here and there round the cottage.

'I'll tell you how it ended. This particular time, I had it hidden under a small heap of gravel that I had in the yard. The oilcloth it was wrapped in had become dirty and muddy, and you'd think it was a bit of old timber if you saw it lying there. I met a farmer from up the hill, who saw the gravel. He was repairing a wall, and I promised him a few stone of it, if he came down for it the following Saturday.

'I declare to God, but when I came back from town the following day, Thursday, there was the farmer's servant boy, in my back yard, with half the gravel loaded into the butt of a donkey car. One look, and I knew that my Webley was in the car as well. I did what I had to do.

'"Unload that gravel," I said to him and be off home with yourself.'

'"But you told the boss," he said.

'"But nothing," I said to him. "I told him Saturday, and today is Thursday."

'He had nothing to do but heel out the gravel, and my heart was crossways for fear he'd see the package. But he didn't. It slid out, nice and aisy, like a small bit of dirty bogdeal. And do you know what the servant boy said when he was out on the road, and well away from me?

'"Jackeen Keane," he said, "it's true what the people say, there's a mad drop in you, somewhere." Then he belted the ass, and galloped away up to Mountmahon.

'That was the end of it, as far as I was concerned. I could see myself, clearer than ever before, behind bars in Limerick Jail. That very night, I took down the gun and ammunition to a good friend of mine, a local T.D. whose name you know, and he said not to worry, he'd take care of it for me, and that's what he did.'

But though the Webley was gone, Jack had two other pieces of artillery to comfort him. One was a double-barrelled shotgun, and the other a shotgun with half of the barrel sawn off. These he kept in a loft, reached by a small stairway, rising up by the wall of the kitchen. He was living alone in his cottage, and felt vaguely vulnerable.

Jack was sitting by the fire in his kitchen, in the small hours of a Monday morning, listening to the roistering of young people passing up the road from a Sunday dance in town. A tap at the door revealed two young men and a woman, all strangers, who, politely enough, asked for a drink of water. As Jack turned to get it, they came in and took over the kitchen. They demanded he make tea, and give them bread and butter. Jack held his nerve, filled the kettle, and put it on the crane hook over the open fire. He said he had to go to the loft, to get a packet of tea. Up the stairs, and two cartridges went into the sawn off shotgun. He came out on the tiny landing and looked down at them. They were sitting round the fire, their backs to him, laughing and joking, and congratulating themselves on their success.

Jack said not a word. He fired both barrels through an opening between them, directly into the burning fire and ashes. The result was astounding. The fire disintegrated, the room filled with ash and smoke and flying particles of turf. The three invaders, untouched by lead, exploded outwards, by the power of their own leg muscles, their faces blacked like mammy-singing minstrels, their bodies hurtling here and there against table, stairs, and wall, a small howling disarrayed rabble who eventually found the sanctuary of the door and the street, and vanished into the dark with speed and confusion.

'That decided me,' said Jack. 'Ever after that, I never answered the door at night, unless I knew who was there, and I never went to bed without a loaded shotgun, clipped upright to the wall, beside the head of my bed. I'd put out my hand, during the night, and give it a couple of pats. It gave me a kind of comfort to have it there.'

After a particularly bad breaking in and beating in the home of and old man, a small shopkeeper selling mostly sweets and cigarettes, a couple of miles away, Jack intensified his fortification. He bored a small hole in the wall of his scullery, big enough to take the barrels of his shotgun, to put himself in a position to repel any raiders from the rear. He also had a phone placed outside his bed, and another extension under hanging coats outside his kitchen, in case he had to retreat suddenly under a frontal assault. From then on also, he was never without a fair-sized dog, with a good loud bark, to alert him of any impending danger.

All this might seem to indicate a man in some sort of unhealthy state. That was far from being the case. For him, this was merely a well planned practical response to the situation as he found it. He remained his old laughing, joking self, full of his old conundrums and riddles and recitations of his latest rhymes and small poems. He took in tired travellers, and put them up for the night in an old caravan at the side of the house that my father had made and bestowed on him when its time on the road was over. He made coffee, and tea, and gave good conversation to hundreds of passing hikers, and he had a special folder full of letters of appreciation, and cards and photographs, sent by young people from many foreign places.

Jack had another peculiar characteristic, that one would more usually find in magpies or jackdaws. He had an active desire to accumulate things that might be on the point of being discarded. An old caravan, an old tent, a pair of shoes, a hammer, a chisel, an old sieve, a lump of iron, or any kind of old bric-à-brac that might catch his eye. He had a particular fondness for old overcoats, and sometimes for coats that were not so old.

He had my mother plagued with questions like: 'Don't you think the Master should throw away that old grey coat he has, a man in his position?'

Inevitably, the opposition was worn down and Jack got what he wanted. In the end he had a fine assortment of old overcoats from our house, and from the houses of nieces and nephews far away from Abbeyfeale.

Jack was rarely without a pony of some kind, down in his half acre at the back of the cottage. It wouldn't do him at all to have a fairly normal animal, like other people. His ponies always seemed afflicted in some way or other, like a white eye or an inclination to bite or buck under the car.

It was Jack and his afflicted pony, with car and butt, and rail, that introduced me to one of the small wonders of my young life, a day in the bog cutting turf with a team of men. This pony was best of them all. She was a mare, light brown in colour, of muscular build and good clean formation. She was made special by the fact that she had four or five acts in her repertory, which she played out whenever the mood took her. She usually behaved like a lamb when the tackling went on. She even stood quietly enough when the shafts came down over the straddle and the traces were tied to the collar. But at the first clack-clack of the tongue for her to move, came the explosion.

The first thing she did was lash the car with her hind legs, and with an intensity that was wondrous to behold. Jack had guarded against this by nailing a large bag filled with hay to the bottom front of the car. Her next act was to buck and rear, lifting her two front legs off the ground and pawing around with a wild look in her eyes. When this was overcome, by a mixture of force and soothing calls, she desisted and went into her final aria. She threw her head around, snorting and screaming, in a tone that was varied, and high in pitch, and when she was tired of this, as a final insult, she urinated in splashes of derision. All this concluded, she settled down and carried out whatever task was set her, with reasonable dedication, apart from an odd snort or attempted bite on anyone close to her. After we saw her for the first time, somebody christened her 'The Pissing Jennet'. It was the name by which we called her ever after, not very much to the amusement of my Uncle Jack.

– 15 –

By the Tinkers' Fire

I HAD a soft place in my heart for the tinkers that came among us from time to time. We all called them tinkers then, and never gave a thought to the name. Nor did it appear to worry them very much, if at all – maybe because they knew they had an honourable trade as tinsmiths going back for countless years, repairing kettles and pans and fashioning the big silver gallons and the small tin drinking mugs that we called three-halfpenny saucepans.

There was a traditional belief too that they carried the good blood of the ancient Irish, from families of Irish chieftains, maybe, driven from their lands by the invaders. Hence the good names of the O'Briens, the O'Connors and others.

Generally, they fitted easily and with little suspicion into the lives of the people. They fed their skewbald and piebald ponies in what we called God's Long Acre, the lush grass that grew along the richly silted roadsides. At times trouble broke out, when they opened gates and drove their small herd into fields without permission from the farmer. Or something missing from a farmyard, after a visit, brought down some fine curses on their heads. Hardly a day passed but a tinkerwoman would come to the door, her big loose bag tied in front of her, a shawl on her shoulders, and a few children close to her skirts.

'The blessings of God on you, Missus, and on everybody in this house,' she'd say, looking hopefully at my mother.

'What are you carrying today, Mary, is it flour or meal, or milk or tea?'

'Wisha, it's flour I'm carrying in the bag, and may Mary herself, look down on you from heaven, from the side of Our Lord.'

'You're in great form with the prayers today, Mary,' said my mother, saucering the white flour into the open bag.

'Its a small cost that a prayer, or a good wish, ever took out of anybody's pocket, and maybe they might do some good in the end.'

The tinkerwoman looked at my mother again. 'Would the goodness be in your heart, Missus, to give me a small scrape of butter for the childer? Nothing went past their mouths all day but dry bread. They say it's a bad thing to have the dry bread lying in their stomachs with nothing to ease it down.'

The butter having been got, the tinkerwoman went on again. 'As sure as God is my judge, Missus, it breaks the heart in me to say more, but St Joseph himself would pray for you above if you could find a draineen of milk for me for the youngest child. Do you see him there with two bow legs on him. They say it's want of milk to put the goodness into his bones, that's the cause of it. The doctor in Rathkeale said it was how it was the rickets he had, God between us and all harm.'

A shadow of impatience passed over my mother's face, but she moved into the scullery and washed an empty whiskey bottle. She filled it from a half-gallon jar of milk, and brought it to the tinkerwoman. She took it gratefully and laid it in a small basket she carried on her arm, beside a small paper parcel of homemade butter and an assortment of other goods she had gathered at other households.

'It was the hand of God that directed me to this house today, Missus. May you or yours never want for anything, in this life or in the next, and in whatever place you find yourself. Amen to all that.'

Having delivered herself of her few final words, the tinker-woman turned, and she and her children were making their way through the front door, when an urgent thought seemed to strike her and she turned round to face me and my mother again. Her face had a look of fear and agitation.

'You know, Missus, I am in the way of having my life taken, if I go back to the camp now the way I am. The last thing himself said to me this morning was not to come back, in danger of my life, without a bit of baccy for his pipe. How could I get baccy for him or anybody else, or even a few Woodbines for myself, without as much as a halfpenny in the bottom of my purse? You wouldn't have a few coppers to spare, Missus, so that I can pay a little visit to the shop and I passing, and I'll be on my knees in your honour, every day for ever more?'

I knew by the look on her face that my mother had come to the end of her tether.

'Well now, Mary,' said she, 'I think you have done enough praying for one day. I have no coppers about me today for baccy or Woodbine. Maybe the next time you call you'll have better luck. Be on your way like a good woman. Hurry on out the gate and be good enough to close it behind you, as I have a cross dog at the back of the house, and I wouldn't want him going out on the road and taking a bite out of anybody that might be passing.'

The tinker woman took the farewell words in good part, and with a final blessing she and her children departed.

It was around this time that I first saw a convoy of tinker families moving in their ponies and cars along the mile-long dusty road that led north from our house, down to the Metal Bridge. There were three carts together, with old men and old women, brown and wrinkled, young men and young women with flaming hair and red faces. There were children of all ages in front of and behind and beside the gay caravan, tripping along and squabbling in a light-hearted way. The young men had places of privilege, sitting in the front of the cars, guiding the ponies, their caps at jaunty angles over the sunburned faces. The old men and old women were sitting in the centre of the cars, like old bundles in human shape.

The younger women were walking behind, some of them with young babies in their shawls, striding along, and I wondered what custom made it so, that they were not in the cars as well. I wondered too why they did not get on the backs of the spare ponies that ambled along on ropes tied at the back.

They looked so colourful, and free from care, that I longed for the kind of freedom that they had and wished that I could be with them, travelling the white roads of the country. Only the romance of their lives could I see. I did not know that most of them might reach little over fifty years, and that in all their sweet living there was pain and hardship too.

At about that time a book came into the house that enhanced for me, even further, the romantic longing for the wandering life. It was called *Lavengro*, by an English writer called George Borrow. He was born of Celtic stock in Norfolk just after 1800, and as a young boy travelled with his father, a Militia man, all over southern England, Scotland and even Ireland, trying to keep England and her possessions safe from possible invasion by Napoleon.

When he was seven or eight years old he met an old snake-catcher and herbalist, who gave him a viper which had its fangs removed. It was this snake that opened the way for him, one day, when he came upon a band of gypsies, who were hostile until he pulled the snake from inside his coat. Now he was treated with reverence, as a sap-engro (snake-catcher), by the band, including a young lad, Jasper, who became his friend for life.

Borrow learned the Romany dialect and became ensnared forever into the gypsy life. He tried his hand at writing in London, but at the age of twenty-three took himself off to travelling the roads of southern England, in a pony and cart and tinker's gear that he bought from a tinker called Slingsby for a sum of £5 10s. Slingsby gave up because he was threatened by a bully called the 'Blazing Tinman', or the 'Flaming Tinman,' who wanted to be king of the road himself.

Borrow came to Staffordshire and installed himself in a deep hollow, 'in the midst of a wide field, with shelfing sides overgrown with trees and bushes, and a steep winding path leading down into its depths'. It was called Mumper's dingle, and it was here that the Flaming Tinman caught up with him, and recognized the pony and cart of his old enemy, Slingsby.

A fight was inevitable, the Flaming Tinman being egged on by one of his two women companions, a stout and vulgar-looking woman, aged about forty. The second of the fighting tinker's companions was a beautiful flaxen-haired girl of eighteen, Isobel Berners, known as Belle, who called for and got fair play for Borrow in the heroic battle of fisticuffs that followed.

When Borrow appeared well beaten, having been knocked down six times, Belle called out to him to use his right hand, which she called the 'Long Melford'.

Borrow described what happened next:

'On the man came again, and aimed a blow which would doubtless have ended the battle, if he had not slipped, and hit a tree with terrific force. Before the Tinman could recover I collected all my strength and struck him below the ear, and then fell to the ground, completely exhausted, and as it so happened, the blow that I struck the tinker, beneath the ear, was a right-handed blow. "Hurray for the Long Melford," I heard Belle exclaim.'

That was the end of what one critic has called the finest description of a fight in English literature. The Tinman went off with his moll, swearing horribly, and Belle remained with Borrow, sitting beside the fire in the dingle.

It was an unfruitful association. Borrow, a strange man by any standard, treated the young girl with little sensitivity, and instead of making love to her tried to teach her to say 'I love you, I love you' in Armenian. Bella broke down crying, and he then suggested they could go off to America and live together in some forest.

The next day, Borrow had arranged to go to a fair with Jasper Petulengro, his sap-engro friend. Borrow describes the parting:

'On arriving at the extremity of the plain, I looked towards the dingle. Isobel Berners stood at the mouth, the beams of the early morning sun shone full on her noble face and figure. I waved my hand towards her. She slowly lifted up her right arm. I turned away, and I never saw Isobel Berners again.'

This parting nearly broke my heart too, and I lived every turn and twist Borrow made on the roads of England, and every quaint adventure that he had. What could match his meeting, while they were both young men, with Jasper Petulengro, the flamboyant gypsy, with his gay waistcoat and mighty whip of whalebone with a brass knob?

'What is your opinion of death?' Jasper Borrow asked, as he sat down beside him.

'My opinion of death, brother. When a man dies he is cast into the earth, and his wife and child sorrow over him. If he has neither wife and child, then his father and mother, I suppose; and if he is quite alone in the world, then he is cast into the earth, and there is an end to the matter.'

'And do you think that is the end of a man?'

'That's the end of him, brother, and more's the pity.'

'Why do you say so?'

'Life is sweet, brother.'

'Do you think so?'

'Think so! There's night and day brother, both sweet things; sun, moon, and stars, brother, all sweet things; there's likewise the wind on the heath. Life is very sweet, brother; who would wish to die?'

Borrow's book enflamed my heart with love and regard for the tinkers. I saw them as being made of the same stuff, and having the same traits, as the gypsies of his time. The tinkers even spoke a dialect of their own, among themselves, which I regretted not having tried to learn. Few real gypsies, with their dark hair and eyes and brown faces, ever passed our way in their colourful, hooped caravans. Those that did looked out at me, I thought, with no friendship in their demeanour. They passed through as wanderers, two or three times, in all the time I was there, with no time to talk about anything they might have on their minds.

Every late spring and early summer I waited each day for the tinkers to come. The families camped in a small enclave of ground, in off the road, and surrounded by high hedges of whitethorn and blackthorn trees, a couple of hundred yards below our house. It was a natural platform of ground, slightly raised, with protection for their ponies and cars, and small rounded sleeping camps. Best of all, on one side, close to a ditch, was a small spring well, with sweet water that overflowed down to the roadside dyke.

I ran to them in joy when I heard the sounds of the work of encampment, coming from what I always thought of as their own small dingle. Usually they were the O'Briens or the Coffeys. What confusion and noise they made in that small space. Shouting at the ponies, and at each other, as they backed the cars in, screaming at the children to get out of the way. The children roistering around, rollicking and rolling on the ground, as if they were on the first day of their holidays. In a way they were, for they stayed in their new home a week or two, and even more.

The ponies were taken out from between the shafts, and the harness taken off. All were fettered with soft ropes to make sure they would not wander off too far. They were driven on to the roadsides to feed. Then the long hazel rods were pulled out, along with the covering for the camps – four rods to a camp, looped over in half circles and driven into the ground; three camps in all, side by side. Then the canvas covers went on, and were held down with heavy stones at the sides and at the back. The fronts were left open for access. Then the carts were further unloaded of bedding and groundsheets, sheets of tin and tinsmiths' hammers, lengths of blackthorn and rough ashplants for treating, buckets and tin-cans and other accoutrements and contrivances.

When the unloading was finished, the three cars were backed again to the windward side of the camps, with their front shafts in the air to ward off, with their bodies, any heavy winds or rain the weather might bring.

The elder children soon came with dry wood, from foraging under nearby ash and other trees, and in a short time a fire was blazing and a kettle full of spring water was hung from a black iron rod, driven slantways into the ground with a crook at the other end.

The evening twilight was around us as we sat by the wood fire, drinking tea and eating white oven bread with a light sprinkling of sugar. There were three old people, one man and two old women. There were two married couples and eight children of various ages, from young teenagers, down to a baby of about one. Each of the two younger women were going to have another baby.

They were talking away between themselves, and of the sixteen miles they had made that day, from the town of Listowel, and the luck they had on the road. Old man O'Brien, a big heavy man with a florid face, seemed to be the dominant man among them, and he talked most of the time. He was badly lame on his left leg, and he nodded forward heavily, every time he took a step on it. As he sat by the fire, he kept moving it around as if it was causing him discomfort. The women hardly spoke at all, but one of them leaned over from time to time to poke the fire or to throw on a bit of fresh wood.

''Pon my sowl,' said the old man, 'as I says before, we had worse days than today. I always says, and I'll compound it again, they're a dacent oul' lot down there, in the town of Abbeyfeale. They have no argifying about a few oul coppers, when they'd see with their eyes that a man was in need of it. And no oul' preaching to you, like would be inclined to come from people I could name, in other places, for fear a man might spend it on an odd pint of porter.'

Nobody said anything to contradict him, but a glance passed between two of the younger women. I sensed that things were not too good between some of them, and that porter might be the reason.

The old man decided to take the bull by the horns. He turned to me and continued: 'Do you know, young lad, I'll tell you something maybe they never larned you, in the school you go to over there across the river. Knockbrack, they call it, isn't it? I know your father well, as dacent a man as trod leather, and a topper to strokeall a salmon, they tell me. What I was saying was that porter did no man harm, if he didn't go over the top of the ditch entirely. I drank as much porter as any man, but there are only two times that come to my mind that it did me, what you could call, a world of harm.

'Do you see that mark I have on my face?' He turned his face to the firelight to show me a long red scar on his face, that ran from his right temple to his lower jaw.

'That happened in a fight in Puck Fair. Done by a Cork tinker, who was mad drunk. A scheming Cork tinker that did it, with a broken pint glass, when I had my head turned. I always admitted it, that it was one of the times that I was too drunk to mind myself. I was three days in hospital with twenty stitches. But I'll tell you the truth, and I'll tell you no more. That was the last time the Cork tinker was seen in Kerry, for O'Brien was known as a fighting man through the length and breadth of the land.'

The old man finished, and had a look around to see what effect he might have caused with the great story he had to tell. But devil a word anybody said, except another couple of looks between the women that were hard to put a name on, though I had a feeling they didn't figure on the right side of agreeing with him, in any case. The two young married men had their hands before their faces to hide smirking looks. The old man decided to continue his tale.

'I'll tell about the second time, that I was talking about, that a sight of drink brung me to the edge of misfortune. We had travelled hard enough to make a fair in Cahirciveen. I had set it before me, do you know, to try and get rid of two oul' piebald ponies that I didn't think too much of. One of them had a spavin, on his right back, that was as big as a small duck egg. But that was ne'er a bother on me, as a good plaster of the right mud, a plaster of the right kind of white clay, do you know, well rubbed in and dried out, on the bad leg, and on the good one as well, and these smart country boyos couldn't tell one leg from the other.'

The old woman stirred herself, and made a deep sound in her throat, that stopped the old man.

'Your soul to a thousand devils, asthore, how do you intend to make it right to translate a story of devilment of this kind, to this young lad, and maybe for it to go raging around the country ahead of us wherever we might pull in the cars?'

The old man turned his head in surprise at the intervention, and kept looking at her.

'Wisha, will you hould your whist, you poor old angishore, and how could it come to you to know anything about the angling and cavorting we do have to bring upon us, and us trying to gather a few honest coppers in trying to sell a good honest piebald against another one that might have a small wakeness in one of his hind legs? Was it Moll Bell, or was it yourself, that told us of the bag of spuds you bought for good money, with a few good ones on the top, and all the ones under that were so small, that 'twould bring shame on you to feed them to a chicken, if you had one?

'And not to spake of anything else, do you think that this young garsoon could be thinking of doing nary a thing better, than to be giving spread to lies and stories about us, for the divarsion of the barony?'

The old man drew himself together in a gesture of aloofness and disdain.

'I'll finish the tale, as I set out to tell it. Where was I now? Yes, yes, to sell the piebalds. Well to tell nothing but the truth, I had a good enough feed of porter, that night, and again the following morning. I thought I was feeling all right, but that can be the worst of all. I was in the middle of the fair, meeting this fella and that, and having a haggle here and a haggle there.

'Once, or twice, we were on the verge of putting a spit on the hand, but some cross-grained hoor would waltz in, pernickitting, and finding fault, and no good was done. I thought the day was going from me, when along comes this small farmer, from behind Castleisland, and we were close enough to doing the bizniss. I was explaining a special fathure of one of the ponies, and was stooping down to give a rub to a leg muscle, to make my point, when I declare to Jaysus but I got this stagger in my head. I put back my hand to save myself, and where did I land it but between the hind legs of an entire horse that had been prancing around the fair all day looking for mares. In one second, he was up in the sky, in a big rear, and where did he come down, with one of his iron shoes, but right across the toes of my left leg. My big toe was gone, and half the one next to it. I did no more trading that day, but off to hospital in Tralee for three weeks, and I was three months more with the crutches, and for six more with the stick.

'The worst of it all was the name they stuck on me, when I threw away the stick. Tip Toe, they called me. To call a man Tip Toe, that could fight his way out of a yardfull of tinkers, or any other kind of men either. But the devil a thing I could do, but swallow my spit and think of what I'd do to them in a bright night, with my back to a good wall, and a blackthorn stick or a good ashplant itself in my hand. But one thing I larnt, and 'twas a good thing to do. I larnt that time clanes everything up, and after a bit, I didn't mind too much about the name. As God is my judge, I would laugh to myself, sometimes, thinking about it, and I still would, if things weren't coming too hard on me.'

The story brought no comment, but everybody looking into the dying red embers of the fire. The old woman roused herself again.

'By all the Glories, the dark of the night is down upon us. Will ye put the childer to bed, or the wet of the dew will get into their bones.'

They did as she said, and they all disappeared into the black holes of camp fronts, like the children of the Pied Piper going over the edge of a cliff.

I was shaking myself to depart when Tip Toe called over to me. 'Toughen a while, for a small while, there's another small story I'll call out, about a tinker man and his wife, that were out for to make their fortune.'

The big ones all settled down again, and Tip Toe went on:

''Twas a story I heard once from a man on my travels, I think he must have got it out of a book, himself, as I never heard it related otherwise. It went like this. A tinker man and his wife were sitting one evening, to take their rest, after a hard day's begging. A full gallon of new milk was sitting out in front of them, as proud as you could wish. "Do you know," said the woman, "I have a bit of an idea, that, I think, could be the makings of us?"

'"'Pon your sowl," said her man, "and what kind of an idea is it that you have, that could do this?"

'"What I was thinking was, if we sold this gallon of new milk, we could buy a hen, and if we could let her run with a cock, in no time at all we'd have a small basket full of hatching eggs. And before the moon would change, we'd have nearly a yard full of chickens, that we could feed on costarwan from the fields, until they grew up to be birds, as fine as you'd seen. Then we'd sell the hens and buy a calf."

'The tinker man could see something coming, and his eyes were out of his head.

'"God be praised," said he, "go on with the story, and what is it that we'll do next."

'"We'll keep the calf, and when it grows up to be a heifer, we'll breed it every year, until we have a fine field of cows."

'"And what'll we do then?" said the husband, and he getting more excited than a young stallion ass.

'"We'll sell the cows," said the wife, "and we'll buy a nice snug little farm, and we'll be fixed for life, for all time."

'"By God, we will," said man, jumping to his feet in excitement. "It is independent farmers we'll be then, and can do what we like. And do you remember that farmer today that set the dogs on us at the gate before we could bid him the time of day. I'll tell you, woman, if ever I meet him on the road, I'll give him such a root in the arse that he won't know for a month, whether the day is Monday, or Tuesday, or any other day. Look at me, woman, this is the kind of lash I'll give him."

'And with that, he drew an almighty kick, and sent the gallon, and the milk, sailing into the next field.'

Now, at last, all around the half-dead fire were together, and threw back their heads and moved their arms about, laughing.

'As God is my judge, but that's a true story. The man that told me about it, on the road, was as honest as a priest, and was never known for his fondness for lies. And the one thing you'd larn from it, is that you should always be extra careful with a full gallon of milk. It could turn sideways on you, if you looked at it anyway crooked at all. A small dog or a young child, or even an ass itself, could spill it in no time. Well, there's one thing sure, anyway, it was an ass that spilt it, in the story I gave to you now.'

Everybody laughed again, and got up to go to bed for the night. I was slouching my own way out, on to the road, reluctant to leave these romantic people of my life.

Tip Toe called out to me, 'Come down tomorrow, after school, and I'll show you how to cut a sheet of tin, and turn the edge on the bottom of a gallon, and rivet a handle on to a three-halfpenny saucepan.'

I waved to him as I turned away and began to parse in my mind what kind of story I'd tell my mother.

Every evening that week I stuck with Tip Toe and his tinker tribe. On the fine days, the sun would still be fairly high in the sky when I'd go down to them. The two old people would be sitting beside the ever-burning fire, the old woman warming her shins and smoking the clay pipe that was seldom out of her hand. Tip Toe was ever busy, fashioning gallons and saucepans of different sizes, turning out the strips of tin with a small cutter, or rounding the bottoms around small wooden patterns on the ground beside him. They sat on small butter boxes, about a foot and a half square, and there was a degree of tranquillity and contentment about the place that made the heart warm.

Tip Toe saw me looking around and examining the openings of the camps.

'You're lookin' for the rest of them,' he said. 'They were well gone by the early mornin'. Gone on the road for themselves, to see what luck the day might bring them. They'll do a sight of travellin' in a bit of a day, with hardly a house they won't make a call on.

The men stay well back on the roads, with the cars. The women and the childer go into the houses. People don't like the men coming in to them, the women do be often inside by themselves. They'd be afraid, some of them, women, with no men in the house. But they like the childer, they do be sorry for them, some say, and they give them nice things like currant bread and jam, if they had it at all. Our crowd will be back now in an hour or two, before the sun starts to go down behind that hill.'

The old man cut the tin sheets with his small shears, and cut out the bottoms. He tapped with his light silversmith hammer, and used his small tools with the skill of a doctor performing an operation.

'If you cut them right, you have no trouble,' he said. 'The worst is turnin' the edges round the bottom. You have to be fierce knacky about that. Another thing is cuttin' a straight line, with maybe a shake on you after a bad night. There were times I'd dread taking the shear in my hand, for the fear of ruinin' a sheet of tin or maybe gougin' a lump out of my finger. Another thing is the rivets, you have to go light on them. If you go too hard, you could leave the sign of the hammer on the side, or maybe drive the whole thing through, in a way that would be a ruination on the job.'

Tip Toe was as good as his word, in trying to make me into a tinsmith. But I'm afraid it was of little use. The furthest I got was experimenting on a few cast-off tin strips, and my teacher held out little hope for my future as a working tinker.

'The way it is,' Tip Toe explained, 'it has to come down to you, in the blood. It was passed to me, from my father, and from his father before, and so on back. It's the same as judging the points of a good animal. Or hidin' the bad ones,' he said, with a loud laugh.

'It's like telling the weather. A tinker could smell the rain comin', or a blowin' of hard wind, by readin' the sky above him. It's from long days on the road, and lookin' around at the world, it's in the blood too, the same thing.'

A black kettle, or more often a burned billy can, hung from the iron crook, ready at any time to be swung in over the fire for the hot tea, to which they were both most partial. Every hour or so a new brew was made, black and strong. No teapot was used, but a fistful of tea, straight into the boiling water. Steaming tin mugfuls, well sweetened with sugar, were quaffed back with many sounds of satisfaction.

The old woman was smoking her pipe again, and she called me over to her.

'Did you ever see the likes of that before,' she said, stretching out her thin legs for me to look at, and rubbing her shins.

She pointed with her finger to an array of broken blue veins showing through the skin, and crossed in many places with thin brown lines and stripes of yellow.

'That's the writin' of the fire,' she said. 'It took many the long year of the burnin' of dry ash, and bog deal, and turf itself, to make the writing as good as that. They say if you had the gift, you could read a life from that writing, and see into the future as well. 'Tisn't many you'd meet, with a second sight like that, in these times, although many's the time we read the palms of fine ladies at fairs and the like, and making up fine stories for them. They liked to hear of well set-up dark men on their way to them, and going over water. If you could see gold or silver on their palms they'd be delighted, to be sure, so you'd tell them that, as often as you could. People in houses get this as well, from hating their shins to the fire, but not as good as we get, I'll warrant, for they do have the shelter, that's not in our way. Do you know what they calls it, the ABC, but not the ABC you do be larning, in your father's school, across the river, I'll bet a silver penny.'

The old woman laughed, then she got up and dragged a small sack of potatoes out from under a car and spilled them on the ground. She washed them in a big black pot, scrubbing them clean.

Then she drew water from the well, and washed them again and again. Then she threw several handfuls of dry wood on the fire, and hung the big pot, on the iron crook. Then she settled down again with her pipe, waiting for her family to come home to her.

They rolled in one after another, with not too much time between them, and with as much noise and confusion as the first evening they came into the dingle.

They set down the gatherings of the day, and before long they were all munching at big floury potatoes, with a sprinkle of salt, and drinking milk from their saucepans, and chattering away about the adventures they had come upon that day.

A week had passed, and the O'Briens had worked with great industry in reaping their own simple harvest. They had garnered in what they could get, and they had decided, perhaps, no more good could come, at this time, from wandering further along the white roads and boreens round this small hilltop village on the eastern side of the Glanaruddery mountains. All the prayers had been said, all blessings that might be of any use to them, or us, had been called down. All the saints in heaven had been stormed, and Mary and Joseph, and the Good Lord Himself, had been called into the battle to bring some small succour into the lives of these small people, who were striving to hold on as best they knew.

Tip Toe told me they were leaving in the morning, after the sun came up. He said they would go south to the town of Castleisland, and west to Tralee, past the Ballyseedy Monument, with the grieving woman showing the dead body of her husband to the child in her arms. After that, they would take the road to Dingle, and then go west again, to Dunquin and Clogher Head, to have another look at the Blasket Islands and the Atlantic Ocean.

I was saddened that they were departing. I asked myself where they were really going. Was it home they were leaving for? But I knew it wasn't home, for there was no home for them, as I knew it, but the open road before them, and their eternal quest for whatever it was that they were seeking. Home for them was their own small caravan of pony cars, their own people, and their children, and whatever small dingle or enticing stretch of green roadside that lured them in there for the night, in whatever place they found themselves.

I went to them early next morning, well before schooltime, to bid them goodbye. The were all hitched up and loaded, and ready to go. This time the smaller children were in the cars, along with the young men and the old people. Tip Toe had pride of place, today, in the right setlock of the car in front.

He waited for me to come up, and I looked at the two pregnant women standing beside the cars. I motioned to him and said: 'What about these, are you going to take them in?'

He seemed surprised, as he looked at me. Then he laughed.

'Yerra, young lad, sure they're rale hardy to be sure, and used to the walkin'. Then he laughed again, and looked over at them.

'Don't ye worry your soul about them, we'll take them in all right, a bit back the road, when they have the stiffness of the night walked out of their bones.'

Tip Toe clacked up his pony, and they pulled out. I stood watching them until they were going out of sight at the bend of the road. There, he turned round, and raised his ashplant stick.

– 16 –

Fishing with My Father

MY FATHER was a small man about five feet six inches in height. From my earliest memory he wore brown horn-rimmed glasses and to me had a forbidding look about him, and I was always well behaved and a little afraid in his presence. The main reason for this was that he said very little, and I did not know what powers he was holding in reserve. Like many a schoolmaster before him, when he gave an order he expected to be obeyed. He had a belief that discipline was good for children, and in moments of unruliness on my part he said quietly: 'Small boys should be seen and not heard.'

It was perhaps relevant that he was born in 1900, one year before Queen Victoria died, after sixty-four years on the throne. She was there long enough for this particular philosophy of her time to percolate down into even so remote a region as Knocknagoshel in the south-west of Ireland. If this was true, then it must of been one of the very few beliefs of Victorian England that he had any time for, although I did hear him on more that one occasion extol the virtue of keeping 'a stiff upper lip' in times of my childish difficulties.

Curiously enough, in his own lifestyle he adopted some of the habits beloved of the upper classes and affluent everywhere, fishing, shooting, hunting and roistering with whiskey and black porter when the occasion arose. I had never any evidence that he included women in the equation.

I was not very old when I began to realize that inside the austerity of demeanour was a heart and a mind concerned with the injustice of the world, and angry with the plight of the downtrodden. Like many a thinking man, he filled bookcases with the complete works of Charles Dickens, and Balzac, and Donn Byrne, and Cassell's *Books of Knowledge*; and his shelves also included the writings of James Connolly. He capped it all by arriving one day with a copy of *The Communist Manifesto*, and a large tome entitled *Das Kapital*. Many years were to elapse before I attempted to read these two books, and before their significance was borne in on me.

Three o'clock and my father rang the school handbell for an end to classes. The students, assigned to clean up the two big classrooms, rushed for their brushes and swept all the dust and bric-à-brac of the day along the floors to the front doors. Particular care was taken to bring out all the small breadcrumbs scattered about, to deny supper to the big brown rats that inhabited the bottoms of the walls, behind the several small black holes in the skirting boards of the old schoolhouse.

At ten past three the doors were locked and we were off, with my mother, who taught the infant classes, at the rear struggling to keep up. Down the boreen to the river, over the footbridge, and up the rising bogland to the Board of Works road, and on to our house. The 'girl' had the dinner ready, more often than not bacon and cabbage or turnip, and potatoes; and in a short time my father was up from the table. The smelly canvas fishing bag was got out, one of the long fishing rods lifted from a row of six-inch nails on the garage wall, and off he went to the river. How often I watched the small figure, with the hat square on his head, dissolve and disappear into the surrounding foliage and shrubbery, until at length only the tip of the rod gave evidence that here was a fisherman, going to his river.

We were free as birds now. We romped and revelled and screamed and fought, in the aura of my mother's benevolent toleration. Isolated at last as the main villain in the uproar, I took off to reconnoitre the possibilities of the surrounding countryside. A visit to Delia's farmyard in search of danger and adventure in the big haggard, tempting the menace of cutting machinery, or teasing a cross sow, or aggravating a bull with provocative whistling, or hurling stones at the vulnerable white cups that carried the telegraph wires. Anything to enliven the tedium and give some spice to a young life.

Slinking back home again, and my mother waiting. We waited with her through the long final hour or two to the approaching twilight, into the deep gloaming of approaching night. Her eyes searched the dark land towards the river, her face troubled.

'He's in Lyre Hole, I'm afraid he is. I told him again and again not to be on the bank of the river in the dark. Do you think he'd take any notice of me? Oh, no. He'd take notice of nobody, only his own selfishness. He's insatiable, fishing and shooting all the time, insatiable. Enough is never enough, only making my head troubled worrying about him. Mother of God, bring him home safe to us, and I'll make a novena.'

I hated my mother for talking like this, the mother I loved with all my heart. Why was she frightening us in this way? Despite all my swagger and vainglory, I was full of fear too. It was only my mother and myself. My two sisters were untroubled. So they might be – it was all for nothing. We heard his heavy steps, and he came in with his old bag, smiling.

'Is that yourself,' he said to me as I came towards him. He threw the bag into my arms. 'I'll tell you what,' he said, 'gut these now, and we'll put them on the pan.'

I did not like gutting fish, with their small bright eyes looking up at me. But my mind was easy now, and anything he'd ask me to do, I'd do for him with much happiness in my heart.

My mother got out the frying pan, and put it on the red coals of the open fire. She took out a jar of cooking fat and spooned some onto the pan. Then she turned round and looked at my father.

'Jim, you shouldn't be frightening me like this, there's no need for it, no need at all.' She said this in a resigned way, without much reproach in her voice.

My father laughed gently. 'Yerra, woman,' he said, 'be rational. Sure I know every inch of that river bank. You shouldn't be worrying about me, there's no need for it at all, no need at all.' He used her own words without rancour.

My mother said no more. She was grateful he was home again. The contentment returned to her face. It was always like this. My mother couldn't control her own imagination, and the fear that it brought on her, and the fear it brought on me as well.

I never asked him, but I wished he'd take me fishing with him. Then one day he arrived back from Abbeyfeale with a bamboo rod for me, with reel and line. There was little water in the river, and I fly-fished with little success.

Then came the heavy rain, and after a night of downpour, we awoke on a Saturday morning to find the Oweveg in full spate with muddy brown water. My father came to my room early.

'Get up', he said, 'and we'll hit the river. The white trout are running today, or I'll eat my hat.'

We went into the orchard in teeming rain, snug and dry in big rubber capes and hats like cowboys in the Wild West. The slickers took the rainwater down over the Wellington boots that came up to my knees. My father's waders went up to his groin.

He dug the rich brown soil under the apple trees, and I picked the worms into empty cocoa tins lined with wet moss. Some of the worms had swollen purple necks, and I feared they would bite my fingers and suck my blood.

'Throw them all in,' my father urged. 'They're the lads for the big fish.'

Other worms had a translucent red look about them, as if they'd been flushed through with clean spring water.

With my fishing rod over my shoulder and pride in my heart, I marched behind my father through Delia's yard, past the front door and down into the long boreen that led to the river. The rain was still coming densely down, splashing off the leaves of the white-thorn and blackthorn trees on either side, and filling to overflowing the cloven imprints of cattle hooves along the way. On each side, in the car wheel ruts, small rivulets flowed. A turn to the right, and we had the first good view of the swollen river. The brown and black water rushed along, bending with its force the dense sally trees on the banks on either side. Uprooted small osiers and pieces of bog oak tumbled in the water along stretches of white foam made by the turbulence of its journey, through the bogland back river.

Worming the hook was not easy for a young apprentice. I held the small red squirmer to pierce in and out just under the head, and in and out again back further in the body. It was still raining as my first bait was cast upstream and let run with the water. My father called over to me: 'Find a quiet side pool where the current is not so fast.'

I found it in an old car passage, now covered over. The whites were ravenous and the take was rich. My father pulled a dozen fish from the water, some of them over a pound weight. In my car passage, the half-pounders were hungry for my small red worms.

Eels up to nine inches long were running too, and I cursed them as they took my bait again and again. Their little eyes had a malevolence, and I feared the sharp white teeth as I took out the hook from the fighting head.

It rained all day as we made our way up river from water hole to water hole, taking fish everywhere. It was still raining as we came home and spilled the silver bodies on the kitchen table. We ate some of the white trout that evening. We ate the eels as well, and I wondered at them turning and twisting on the hot pan as the muscles spasmed in their dead bodies.

But pulling sea trout from river floods was not my father's main preoccupation. It was salmon that were mostly on his mind during the spring and summer runs. On bright Saturday mornings he sat for long periods in front of the house examining his collection of artificial bait and thinking up schemes for luring this strangest of fish on to his hooks. Most days of the week he spent long evenings on the banks of the river Feale, hunched over his long rod, hiding, in cover, from the eyes of the wary fish, and enticing them with silver spinners and prawns and salmon roe. He never caught more than a few each season, but there was great glory and wonder for me in the house when he came in and threw an eight- or ten-pounder on the table.

I never became a real fisherman, and mused on this strange obsession that some men had for being on the river in search of salmon.

'Nobody knows', my father said, 'why they travel back to the river where they were born. They never eat in fresh water, you know, so why do they take a lure? Nobody knows that either. Maybe some kind of curiosity. It's a mystery.'

At that time there was a returned Yank living two miles from us, up river from Feale's Bridge. He told how he worked for forty years in New York, and saved his money to come home.

His main hobby in exile was thinking about salmon, and studying books on the best and most scientific ways of catching them under different conditions. He studied the life history of the salmon, and how they behaved at different temperatures, in currents and still water. He returned home at last, with his books and thermometers, and bought his little home on the river bank. My father told me the story:

'He was on the Feale for several months, and he had more equipment than a scientific expedition to the Arctic regions. He had an American holdall bag, full of books and fishing magazines and thermometers. He had three fishing rods and two different kinds of gaffs, with short handles and long handles, and several nets. Every day he brought the whole lot with them to the river. He was months at it, and every day that passed he got more tormented. Above him and below him there were fish being taken, but never a one did he get.

'He came to me and several others asking for advice, and we did the best we could with him. I told him to forget the books and the thermometers, to take one rod with him, and at most one or two different lures, and showed him the holes and the salmon lays. But I might as well have been talking to the wall. Such was his faith in science that he could see nothing else. He went on like that, the same way, until at last it happened. He was about to pack up one evening, shortly after dark, and was reeling in his spinner, when a salmon struck. He got the fright of his life, and his face was still pale when he was telling me the story, a day or two later. No matter what he did he couldn't bring the salmon close enough for the gaff or the net. The best he could do was to hold the tip of the rod up, to keep the salmon from going off the hook.

'It went on like that through the whole live-long night. The dawn came about half past five, and three hours later he was still sitting there, looking at the water, his rod up in the air. He heard the horse cars and ass cars crossing the road above, going to Feale's Bridge creamery with the milk, but if he was shouting still, none of them could hear him.

'In the end it was a young boy, going along the river bank to school, that rescued him. He asked him to go to the creamery, a good mile away, to send down a fisherman. At first the schoolboy refused, but he agreed after he was given a half crown, a lot of money at that time. About ten of them made for the river and left their ponies and asses tied to whitethorn bushes on the main road. You could hear them laughing and shouting a quarter of a mile away. 'Twas the greatest sport they had in a long time. They got out the fish, he weighed over twelve pounds, and they were talking about it from here to Clare for a month afterwards. He gave up fishing for a week or two, with the nerves, but went at it again and caught one or two more salmon before he died.'

Apart from salmon fishing, my father always said that the best sport on the river was going after white trout with the fly, after dusk of a summer's evening. I went with him a couple of times, and the experience remained strongly with me throughout my life.

The sun was long gone down and the land was still warm after a hot day as we made our way to the river. The land was going dark about us, and the orange and pink and white of the western sky had given way to a more sombre aspect, with odd last shafts of light still brightening the few dark clouds that trailed across, low on the horizon. I looked at my father's hat as he walked beside me, rod on shoulder, and tried in vain to make out the shapes and colours of the fishing flies that decorated the band of his old hat. I could not see them clearly in the failing light, but I knew they were there, and I knew, too, many of their names – 'Wickham's Fancy', 'Greenwell's Glory', 'Dusty Miller', 'Blue and Silver Devon', 'Silver Dragon.'

We made our way down to the water, below the old Metal Bridge and under the shadow of the big dark structure of Shaughnessey's Woollen Mills. This was the river place we were looking for, our water dell of plenty. The fishing hole was warmed on both sides by dense masses of willow and ash and fern, entwined with whitethorn and blackthorn, and hazel bushes, and river plants, and flowering shrubbery. From this small forest of life came myriads of insects of all kinds, filling the air with the intensity of their life and the faint music of their wings. They came down over the water, full of allure and enticement, until the white trout rose to meet them, first in ones and two, in widening water circles, and then in masses that churned the water in their excitement.

It was in the slipstream of this frenzy that we entered on the scene and reaped our harvest. The fish did not discriminate between the sweet manna of nature falling from the warm air, and the sharp hooks of 'Wickham's Fancy' or 'Greenwell's Glory', couched and wrapped within the small feathers of coloured birds.

'I wonder is it right what we're doing,' my father said. 'We're giving them no chance.'

He did not appear to expect an answer, nor did he wait for one, but cast his fly over the water, and then again, and again, and again.

- 17 -

Guns in the House

FROM MY EARLIEST MEMORY my father had guns in the house. First double-barrelled shotguns and later a semi-automatic .22 rifle that fired eighteen bullets from a magazine laid along the barrel. They had for me a dreadful fascination, and despite my father's warnings I found them and examined them in secrecy, opening and closing the breach, putting the safety catch on and off, aiming at imaginary targets, animal and human.

In daring moments, full of guilt and trepidation, I loaded the guns with live cartridges and bullets and carried out my fantasy of warfare against man and beast. I even loaded six bullets into the chambers of the big Webley revolver my father kept in the drawer of a dressing-table in his bedroom. The reason he kept the revolver there, I did not question at the time. Nor did I question, then, the twisted and crushed lead of a fired bullet that I found in the same dressing-table, wrapped carefully in white tissue paper.

The 12th of August, the opening of the grouse-shooting season, was the day for the guns. From dawn of that morning I heard the distant small explosions coming through my open bedroom window from surrounding moorlands. Pop, Pop, Pop, from all around, each pop signifying a flurry of feathers and a grouse falling to the ground. This was life, and excitement ran through me. I did not spare a single thought, then, for the poor broken birds and the orphans they left behind them, running through the heather.

If my father had any doubts about the killing, he never spoke about it. His only scruple was a determination that no shot bird or animal should suffer without need.

'Put it out of pain,' he shouted at me when this arose. He or I dispatched the fish or animal or bird with lethal concussive blows.

On the 12th of August he was out of bed at dawn, like the others, called his gun-dogs to his side, and was off to the mountain. I tramped many a mountain by his side, rising grouse from the heather or snipe from wet bogland. Grouse were easy targets, but snipe were different. They rose in great hurry and anxiety, and made off in a series of twists and zigzags.

'Wait for the third turn before you fire,' my father coached.

It was a discipline I never mastered, and the fleeing snipe were never in too much danger from me. They were only a small meal, in any case, only a bite or two when roasted. I might have said that to myself, as a kind of salve to the shame of the lack of this particular skill.

Woodcock were different. They were fat and juicy for the roasting pot. We flushed them from the brakes of hazel and sally, and ate them with relish.

It was with sadness in my heart that I saw the beautiful cock pheasant come down. For exquisite form and colour, what could match this perfection of nature, with the long feathered tail? It was a mortal sin to shoot a hen pheasant, although I knew some were guilty of this, and they escaped without punishment.

No bird fought for its life with as much determination and instinct for life. The wounded pheasant always dived for cover over the nearest ditch. If his legs were intact, and they often were, he struck for his freedom and ran. A running pheasant broke the heart. He did not know it, but his beauty, borne along at the speed of a racing horse, was about to be destroyed. His noble effort was in vain. The small black lead shot broke his tissue and drew his blood, the strength drained from his tiring legs, and in the end he fell over on the ground and died.

Our killing was all so planned and deadly. We played no fair games. Not for us to walk openly into a cornfield or a turnip patch, flush the birds from their cover, and give them their chance in the air. We had with us two deadly weapons. One was called Rose, and the other Toby.

Rose was the first of many Irish red setters that dwelt in our house. They were all treated royally, and their feeding and health carefully seen to. They were so finely bred that their slim bodies, in their shining red coats, shivered with nervousness and sensitivity. They winced at any sudden noise, an accusing look in their eyes. Their bodies were rubbed with old towels after a day on a wet mountain, and they dried out in a favoured spot on the hearth of the open fire to prevent them getting the sniffles.

New heights in care and attention were reached when Toby arrived. My father brought him home in his hands, a small white bundle of fur with black spots all over. He was no more than six weeks old, and weighed only a few pounds. He was the aristocrat of all gun dogs, an English pointer. We fed him on 'goodie', a mixture of bread and warm milk, and 'pandy', mashed potatoes, also with warm milk, and supplemented with portions of mashed vegetables, and scraps of well-cut meat. His bed was a wicker basket, lined with woollen cloth, not too far from the fire.

When he got good and strong, all this changed. He was banished from all human and other society, other than my father. The time had come to begin his training for the purposes for which he was born, to set and point out hidden birds from their scent. He had to be removed from all temptations and contaminations, and from any bad habits he might pick up that would interfere with his mission in life. Until he emerged as a fully trained gun dog, he was my father's dog and his alone.

It was at this time there appeared in the house a most curious book. It was entitled *The Scientific Education of Dogs for the Gun*. The man who wrote it was a person of some modesty. He did not append his name, and the title page merely said 'By H.H.' It was published in London, a green hardback book with gold inset print on the front cover, and ran to 217 pages. It had no publishing date, and the only clues to its history were writings in pen and ink on the front dust page.

I know it was published during the reign of Queen Victoria, as one of the subscriptions said simply, 'G. Elliot Price, 1901'. Another said: 'Dr. G.M. Vivers, Hon. Sec. and Treasurer, Zoological B.T. Club, Society of London, N.W.8.' A third said: 'M.J. O'Connor, Resident Surgeon, Dr. Steevens' Hospital, Dublin, July 1919.' How it came into my father's possession, I have forgotten, or I never knew. In any case it removed Toby, for several months, from all the joys and satisfactions that any normal dog might expect in the young days of his life. My father, a stickler for detail, unrelentingly carried out all the disciplines of this scientific book.

Toby emerged from his purgatory an animal of great distinction. He was tall and well formed, with a bearing and disdain befitting an aristocrat. All over his body his black spots shone like dark orbs through his snow-white coat. To cap it all he was very good at his job. My father said once, in a rare moment of self praise: 'This is the best grouse and pheasant dog in the whole of Kerry. He has a nose for a bird like I never came across before, he's as steady as the Virgin Rock of Ballybunion, and he'll go or stay on a sign from your little finger.'

These were the secret weapons, then, that my father took with him into the fowling places. No safety or privacy for the beautiful cock birds. Sought out and identified from a distance through the miraculous scenting powers of Toby's nose, then stalked silently, with slow and deliberate goosesteps, and finally pointed out from a few yards, and condemned. Curiously, I saw nothing wrong in these destructive things. It was all part of the wonder of the glorious life that I was living.

It was a frosty December night in the middle thirties when my father took me on a wild goose shoot. Just himself and me, and Jessie, our brown retriever with long ears and white spots on his back. In the blue Baby Ford we headed west, about an hour before midnight, along the side slopes of the Glanaruddery mountains. We were making for a small plateau, high up and with a number of small lakes no more than fifty feet across. A bright moon was shining, displaying the surrounding mountain tops for a good distance. The stars were twinkling with a luminousness I had never seen before. We walked the last half mile to the lake and found a dugout that had been made for our very purpose. It was hewn out of raw bog at the lakeside, and covered and hidden with tree branches and heather.

We got inside on our groundsheets and old rugs, and settled down to wait, well out of sight, with only the tip of my father's shotgun visible. The retriever was lying beside us, panting quickly, but very still.

'They'll come all right,' my father said, looking through the old branches to the north over the moonlit mountain.

We waited for a long long time, and I had gone past regret that I had agreed to come with him in the first place. I was very cold and I was blowing into my hands.

'Hold it,' said my father, and he turned his head. 'Do you hear them?'

Then it came to me, a faint sound from far to the north, repeated again and again. It was the honking of a flock of wild geese, getting louder and louder, and approaching fast. In a minute or two they glided on to the lake in front of us. We watched them for a short while as they gently swam around. They were making little noise, except for a slight lapping of the water.

'I'm going to rise them now,' my father said, and he clapped his hands loudly. They rose as one body, and wheeled to make away. The air was full of the sound of their flapping wings and their frightened honking. My father fired one barrel, followed immediately by the other. One further moment of confusion and the geese were gone, their sound draining away into the distance.

'There's nothing in the water,' my father said. 'I declare to God, I missed them all. I don't believe it, I don't believe it. I'll send in the dog anyway.'

My father was right, he had missed them all. He had fired both barrels into a bunched flock of fifty geese at forty feet, and missed them all. The dog searched around for several minutes, but no goose did he find. He came in at last with something in his mouth. It was a dead wild duck. He went back again and brought out another one. Killing without intent. Would it be a good defence, if somebody brought it home to us that we killed two wild duck, innocently feeding at midnight, on a mountain lake?

I did not think of it then, but my father certainly knew that a number of the fleeing geese were carrying shot in their bodies. Some might make it, to the other side of the mountain or farther, before sinking down to die alone. Others, slightly wounded, would recover, and carry their healed scars back to their first home, in Iceland or some other place.

My father said nothing about the thoughts that were in his mind.

Perhaps he was reluctant, just then, to worry my young head with these unpleasant thoughts. Perhaps he did not wish to disturb the close bond that held us close together, the father and the son, the master and the pupil, forging new links of experience in the passage we were voyaging on at that time.

*

With the hardening of the heart that came with the passing years, rabbits became primary targets of my hunting instincts. Gone was the pity of the very young boy, when I gently held baby rabbits in my hands and felt their frightened hearts beating under my fingers. The pitiless things of nature as I saw it, day after day, had washed away the young sensitivity. The hawk turned on the small birds and rended their flesh. The fox smote the rabbit. The big fish smote the little fishes, and the otter smote it in its turn.

Our first two hunting dogs were a small gamey wire-haired fox terrier called Terry, and a hapless greyhound bitch called Pup. These were the eager accomplices of my early predations among the rabbit fields of the surrounding countryside. Terry was full of enthusiasm that was not matched by the speed of his short legs. But he gave limitless encouragement to Pup, from the rear, with ferocious barking, as she was in full pursuit, mostly unsuccessful, of jinking rabbits. Pup was bought in high hopes, which were never realized. She was short of real pace, and was not as full-hearted as we might have wished. Her social standing in our household diminished as the years went by, although she was still treated with a good deal of affection.

My father, on his way home from the mountain with his shotgun, would often come across the odd rabbit and bag it for the table. It came well from the pot, with flesh as sweet as that of a young chicken. He had to be careful about this, as sometimes he shot a rabbit that was infested with fleas. If one rabbit had a heavy infestation, then as sure as God made sour milk the whole colony would be likewise. And woe betide him if he brought an infected animal inside my mother's door.

At about that time, my life was being made miserable on a number of fronts. At the end of each month my father had to fill forms, for himself and my mother, and another teacher, Mrs Curtin, setting out the activity of the school for the period. These reports, called the 'Returns', had then to be brought to the parish priest, the manager of the National Schools, for his signature, and posted off to the Department of Education in Dublin. No Returns, and no pay, so this was a fairly serious matter.

Inevitably, and always at the last minute, I was called in to be the messenger to the Presbytery in the village. To say I did not take kindly to this would be to put it very mildly indeed. I usually kept a stiff upper lip in the presence of my father, but once on the way I decorated the surrounding air with a string of childish blasphemies, or worse, if I could think of it.

So aggravated was I by my misfortune that, at times, I cried a good part of the way. At the last ditch, I cleaned my face with wet grass before going out into the road and striking up the village before all the people. The man who was my objective, and whose services I wished to use, was the parish priest, Father Byrne. He was a man of more than medium height, and well into his sixties. He had a stout comeliness of body that was pleasing to the eye. He had pure white hair, grown long and brushed close into his well-shaped head. All in all, he had the bearing of a man who would look at home in a synod of bishops or in the House of Lords itself. He was gentle of manner and speech, and had the demeanour of a man who was not too disconcerted by the troublesome facets of his own and other people's lives as he came in contact with them. With head bent and a pleasant look on his face, he listened to the tales of his parishioners, good and bad, in the same way. Whatever was said to him, he always replied with the same phrase, usually repeated twice: 'My, my, back to the old times again. My, my, back to the old times again.'

Before I could get Father Byrne's signatures, I had to go through his middle-aged housekeeper, Kate Culnane. She was a woman of great curiosity and directness of character, and perhaps, in some ways, regarded herself as equal, if not superior, to the parish priest, in protecting the functions of his office.

As always, she met me at the door with a cold look in her eye.

'Oh, it's you again,' she said, as she looked me over, with a certain disapproval in her countenance.

She escorted me into her hot kitchen, and put me sitting down on a hard chair. Over across from me and close to the warm range was a small black Pomeranian dog, lying on a tasselled cushion on another chair. He sent out a few faint strangled barks in my direction, and seemed to regard me with no greater approval than that afforded me by his mistress. I knew the Pomeranian well, and by all repute he was the most pampered dog in the six parishes. His name was Nixie, and every week a poor young fellow, called Manny Cud, from behind the village, was shanghaied into giving him a wash with scented soap in a small white enamelled bath, and never a thruppence changed hands.

Kate informed me, as usually happened, that the parish priest was out, and I'd have to wait. Then she proceeded to question me closely, on a range of issues.

'Did your mother go to town lately? Did she go on the bicycle, or did your father take her in the Baby Ford? Did she buy any new style? I was told Mrs Curtin was out with the flu, and was supposed to have blisters all over her face. Did you see any on her when she came back? I suppose you would not see them anyway, with all the paint and powder she do have on her face. How is her white pony? They say he is nearly foundered with age, and has her late for school every day. Does she still skelp the children with a sally rod, and beat the legs from under them?

'Did ye hear that Master Heffernan's brother was made a bishop? Pull, I suppose, but that's the way the world is nowadays. Was your father fishing lately? Did he get any salmon or even white trout? Was he shooting at all? Did he bag any grouse or woodcock, or a rabbit, or a snipe itself? Tell him you're not to come again without some little dainty in your bag, for the priest.'

I stonewalled her questions as best I could, and certainly gave no confirmation about poor Mrs Curtin, who was doing the best she could. The priest eventually came home, greeted me with his usual 'My, my,' signed the Returns, and I was away with myself.

My father was not the kind of man to respond to solicitations for bribery, but he gave me the odd woodcock or white trout or rabbit or brace of snipe to bring to Kate Culnane, to keep on the good side of her. Once I ferried her a wild goose, and she appeared pleased enough. The only reason that happened was that nobody in our house, except my father, would eat it, as it tasted strongly of fish.

Things rested so until one day, my father was on the way home from the mountain and he shot a fine fat rabbit. He quickly discovered the animal was heavily infested with a crop of black fleas, and he put him into a big black paper sugar bag and tied the top securely, with a bit of old cord. He called on me to take the bag to Kate with all speed.

I brought the rabbit to Kate, in my usual complaining mood, and in complete innocence of his dastardly plot, although if I had known I would have been more than a willing accomplice.

Kate received the present with a moderate degree of thankfulness, and being in the middle of some other job she hung it on a nail beside the red-hot range, close to where Nixie was reclining. The fleas, uncomfortable in their new environment, decided, apparently, to seek another abode, and left the dead rabbit en masse. How long it took nobody was quite sure. But the apocryphal version was widely told. The final scene had Nixie going entirely mad, and running so wildly round the kitchen that Kate had to let him off through the back door, along the village back lane, to run himself to death behind Boola on the foothills of the Glanaruddery mountains. Whatever happened, neither God nor man would induce me ever to darken her door again, and I never again came face to face with her, or Nixie, if in fact the dog survived. My father had to be his own messenger, or he called in my elder sister, Eileen, who, no doubt, carried out her duties with the same enthusiasm that I had hitherto shown.

Some time after that, my father worked out a scheme that stopped all visits to the Presbytery for a fair good while. Whether in collusion with the parish priest or not, I never knew, but he solved the problem by forging Father Byrne's signature on the monthly Returns.

The tribulations of a child were often overlooked by grown-ups, perhaps because of lack of sensitivity or imagination, or because they forgot how it was when they were young themselves. Fear was a great element in my childhood, fear of animals, and people, fear of the things of nature itself.

Fear of strangers coming to the house, lest they take me away like the old cows that were taken away to the factory in Roscrea and put into grinding machines for corned beef. Strange figures coming up the walk from the gate sent me flying into the back scullery until the situation was clarified. An unknown man, approaching along the road, forced me to leap the ditch into the nearest field until he had passed by.

I was hardly six when I was first sent to the village for messages. Going round the road was bad enough, but it was much longer, and my father said: 'Take the shortcut, up Kate's boreen.'

To my mind, Kate's boreen was a place of mystery and danger. It ran a quarter of a mile in one direction, and then, at right angles, for as long again. It had high ditches, and tall growths of shrubbery. The big growths leant in over the boreen, creating a dark half tunnel where the sun never penetrated except at noontime. This forbidding atmosphere was heightened by the constant noises of small life coming at me from both sides. All around, a low faint humming, and tiny murmurings and breathings, as if small beings whispered to me from a fairy world. In my mind, I saw them with their green jackets and red hats, and spectral women with red eyes stared at me through openings in the undergrowth. Here I was, alone, and open prey to witches or ghosts or any other thing that might come along. My body was stiff, and my heart pounded with dread.

I pulled myself together and back to earth, and thought of Kate's two great horses, a brown mare and a wild red gelding, that thundered down the boreen in full gallop whenever it crossed their minds. No escape from them over the high hedgerows, except to throw oneself into the thorny undergrowth at the base of the ditch. No escape either if Kate's herd of bony cows were to follow the example of the horses, and go into a stampede along the boreen.

Inevitably, these imaginings took some time, and slowed my progress. I was delayed further when, sometimes, I retreated in disorder and made the trip to the village around the road.

My father was not too pleased with these flights of my imagination, although he generally accepted them with some toleration and a half smile on his face. But he showed no toleration on a Saturday he sent me for a Mac's Smile razor blade, to shave himself before going to Tralee for the monthly meeting of the Fianna Fáil Party County Committee. I decided to avoid the trauma of Kate's boreen by diverting a new way. This took me into a field, with newly made-up haycocks. I was going along, in good order and speed, until there descended on me, from the other side of the field, a herd of young pigs that had been let out of their cabins that day. They came at me wildly, snorting and cavorting and menacing, so that I thought my last hour had come. I took immediate refuge on top of one of the fine cocks of hay, and began to consider my position, while the crazed pigs circled me like a band of red Indians round beleaguered wagons.

I was still considering my position half an hour later, when at last the pigs lost interest in me and departed up the field. I arrived home to find my father had left half an hour late for his meeting, having shaved with a blunt old blade. He left behind some threats of what lay in store for me on his return. These he carried out half-heartedly with a strap on the bottom later that evening.

– 18 –

My Father in Peace and Pain

MY FATHER first saw the light of day in 1900, in a thatched house in a poor and boggy farm on an open hillside a half mile from the village of Knocknagoshel. His great-grandfather had come from the west one hundred years before and got one hundred and fifty acres of bad land from the local landlord. His name was Seamus, too, or James in the English language. He had four cows to start on this bogland, but a lifetime of work turned some of it into good earth. He had four sons, White Daniel, Red Con, Maurice, and my father's grandfather William.

When great-grandfather's time had come, he divided the farm between his three fine sons, fifty acres each, and two more thatched houses were built on the hillside. Such was their potency that they each had nine children, twenty-seven in all, among them my father's father, another James, who died when my father was a child.

William had gone to America and fought as a major in the Union army of Abraham Lincoln. He wrote home descriptions of life and civil war engagements in most beautiful copperplate writing. These letters my father cherished, until a well-intentioned vandal uncle of his destroyed them, on the death of his father.

They called their settlement the 'village'. They were fiery and forthright, and the little place teemed with the emotions of love and jealousy and human conflict, common among the simple people of the world, and others, forced by circumstances, to live suffocating lives too close to each other. It was in this place that my father was found, under a head of cabbage, he was told, the year before Victoria died.

Amongst the three families, eccentrics were liberally sprinkled. In one of the thatched houses, lived two unmarried uncles, Jack Cruhoor and Con the Lady. Jack was a small round man with a red happy face. He was illiterate, but nevertheless had a most pungent wit and a wonderful command of words. At times the air was filled with barrages of purple and abusive language that he flung at his current victim. He was a martyr to drink, and at times would stay away boozing for two or three days.

Con was well educated, having remained at school until he was seventeen years old. He was tall, quiet, gentle, and well spoken. From this came his name, Con the Lady. He also had a weakness for black porter, and nearly every Sunday remained in Knocknagoshel after Mass and came home in the evening drunk and morose. The two brothers hardly ever spoke except in acrimony, Con criticizing the rough-hewn Jack for his shortcomings, and Jack jeering the sensitive Con, telling him: 'I must find a woman for you, one of these days.'

With Con and Jack lived Mag Mahony, the servant girl, and the most remarkable member of the household. She was dark and gaunt, with ribs of hair growing on her face. She came when she was twenty, and remained for forty years until the brothers died. She ran the house, inside and out, and aggravated their lives, talking continuously and listening to nobody. In exasperation Jack shouted at her: 'Silence, you hairy bitch!' She took no heed. She slept in a settle bed in the kitchen, a bed by night and a settee by day, and Jack and Con each had a double bed, placed back to back, in the only bedroom of the single-storey house.

This remained the sleeping arrangement until the night of a big thunder storm, when Mag was so frightened that she left her settle bed and jumped into bed with Jack. Con, alarmed for her welfare, got Mag into his own bed, and went to Mag's bed in the kitchen.

My father told what happened in his memoir *Tomorrow Was Another Day*, published in 1970: 'The strange part is that Con remained in the settle bed, and Mag slept in the room with Jack, for the remaining thirty years she remained in the house, and although they shared the same chamber pot, in my time at least (they were fairly old then), I believe there was never anything further between them, and that Mag kept herself intact to the last.'

Jack always kept at least three bulls, to service his own and his neighbours' cows. They were badly fed animals, small in stature, weak and miserable, and badly equipped to perform their duties in life. To complicate matters, it was believed at the time that a cow would not be properly serviced unless she got two jumps. Jack had a little platform built, of stone and mud, for the small bulls to stand on, while the cows were set back underneath and firmly held. Full of guile and resource, he also had a special bar of music of about six notes that he whistled to provide exhilaration for the undernourished bulls, and this never failed eventually to fulfil its purpose, even for the second jump.

Another difficulty was fear of a white calf, which was of little value. Jack dealt with this also, and always drove a cow of rich red colour in front of the mating animals at the crucial moment.

This, he declared, would remove the possibility of a white off-spring.

Such was the rich vein of life in which my father lived in the early part of this century. He slept with his rheumatic uncle, John the Yank, who filled his mind with stories of rapacious landlords, and the cruel and degrading Royal Irish Constabulary; of the small bands of agrarian revolutionaries, the Whiteboys and the Moonlighters, who carried out unremitting warfare to win back the precious land; and the failure after failure of the rebellious Irish in their many uprisings.

My father had uncles who were religious Brothers in the de La Salle Order, and they quickly took charge of his education. He did the teacher entrance exam called the King's Scholarship in Killarney, the week of the 1916 Rising, and in the autumn of that year found himself in the teacher-training college in Dungarvan, County Waterford, for a two-year course. He was discovered to be two years too young, and was promptly expelled. One of his overzealous uncles had changed his birth certificate from 1900 to 1898, and was caught out. Two years of further schooling with his contrite uncle in Dungannon and Enniskillen saw him back in de La Salle, to emerge in 1920 with his National Teacher's Diploma.

After a year of so teaching in Knockbrack National School, Knocknagoshel, he left in June 1922, at the outbreak of the civil war. It was three years before he returned again to teach in his old job.

The intervening period he had spent on the run in Ireland, fighting on the Republican side, then in England, then a year in America under a false passport and name. It had included capture and imprisonment in Newbridge, County Kildare, tunnelling to freedom and walking back to Kerry at night over the mountains.

When the war was over he fled, as he believed he would be shot on capture. The reason he was such hot property was that he, with others, was blamed for the Knocknagoshel trap mine in which two Free State captains, a lieutenant, and two privates were killed.

It was grim fortune indeed that a number of what might have seemed fairly unimportant events at the time should have resulted in the placing of the Knocknagoshel mine with all its deadly consequences.

It was the autumn of 1922. The civil war was at its height and thousands of Republican fighters throughout the country were resisting in arms the government of the new Free State, over the signing of the Treaty with Britain. Nowhere was opposition more implacable than in County Kerry, and in places such as the village of Knocknagoshel.

An overzealous IRA local battalion officer one day visited the home of an old man named O'Connor, a farmer in the nearby parish of Castleisland, whose sympathies were on the Free State side. The old man thought he was talking to a Free State officer, and gave away some information about the Republicans. The farmer was later tried by a Republican court and fined a hundred pounds. He refused to pay and his cattle were taken away and offered for sale.

The old man's son, filled with anger, joined the Free State army and was appointed intelligence officer. He was blamed by Republicans for what they considered to be gross ill-treatment of captured men. The Republicans were also inflamed by stories, coming from other Kerry areas, that a number of captured and disarmed men had been taken out and shot, and their bodies found in fields and ditches.

It was now the early spring of 1923, and the prospect of victory for the Republicans was receding by the day. The Free State forces had come into Kerry by sea, and the main towns were in their hands. The war was lost and soon the leader, Eamon de Valera, would issue his famous order of the day to his 'Soldiers of the Legion of the Rearguard', to lay down their arms.

This was the political atmosphere at the end of February 1923. But there was one last tragic drama to be enacted. Reports of beating and torture of prisoners were still coming in. The IRA Battalion OC decided the Castleisland intelligence officer should be removed by trap mine.

My father and another battalion officer, Mick McGlynn, who was an expert in machine-guns and explosives, were reluctant to set the mine, and offered to enter the town of Castleisland and machine-gun the Free State officers through the windows of a hotel where they lunched at midday.

McGlynn started to prepare a motor car, putting up steel shutters to run the gauntlet through the main street of the town.

Another small event changed the situation, and delivered the means to lure the officers into ambush. Two friendly girls in the local post office were in the habit of giving all outgoing letters to the IRA for perusal. They made an astonishing discovery. A woman living near the village was sending written reports to the Free State intelligence officer in Castleisland about their movements.

McGlynn later made a brief written report: 'A decision was taken to do a trap mine operation on the Castleisland intelligence officer. We set up what looked like an underground dugout, on the Walsh farm at Clasnagough, about two miles from the village, and near where the lady informer lived. We mined the dugout with a powerful mine made from a United States formula of explosives. Johnny Nolan and I set the equipment for instantaneous explosion.'

A forged letter in the writing of the informer was sent by lady courier to the intelligence officer in Castleisland, telling him about the 'dugout'. It was Johnny Nolan, too, a skilled penman, who forged the fatal letter.

Within a couple of days, in the small hours of the morning, the intelligence officer and a large party of officers and men surrounded the 'dugout' and began to search. They came upon a wooden box which contained the mine, and it blew up. Among the five dead was the intelligence officer.

The night the mine went off there were men lying in bogs and fields and other places waiting for the blast. My father wrote of the scene where he was in hiding:

'That night four of us were sleeping in a dug-out in a rick of turf, about a mile from where the mine was sited. To fall asleep and remain so was always the least of our troubles, no matter where we were. At all times, no sooner did we lay down than we fell asleep and remained so until somebody woke us up the following morning.

'We might wake with the cold, if somebody grabbed all the clothes. Seldom this happened, but it happened this night. We were awake maybe five minutes, grumbling and re-adjusting, when we heard the mine go off. Somebody said, 'The mine.' I said, 'The Lord have mercy on their souls.' I struck a match, and looked at the watch. It was two o'clock. Then we all turned over and fell asleep. Our falling asleep immediately may now look dreadfully callous on our part, but, by this time, it would be difficult to surprise or shock us. We were living from day to day, fatalistically untroubled, and not thinking what the next hour might hold, though the instinct for survival was, perhaps, as strong as ever.

'The following morning, about nine o'clock, we were all awakened by Charlie O'Donohue, calling from the outside, "Get out, the village is full of soldiers." We then remembered the cause.'

The Free State reprisals matched the mine in all its horror. Nine prisoners were brought from Tralee to Ballyseedy, tied around a mine and blown up. The bodies were blown into fragments, but one man, Stephen Fuller, in a manner that nobody could ever explain, escaped and crawled to safety. On the same night four prisoners were killed in a similar fashion at Countess Bridge, Killarney, and here also, one, Tadhg Coffey, escaped.

Five nights later, five others died in like manner at a bridge near Cahirciveen. In all nineteen Republican prisoners died that week in Kerry, and others were to follow.

But the killing that was closest to home was the shooting of a young local blacksmith, Dan 'the Bird' Murphy, who was blamed for helping to make the Knocknagoshel mine. He was taken from his forge to the scene of the explosion, and shot dead by a Free State officer.

That night, after a day on the run, my father came down from the hills in the small hours, and entered the house where Dan Murphy's corpse was laid out on his own bed. Examining his wounds he found a spent bullet breaking through the skin on the front of his shoulder. It was a Peter the Painter bullet, its top flattened by a bone. He had been shot from behind.

That was the bullet my father had wrapped in tissue paper, and kept for many years in a chest of drawers in his bedroom, and which I had secretly examined from time to time, along with his big Webley revolver.

*

The Troubles had been over for five years when I was born in 1928, but they continued to cast shadows over our lives. My father stayed with de Valera after Fianna Fáil was founded. When I was a small boy, before and after de Valera came to power in the early thirties, I knew there was trouble about.

In the dark of winter nights, men came to our door, and there was long and sometimes loud talk in the small hallway. That was as far as they came, and the talking would go on for a long time. My mother sat in the kitchen with her hands joined and her face pale with anxiety.

It was after one of these visits that I saw my father go to his bedroom and put the big Webley into the pocket of his jacket. My mother argued with him but he quietly put her aside and went to the pub as he did most nights.

It was then began my nightly vigil of waiting that went on for years in my small room at the back of the house. Dogs barked from long distances away through the frosty nights, and others answered in challenge from across the parish. Now and then the headlights of faraway cars passed like ghosts across the room. But for me no sleep would come, nor fear pass away until I heard his heavy foot-steps beating out, faintly at first, and then louder and louder. Then the opening and closing of the big front door, the stockinged feet on the stairs, and the opening and closing of the bedroom door. Then contentment and sleep until morning.

I did not know what was wrong. I did not know that he came through roads late at night with his big loaded Webley thrust out in front of him. I did not know that it was some of the Tralee Republicans, who called themselves the New IRA that were angry with him for going with de Valera, angry to the point of threats and danger.

My Uncle Jack thought he would act as my father's protector. He fashioned himself a most lethal weapon of hard wood lined with lead, and attached to his wrist with a stout strip of leather. He took to patrolling our small half-acre plot, stealing round the little orchard at the back of the house, or moving in and out of the shadows of the many pine trees and macrocarpas around the homestead.

*

I saw it all from my place on my father's shoulders, at the bottom of a village, full of flame and shadows. Men and women and children assembled to celebrate a victory, and the air around filled with the noise and intensity of their feelings. They waited for the march, to vindicate their arrival at the end of the long road they had travelled. They wanted to do this with stamping feet, raised voices shouting out their slogans, with cheering and singing, and raised arms in salute and defiance, in tune with martial music and triumphalism.

In front was the big drummer, sticks tied to his wrists with rubber thongs, and his drum, high and broad, hoisted on his chest. Behind, the fife and flute players, the kettle drummers, and the bagpipe players.

A hundred men or more were assembled in marching formation, many holding aloft blazing torches of paraffin-soaked turf sods impaled on two or three prong pikes.

As they waited the band played the familiar airs and the people sang. 'Let Erin remember the days of old ere her faithless sons betrayed her.' 'Wrap the green flag round me boys, to die were far more sweet, with Erin's noble emblem, boys, to be my winding sheet.' At the end of each song there was massed cheering, with one single slogan being repeated everywhere, over and over again. 'Up Dev', they shouted, 'Up Dev', and the cry was taken up and repeated at all points, and the cheering swept the excited gathering again and again.

They marched up the village casting their light and shadows around, celebrating for the first time the election to power of a government which most of them had voted for. They jeered at those who were their political enemies, taunting them in their houses, invoking acts of killing and atrocity, and shouting out the slogans of the day: 'What about Ballyseedy?', or 'What about the Seventy-Seven?'

Pictures of their hero, Eamon de Valera, were held up. In the centre of the village the marchers stopped outside the door of a supporter of the defeated Free State government. An effigy of the Free State leader, William T. Cosgrave, was produced, doused with paraffin, set alight, and burned on the pathway.

For many elections after that the victory parades were repeated, but the passion became less fervent, and they stopped the burning of effigies. For sixteen years they had victory, and they no longer felt like beggars on horseback, and they forgot the need of riding to the devil over the bodies of the defeated. But after the sixteen years they were defeated too, and they licked their wounds inside their houses. Others did the marching now, until they were back again, and round and round they went, in the merry-go-round of victory and defeat.

The terrible things that happened in the four years or so of the Troubles lay heavily on my father's mind for the rest of his life. Twice later the burden became so heavy that he broke down in mental worry, and had to leave his teaching at Knockbrack School for periods of six months each time.

Even when he appeared well, there was an ongoing preoccupation with the state of his mind. He searched for new psychological therapies. I remember a series of slim grey books arriving by post from England with the general title of 'Pelmanism'. These set out to improve the mental condition by exercises in such things as Concentration, Observation, and Meditation, in a number of lessons. For some years too I had seen in the press in the kitchen, jars of a white powder that he took in water several times a week. On the jars was written the name 'Sanatogen', a medicine for the strengthening of the nerves.

When the crisis came on him, there was no change in his normal calm demeanour. But I knew he was not sleeping and I knew that my mother was troubled. He stopped going to school and in a weak moment my mother told me it was the things that happened when was out on the run that were on his mind.

He set about his own way of curing himself. Every day he hit out for the mountain with his dog and gun, a flask of tea and hard egg sandwiches. He walked all day over miles of rough ground seeking to tire himself before evening, so that at night he might get some rest and sleep. He found the wheels and back axle of an old motor car, and bought timber and plywood and all the other things that were necessary to build a caravan. I was his chief apprentice, and we toiled together for many weeks on the concrete surround at the back of the house. Our main difficulty was shaping the long timber joists into curves for the roof and the front and rear. But we solved that too. We burned turf under a long zinc vat, until the water boiled and steamed. We hot-steamed the long rods until they were saturated and flexible, and nailed them in curves to wide boards to dry out in the shape we wanted. That summer the family had a new caravan and an old Model T Ford car to pull it along. But best of all my father was cured after his long dark night.

That my father had survived for so long was in itself something remarkable. The years on the run took a heavy toll on many of his comrades. Months in the open in hard weather, often wet to the skin, for long periods, sleeping in bogland dugouts on wet blankets, lack of sleep and regular rest, these and other things weakened their bodies, and some succumbed to tuberculosis, pneumonia and other diseases. In 1924, having escaped to America for a year, he returned in a very doubtful state of health. He recalled this episode of his life in his own words. He was not yet twenty-five years old.

'Two years after returning from America I got completely debilitated. I lost all appetite for food, fell to seven and a half stone weight, got very weak and when walking, had to rest every couple of hundred yards. My wife made a red flannel woollen garment for me, to be worn next to the skin, to keep me warm (there was supposed to be a cure in red flannel). I had also five or six other woollen garments on. The result was my skin got quite green and I looked like a corpse, and as if I was in the last stages of consumption (there was no X-Ray diagnosis at the time).

'I went to a doctor in Castleisland. When he saw all the garments, he said I should discard three or four of them, including the red flannel, as my skin had ceased to function. "If I do I'll die with the cold," I said.

' "I'll show you how," he said. "Tomorrow, jump into a hole in the river, and out again immediately. Dry yourself well and then discard one."

' "I'll die of heart failure," said I (it was the month of April).

' "Have somebody with you to help you out in case," he said. "The way you are, you'll die anyway. Repeat that every couple of days, until you are down to four."

'I did as he told me and survived, and went to see him again, though, if anything, physically worse. "Go to the seaside," he said, "and jump into the seawater, and out again immediately, and allow the water to dry on you, under the sun. After half an hour repeat this, and do it several times a day." He told me how to gradually initiate myself into sunbathing.

'My wife and I went to Kilkee, and it happened to be a beautiful summer (1926), and after six weeks of this treatment I became completely transformed and when I came home those who knew me would hardly recognize me. I never looked back after that and have practised river and sea bathing and sunbathing ever since. I may add that in that year, there was only one other sunbather – an English naval man – and he and I drew a lot of attention on ourselves by taking the sun. It transpired afterwards that I had no consumption, and if I had, the sun treatment would only have hastened my death.'

If the body was healed, the mind was still in difficulty. I was later to know that it was the Knocknagoshel mine casualties and the subsequent reprisal killings that caused the main disturbance within.

– 19 –

Going to the Ocean

GOING TO SEE the ocean for the first time, at Ballybunion. Walking down the wide street, between the coloured houses, the pavement flags warm under bare feet. Public houses on every side, painted gargoyles grinning down. In between, windows big and small alight with colour. Gold and red and blue chocolate boxes, trays of buns and cakes and sweet bread, sticks of rock, small bags of sherbet with white powder, acid and sweet, small black pipes of liquorice crowned with tiny red cherries, green and red apples, oranges and yellow bananas. Silver churns of ice-cream, dispensed in thin wafers by smiling girls. Here and there old women at their small stalls selling periwinkles and purple sea grass and small paper bags of carrageen moss.

Down farther on the right, Cissie Mac's, the old curiosity shop. Frail-looking kites and spinning tops, baskets of beach balls, and artificial coloured birds on thin sticks on the low walls, turning and chirping in the light breeze.

Inside, Cissie herself, flamboyant of demeanour and dress, handing out her special things from the bedecked counters and walls around. Scarves and bathing suits, carved figures and card games, small statues of the saints of heaven, and silver lamps with red globes in honour of the Sacred Heart. Pencils and puzzles and fairy-tale books, bows and arrows for young Red Indian braves, metal toy handguns and belts and broad-brimmed hats, tin rifles and timber horses for the cowboys coming in. There was no end to things in this parlour of delight.

Farther down still towards the sea, the Castle Hotel, a large long two-storey building, the special holiday place for the special people who had made good in life in the big towns of Kerry and Limerick, and lawyers and doctors and other rich people from Dublin and other faraway places. This place that was outside my life, standing on a huge green lawn, and looking west, in the heart of the old town. From the street and over the wall, I looked in at the big dining-room, arrayed with tables covered in white linen and decked with glittering cutlery and china. Up high the large windows open to sunlight and air, festooned with drying bathing suits and towelling, red and blue and white and yellow. What kind of people were these? What were their lives? Did they walk through life in a dream of happiness and contentment? Were they protected against trouble and misfortune? How did they get on this sheltered long white road; how did it happen to them?

I passed on and then I saw the ocean, the wide blue infinity that stilled the heart. Snatches of old poems and songs tumbled through the mind. 'Roll on thou deep and dark blue ocean roll, ten thousand fleets sweep over thee in vain.' 'When you go to your home by the ocean, I will never forget those sweet hours, that we spent in the Red River Valley, mid the green mossy banks and wild flowers.' 'Red Sails in the Sunset far out to sea, you'll carry my loved one home safely to me.'

From my earliest times I knew there were two beaches in Bally-bunion, the Men's Beach on the left looking out to sea, and the Ladies' Beach on the right. The two large beaches were divided by the green promontory of the Castle Green, about fifty yards wide. I never gave the matter too much thought except to wonder, as the women had their own beach, why most of them were over on the men's place. However, there was another person who was giving considerable attention to the matter. He was the parish priest, Father William Behan, who came to the place just after the middle thirties and who had a reputation as a man of action. He was also a man aware of the dangers of the proximity of the two sexes, especially when they were scantily clad.

The summer was upon him and he spoke from the altar in a series of sermons about the avoidance of sinful temptations and the pleasures of the flesh, and advocated with all the passion he could muster that the sexes should keep to their own beaches. Nothing happened and he played what should have been a trump card. One Sunday, he solemnly banned mixed bathing from the beaches of Ballybunion. Normally an edict of this nature would be expected to have an effect similar to a message from Rome. But to his surprise, perhaps horror, there was no improvement. In fact the situation worsened with the arrival of large numbers of the summer people.

He took action. He had a line of stakes driven down the middle of the Men's Beach. He decreed that henceforth the women should remain on the left-hand side, and the men on the right, with no exceptions. Lo and behold, the plan worked. Husbands were divorced from their wives and families, and contented themselves with the much more favourable part of the beach. They sat with their backs against the warm rocks of the Castle Green promontory, or perched themselves on the face on small ledges, sheltered from any chill winds that might be blowing down the river Shannon. Among them were a liberal sprinkling of priests in their new domain.

They called it the Behan Line. The bathers entered into the spirit of the arrangement, and howled in mock outrage should any hapless person accidentally wander across the blessed divide. There was an occasional incident, and I was informed, without verification, that one day the priest was struck by an enraged father who revolted against being parted from his family. Things rested so for a fair time until one night some adventurous young blades soaked the timber stakes with petrol and burned them to the ground. The women came back, timidly at first, and then the flood, right up to bikini time, when female bodies could be seen in all parts of the Men's Beach, the Castle Green cliff face included. The Behan Line, as happened later to the Maginot and Siegfried Lines in France and Germany, was gone forever.

When things had loosened out and we were all together again on the beach, with the exception of my father who was sunbathing on the cliff face, a man called Peter Browne joined us. He was a tall man of serious demeanor, with a square jaw and a contemplative face. He had been out on the run with my father in the Black and Tan war, and was now in the Irish Army, with the rank of Captain. In an interlude after the Troubles he had spent a period in America on a ranch in Arizona punching cattle. He gave full consideration to anything that was being said, and paused for several seconds before replying to any question that was directed to him. He smoked cigarettes with great deliberation, slowly raising his hand to his mouth and down again, then pulling back his lips and exhaling the smoke as if in slight pain. He was also a man of great courtesy, and when he visited our house, as he often did from his home in Tralee, he never came inside without a careful examination of all the flowers from the front gate to the doorway, a distance of some sixty feet. He did this to avoid catching my mother by surprise, and to give her adequate time to prepare the kitchen for his entrance.

He had the gifts of a diviner, and could find water and things that were hidden underground. He used a small forked rod of hazel or sally, one end held in each hand. When he came over the thing being searched for the, rod was pulled downwards and pointed to the exact spot.

On the beach that day my mother was wearing her gold wedding ring, and after some time Peter indicated he could locate the ring if it was hidden in the sand. My mother gave me the ring with a severe admonition not to lose it. Peter turned his back and my mother watched Peter to make sure he wasn't looking. I quickly buried the ring in dry sand about four inches down, and a fair distance away. Peter set about the recovery with great confidence, and moved up and down over the place indicated. After a good while had elapsed, it became clear that if he was there until Christmas he wouldn't find the ring. My mother in increasing alarm finally gave up patience and said to me, 'Rory where did you hide my wedding ring, get it for me at once.' I did my best, but between the jigs and the reels, and all the excitement and all the sand about, I couldn't find the exact place nor the ring, no matter how I searched.

Peter was mortified, and my mother was pale with anxiety. I said I'd get my father, and brought him back from his cliff perch, where he was stretched out sunning himself like a large brown seal. He took charge like a general. 'Show me the place where you think you put it.' With an old stick, he drew lines on the sand eight feet across and set us to search with military thoroughness. Line upon line, up and down we went. Within twenty minutes or so the ring was found and returned to my poor mother.

*

It was evening time in golden light, and the sun was dipping towards the horizon in the west, sending silver shafts over the ocean before my eyes. A million diamonds shimmered and sparkled on the broad expanse of sea, and the low sky was red and purple and blue and pink, with wreaths and scarves of gold, intermingled in the scene of glory. There was no air moving, and the white and brown figures that dipped and frolicked along the fringes of the small waves seemed to make little noise in this place of dreams. The light sounds of splashes and the low tingles of laughter rose and fell, all round, over the yellow beaches that stretched on either side. And the sea moved and sighed and moved again and again.

Far away to the south were the shadowy outlines of the Kerry mountains, of Mount Brandon and Slieve Mish, and farther away still, and more shadowy still, the peaks of Carrauntwohill. Across the broad opening of the Shannon mouth, the outlines of the Clare coast and the small faraway white tower of Loop Head lighthouse, standing on the edge of the land.

Here was the holiday place that was ours, and to which we returned each summer for all our lives. It was nine miles of a stretch of dead straight road, west from the town of Listowel, and one mile north of a place called the Cashen, where the salmon river of the Feale flowed into the sea.

But this heavenly place had other faces at other times. Thousands of years of storms and fierce Atlantic waves had sculped and honed the stone land into high cliffs, and long dark caves entered each stormy tide by pounding waves that howled deep underground with dreadful menace. Thousands of years too had sculpted and honed the folk memories and folk tales that surround the place. Pirates and smugglers of wine and brandy with their broad cutlasses and black headbands and bright red neckcloths used the long dark caves as their fearsome lairs. In the dark of night they moved their boats through long caves, and sea passages, without once entering the open sea. One cave, called the 'Pigeon Cave', is eighty feet high and is celebrated for the splendour of its roof.

The English poet Tennyson visited the place in 1842, four years before the Famine, and was moved to write:

> So dark a forethought rolles about his brain
> As on a dull day in an ocean cave,
> The blind wave feeling round his long sea hell

Up along the cliff walks to the north there is a deep round opening on the cliff top, and fifty feet below the thrashing sea rages and growls in anger. It is called 'The Nine Daughters Hole'. The folk legend says that a thousand years ago raiding Norsemen pulled in their boats here and charmed the nine daughters of a local chieftain, who agreed to elope with the blond warriors. Their enraged father thwarted their plan, and the daughters were brought to the clifftop and hurled to their deaths, into the waters deep below.

Another version has it that the youngest daughter escaped. She was the last in the line, and begged her father, in modesty, to turn his back while she disrobed. He did so and the resourceful young woman pushed him over the edge and kept her life.

Overlooking the beaches on a green promontory stands the eastern wall of Ballybunion Castle, built by the Geraldine branch of the Norman invaders five hundred years ago. The old castle, battered by numerous sieges and by the Atlantic Ocean, lost its seaward walls. The remains of the once-great edifice stand forty feet high.

The old Irish tribes who inhabited this place six thousand years ago have left their footprints in the sand. Traces of primitive hearths and kitchen middens, where the people cooked fish and the flesh of deer and wild boar, have been found among the ancient sand dunes where the famed Ballybunion Golf Course is now set out. Some of these people lived by a stream that still flows through the sandhills. They sheltered in caves and tents made from animal skins, and sewed their clothing together with bone needles and the sinews of the wild pig and deer they chased. They heated stones and dropped them into vats dug out in the ground until the water boiled.

If you walk along the oceanside on a still evening just as the light has faded, and you listen closely with wonder and faith in your heart, you can still feel their ghosts about you, and hear the rustle of their movements in the light air.

A half mile or so farther south just beyond the Cashen mouth more wonder awaits, and more ghosts walk. It was here, on Ballyeagh Strand, at a race meeting in the summer of 1834, that the spleen of ancient feuding between two families, the Cooleens and the Mulvihills, spilled over in fury and bitterness. Thousands of people thronged the beach decked out for carnival enjoyment. The old feud had, on the face of it, been long forgotten, when a spark of animosity set it alight again. At the height of the battle three thousand people flung themselves on each other with any weapons they could lay hands on. Soldiers and police on foot and on horseback were unable to stem the fighting. Some were killed with terrible body wounds and other were driven into a gut of sea water and drowned.

At the end the strand was littered with the dead and maimed. The dead numbered between sixteen and twenty, and further scores were injured. It was the end of Ballyeagh Races, which were banned by the authorities. But it was the beginning for another local town, Listowel, to which the races were transferred some years later.

Some local people will tell you the strand is haunted from end to end, and that you shouldn't go near the place after the fall of night. And there is this place where you should never walk when the moon is full, lest powerful and mysterious forces drag you to the water.

I never saw the ghosts nor felt the mysterious forces near the mouth of the Cashen. But in the month of July I did see the net fishermen pulling mightily on their oars as they made the big circle to trap the incoming salmon on a falling tide. Out into the flow of the water, with the net end held tight on land and the rest spewing out from the boat. Lead on the bottom and cork on the top. Keep our, keep out into the water, and turn with the falling tide, flowing down the gut. Turn in and row for the shore. They lay on their oars, to rest for a few moments, knowing well that if they gave them a bit of time, a few more salmon might move up into the trap. They know too that this is not in the rules of the game.

The salmon harvest is poor, with some draws showing only a fish or two. They curse quietly the farmers and factories, sometimes spilling their poisoned brew into the spawning beds up river, choking the life out of the young fry and salmon parr. And worst of all, choking the life out of the growing smolt on their way to the sea for the first time, making for the Faroe Islands of their forebears to feed and mature for a few years, and then back to the small rivers of their birth, there to spawn and begin again the great cycle of mystery. Most of all they curse the deep-sea spoilers with their miles of drift netting, from Donegal down the coast, sweeping the runs out of the sea; and the government for failing to keep these trawling predators under some kind of control.

Lying on the thick scutch grass of the Ballybunion cliff tops, I spent time gazing out to the west, looking for something magical. From the slopes of the Glanaruddery mountains, near my home inland, I could never hope to see Atlantis, the famed and mythical island of the Atlantic ocean. Nor could I see from there 'Hy Brasail' the Ireland's own beautiful island of myth and the inner heart, the isle of the Blest. The poet said:

> On the ocean that hollows the rocks where ye dwell,
> A shadowy land has appeared as they tell,
> Men thought a region of sunshine and rest,
> And they called it Hy Brasail, the isle of the blest.

From Ballybunion, I could see it. They told me I could see it, and I spoke to one who had.

Out near the promontory point of Loop Head in Clare, was the Head of the Leap, named for the leap made by Cuchulain, the great Ulster folk hero, in his successful attempt to escape the clutches of a woman who had become enamoured of him. It had been seen out there many's the time, and I could see it too, if I looked, and looked, and looked.

If I see it am I seeking an end to my own life? For tradition says that those who see it will die within seven years. In this place they have named this vision 'Killsaheen'. It appears on a calm day, way out near the Head of the Leap. It's a scene of a village with people walking around as if at a fair, and an old woman selling her goods from a cart. There is a large arch as in a bridge, and the spire of a church. Sometimes it appears as if turned upside down. It lasts for a long time, they say, sometimes for as long as twelve minutes, before it fades away back into the ocean. Some say it is a reflection of the light from a faraway place, a mirage like on the desert, where thirsty travellers see a green and palm-covered oasis, rising in the distance over the sand and then dissolving away.

I never saw my Hy Brasail. I only saw the lighthouse winking at me over the water, from the coast of Clare, in the darkness of summer evenings. I wondered if I was lucky perhaps that this was so.

Two miles travelling north along the coast road, from Ballybunion, there is a legendary hill. It is just over 800 feet high, and it is named 'Knockanure', translated, variously, as the Hill of Gold, the Hill of the Harvest, or the Hill of the Slaughter. I like the Hill of the Slaughter best, as it fits the picture.

Two thousand years ago, a band of warriors, called the Fianna, defended Ireland against its enemies. The warriors, famed for their chivalry, and glory, were led by a renowned champion, Fionn MacCumhail. They traversed far and wide, and hunted wild deer and pig in the forests, with spears and hounds.

A Greek princess fled to Ireland for protection, when her father was forcing her to marry Tailc Mac Trean, a great champion, who was monstrously deformed by an enchantment. He was of huge stature, with dark skin, and the head, ears and tail of a cat.

Tailc travelled to Ireland in fierce pursuit of the princess, and Fionn and the Fianna swore to defend her honour to the last man. On the slopes of the Hill of the Slaughter, the battle took place and Tailc killed one thousand of the Fianna warriors.

Oscar, grandson of Fionn, then threw down a challenge. He fought Tailc on the hill for three days, and eventually slew him. When he died his body changed into that of a most handsome man. The Greek princess, when she saw this, and conscious of the slaughter she had caused, sighed deeply and died in her grief.

*

The boarding house where we stayed, that I first remember, was called 'Sea Haven'. It was a double house with two front doors and two stairs and landings. It had a pink and grey pebble-dashed front, and overlooked a small old Protestant church and the minister's rectory. It was a mere hundred yards from the roadway that led down to the beaches and was close to the centre of the holiday village. The front upstairs windows looked out on the ocean, the Castle Green, and to the north the cliff faces and clifftop walks. In front to the left and south was a tennis court with netting and a hard surface. I had never seen anything like it, and with great wonder I watched the tennis players in their white shorts and shirts. At the back of the houses was a wide kitchen garden that smelt of the roots of old cabbage heads and the discarded leaves of long-gone parsnips and carrots.

The owner of the house was a Mrs Enright, who lived there with her son Jack, a youth of sixteen years, and of eccentric character. Another permanent resident was a retired British Army soldier, called Sergeant Pat. In all there were perhaps twenty people in the two houses between adults and children. All the boarders brought in their own food, and deposited the durables, like potatoes, and bacon and eggs, turnips and bread and butter, with Mrs Enright in the kitchen, on day one, for cooking at the various meals. More perishable food, like chops or steak, or cream buns, or milk, were brought in on a daily basis. Each family had their own large food box, stored in a big kitchen cupboard. The tables were carefully laid out in a large dining-room on the ground floor, covered with clean white tablecloths and good chinaware and cutlery. The bedrooms were clean with tarpaulin carpets, and good white bed linen. I was quite taken with everything. It looked to my untutored eye like something a nice hotel might be.

It was not long before Sergeant Pat made his presence felt. It was the end of July and he had just received his pension from the British government. As apparently always happened at this time, he went on a drinking spree. The first night he came in late, and loudly muttered and damned his way up the stairs to his bedroom, right next to ours. Every now and then he broke out into loud song, followed by snatches of swearing and cursing at some imaginary enemies. A short silence was followed by a loud outburst of 'It's a Long Way to Tipperary, It's a Long Way to Go', followed by a medley of imprecations, such as 'God blast him, the son of a hoor', or 'May the devil in hell sweep him and all belonging to him'. And on it went until my father, a bad sleeper, had to take measures.

He began moderately enough, with shouts of 'Be quiet over there,' 'Be quiet,' 'Be quiet, I tell you.' This was met by loud guffaws, and hooting and jeering. My father got out of bed and, seizing his shoe, attacked the wooden partition wall between us with such ferocity that I thought he'd have it down around us.

Sergeant Pat was not a man to be intimidated by a thumping shoe on the wall from another room, and made it clear what he thought of such lily-livered interventions. And so the altercation continued for what seemed to me a long time. It only came to an end when my father told him that there would be more that a shoe involved in the affair. Sergeant Pat began to take notice when the name of a certain weapon was introduced. Only a little over ten years had elapsed since the weapon concerned had been common currency among the populace. The weapon was still held in a certain place in many a household. Drunk as he was, Sergeant Pat knew this well. Peace soon reigned again over the first night of our summer holidays, and we all lived to fight another day.

There was another war simmering in the boarding house that I shortly became aware of. It was in the kitchen, where Mrs Enright herself was chief cook and manager in charge. Her help there consisted of her rebellious son Jack, and a young girl with a white apron, who among her other duties waited at table. Jack was so disaffected that he insisted on getting the most precise instructions when asked to perform the most simple task. A request like filling a jug of water, or turning down gas under the cabbage pot, would lead to protracted argument and altercation.

I witnessed an episode one day while looking into the kitchen from a corridor outside. Mrs Enright had completed the cooking of the boarders' midday meal, and requested Jack to bring to her a stack of a dozen or so dinner plates from a table across the kitchen.

'I can't, Ma,' said Jack.

'Why can't you,' said his mother.

'Because I can't, that's why,' said Jack.

'For Goodness sake,' said his mother 'bring over those plates at once, or I'll crack you on the head with the scrubbing brush.' Jack appeared to break under this threat. He took up the stack of plates and walked to the middle of the kitchen. There he stopped and dropped the stack onto the cement floor. He looked at his mother, and shouted at her: 'I told you I couldn't do it, Ma.' Then he made for the door.

It was at 'Sea Haven', that I first encountered some people who might be said to belong to another class. I didn't know if they fitted into what my father used to call the 'blue bloods', but it seemed to me they weren't too far away from that description. They were a little girl and a little boy travelling under the care of a tall, dark, imposing young woman whom they told me was their governess.

They were of the Webb family from Nenagh, County Tipperary, and their names were Rosemary and David. Rosemary was an exquisite doll of a girl, with long golden tresses and a pink and white complexion. David was perhaps a year older, and came from the same mould, his blond hair well-combed and brushed smartly back. Both spoke with strange accents that intrigued me, clear and sweet with cadence and stress that was most pleasant. They always spoke out strongly and coherently, their words put together in an ordered way. Everything they did was courteous, and well-mannered, and quietly restrained, with no spark of devilment showing.

I was particularly taken by the girl, as I had never seen the likes of her before. I could not help gazing, whenever possible, at her lightly tanned beautiful face. It was clear to me that something was happening to me, but I did not know just what. There was a song that I knew a few lines of and I found myself humming them silently in my mind over and over again. 'Oh Rosemary, I love you; I'm always dreaming of you; some times I wish that I had never met you; and yet if I should lose you, 'twould mean my very life to me; of all the girls I ever met, I choose you; you are my Rosemary.' It was a quite an extraordinary situation for a boy of seven to find himself in. At times it was a quite pleasant feeling, but there were times of strange anxiety when the governess, who was always hovering about, moved in and whisked her away somewhere.

I had the feeling that the governess looked on me with a certain degree of disapproval, as if my slightly rough and fairly unsophisticated ways might possibly tarnish her young charges in some way or another. In a way she was right. It was not too long before we became adept at giving her the slip, and rushed off to live our own wild childish ways. If they lived with decorum and without too much danger before, it was not long before they were cured of this awful disability. We ranged over sand and sandhill like young heathens, climbed high cliffs, and visited long dark caves with the water lapping to our knees. We caught small fish in the pools, and went deep over the barriers of black rocks to catch red crabs in their lairs. We captured straying donkeys and rode them without blinkers or bridle. They were out of their shells, their eyes bright, and game for anything the day might bring. They told me about their home in a big house with maidservants, their stable with ponies, and most enthralling of all, their houseboat on a river.

My mother was well aware of my new enamoured condition, and viewed the situation with small tolerant smiles. Then one day she said to me: 'Do you know, Rory, I think you've changed.'

'What?' I said in mild shame, my antennae up in defence.

'It's your accent, you have an English accent.'

'I have no English accent, that's an awful thing to say.'

I could feel my feet sinking into the hole that was opening in ground under me. I was glad she had not mentioned the girl. But she was right about the accent, I was beginning to speak like the Webbs in certain ways. I understood it later. In my efforts to be taken in and accepted in the small golden circle, I was adopting their intonations and phrasing. Ever after, I never accepted the criticisms of those who jeered at emigrants returned from America, or England, who now spoke with the intonations of the foreigners amongst whom they had lived, even for a fairly short time. I knew they had changed in their attempts to be accepted and better under-stood by their new neighbours and fellow workers. They did so because they were sensitive, and not because they were weak-minded or compliant to excess.

The Webbs and I exchanged letters for a number of years. Bally-bawn, Nenagh, County Tipperary. Why they came out of the blue with their governess to a boarding house in Ballybunion for a two-week holiday, I never knew, or if I did, I have forgotten. I only know our meeting was a high point of my young life, and fortune being what it is, I never laid eyes on them again.

− 20 −

Sex Drive on the Land

IT WAS a bright day late in spring, and I was driving my new ass and cart back the road from my father's house. I was sitting on the setlock of the cart, my two bare legs hanging down, my head full of romantic notions. It was the month of April, for I had just thrown off the shoes for the first time that year to run in freedom until the first cold started to come in the early autumn. My heart was full of joy and images ran through my mind of who I really might be, driving along with my ashplant in my hand. Maybe I was Tip Toe the Tinker, going to the fair when he was young long ago, or maybe I was George Borrow, traversing the lanes of England in the last century, looking for adventure and watching out along the curve of the road for my deadly enemy, the Flaming Tinman.

It had all come together that morning. The young trembling female ass with all her new harness on for the first time. The brand new car, made by Greaney the carpenter, painted a bright red, and fastened to two motor-car wheels, with springs from an old horse trap. On the side of the right shaft, the family name printed in clear lettering of blue. It was my father's present to me, recognizing the new area of responsibility that I was entering at this time of my life.

I had trained the young ass as well as I could for a few weeks, with the tackling and car of Delia's old donkey. But she was wild of nature, and took badly to any kind of restraint. She too was seeking to be free, to roam unfettered as she wished through any place.

It wasn't the Flaming Tinman that I met, but something that was just as fearsome. When I saw the grey face and white eyes coming towards me, I felt I could be in some trouble. It was Nolan's stallion ass, out on the rampage, and he came in on me and my little donkey with great determination. He threw his head around and bit her on the flank. Then he seized her from the side by her dugs between her legs, and tried to raise her in the air. He got no encouragement from my little ass, but he cared little about what she wanted. I struck ashplant blows on his head, but he paid them as little regard as he would to the bites of passing horseflies. He raised himself on his hind legs, and pawed the air in front of him. Then he leaped on to the rear of my ass and ended up straddled over everything, donkey, shafts and all.

But salvation was at hand in the person of my neighbour Tadhg Doody, armed with the handle of an old spade. He untackled my little ass from the car, and drove the incensed stallion from the scene with mighty blows.

Tadhg put the shaft back over the straddle, linked up the traces, and put me back on the road. The ass was full of wildness after her ordeal, and pulled on ahead at her fastest speed. She went as if she were possessed by small demons goading her on. She gave no response to tightened reins or the bridle curb.

I had to let her have her head, there was no other way. On through Thady's Cross and back Boola road, and on towards the foothill of the mountain, with cut bogs on either side. I was a well-chastened knight of the road, full of anxiety, all romantic notions gone, when tiredness slowed her down. She pulled into the side, flanks heaving and head held down. I cursed the demon jackass that had caused my trouble.

Of all the animals I knew, nothing outdid the stallion ass for the violence of its sex drive. It mattered not whether the female was in or out of season. I have seen a jackass badgering an unwilling mare over rough terrain, and chasing her into dyke and over ditch, and in and out of boggy fields, until she ended up broken and bedraggled, worn out by the fighting.

Now a pig was a different thing entirely.

'Come on,' said Mossie to me in the yard. 'We'll take the sow to the boar.' We brought the sow out with a rope round her upper snout. We lowered the back of the horse cart with a high rail until the short back shafts were on the ground, and Mossie and two other men bundled her in. She came without too much protest, apart from a grunt or two, and she stood up there inside the rail looking around as if she was going on a holiday.

A couple of miles back we came into this yard and the man came out. He said little, as if he wanted to get on about the business. 'I hope she's in,' he said. 'Oh she's in all right,' said Mossie. 'Right so,' said the man and made for the cabin door.

I had never seen a boar before and he was something remarkable. He was twice the size of a sow, with big testicles pushing out under his backside. He had as ugly a head as I had ever seen, with a big snout pointing upwards from his jaws. He had small eyes full of malevolence, and gave out a series of threatening sounds, halfway between grunts and the growling of a lion or a tiger.

He waddled his big fat body forward, and minding nobody he got down to his business. His appurtenance was the strangest I had ever seen, being fashioned like a big pink corkscrew. Strangest of all was the length of time he took. He lay on the poor sow, who had her feet strutted out to keep upright. At times he would not move for a minute or two, and gave the appearance of being asleep. Then he'd move again and take another rest. On and on it went, until it appeared to me that best of half an hour had gone by. How he knew he was finished I never knew. There was no signal given, but in the end, he heaved himself off and growled his way back into the cabin.

The act of reproduction on the farm was not unfamiliar to me. In many farms, the bull ran free with the cows. Always there was a cock with the hens, a drake with the ducks, and a gander with the geese. Taking a cow to a bull or a mare to a stallion was a matter of little wonder. It was all part of the husbandry around which people lived their lives, just as the air they breathed and the rain that came down.

When the time came for the pig to have her bonhams, special preparations had to be made. If the weather was cold the pig would have to be brought into the house, usually in the kitchen. This was often a subject of derision among people who did not know any better. The loss of a sow and her litter could not be lightly dismissed with the Sign of the Cross and the prayer, 'May the troubles of the year go with them.' They blessed themselves all right, and they said the prayer. But they did so with sadness, and sometimes fear for the coming winter.

For me the pig in the kitchen was something of a gladness. Out went the table to another room, and in came a barth of clean straw, and a thick stave of timber to keep her from the wall. Then a long wait for the bonhams to be born. I had heard much of the wonder of sitting up with the pig through the night, and at last my time came. I was not alone, I had Joseph Thompson from across the river with me. But it was a badge of my growth, and a recognition that childhood was being left behind.

We settled in snug in the warmth of the kitchen, when all the others had gone to bed. It was midnight in the light of the lamp and the small flames of the turf fire. It was time for the ghost to walk, but we were snug and safe, waiting. They came at last, the small bonhams, one after another, until a dozen small bodies were moving and writhing about, seeking the teats of their mother, who lay back yielding to her young.

There he was, the runt that always came in a litter, one small weakling who couldn't fight for a teat of his own and who squealed in small anguish at his failures. He was gently guided and protected until he could settle in with the rest.

At around four o'clock the flitch of bacon was taken down and sliced with the butcher's knife. The bowl of eggs and the big iron pan was found, and the soda bread, and the ritual feast was held. It was the first time I had food in the late small hours, but it was as sweet as any I had ever taken.

We watched the sow for any sign of the killer instinct that afflicts some sows after birthing, and drives them to eat their own young. But this mother was benign and caring, and the household got up to a new day and acknowledged the blessing that had come during the night.

– 21 –

Digging for Turf

IT WAS the month of June, and my father arranged that Jack and Tadhg Doody, and another man, would cut turf on Nolan's bog, a small one-eighth-acre bank of peatland we owned two miles to the west, in the foothills of the Glanaruddery mountains. Jack had stripped the bog the day before. This entailed removing, with a spade, a sod of hard dry surface about four inches deep and two feet wide, to get down to the soft wet peat on a bank about five sods deep.

Jack stayed at our house the night before, damp bed or no. My father had agreed that I could get a day off from school. For me, the house was full of excitement. The mad pony was out in the orchard, cropping grass. A big fire was burning on the open hearth, and raked out wide and deep. My mother was baking cakes of bread in the oven and on the griddle, and boiling a dozen eggs and a large cut from a flitch of bacon. A wicker basket was dressed with a white cloth, empty cocoa canisters filled with tea and sugar, milk poured into two pint bottles, and yellow butter wrapped in grease paper. Mugs were stuffed with old newspapers, and a sweetgallon scoured for the boiling of the water. The air of the kitchen was hot and sweet-smelling, and my heart was full of expectation for the coming day, like the night before going on holidays to Ballybunion or waiting for Santa Claus to come.

The next morning we were on the road early, the risen sun hot on our backs, the car full of our goodies for the coming picnic and the implements for the day's hard work. Three triple-pronged pikes lay side by side, inside the butt, and rattled together as the Pissing Jennet's iron shoes knocked sparks off the stones on the dry road.

A thought of excitement and alarm struck me as I looked around the car. 'You've no sleán, Jack,' I shouted over the noise of the car. 'There'll be no turf cut today.'

'Well now, aren't you the smart little man,' said he, looking at me and laughing. 'Will Tadhg Doody have a sleán, will he?' and he said no more. We saw the two figures waiting for us at Thady's Cross, and neither of them had a sleán in his hand. Jack looked across at me.

'Hold your whist, and don't say a word to them,' said Jack as we pulled up. 'Good morrow, men,' he called, 'it's a great day, jump in the car.' He said nothing about the sleán, and I knew it was his own mistake.

We went back the road, without a care. Jack was whistling, but I knew he was thinking fairly hard. We were nearing Boola, when Jack stopped the pony.

'We're getting McAuliffe's sleán for the day,' he announced. 'Rory, will you run up the boreen there, and get it. Keep it on your shoulder, with the iron up, on the way down.'

I didn't move. I knew the game he was playing with me as Send the Fool Farther. In the end he went himself, and arrived back whistling, with the sleán up in the air. 'The luck was with you today, my boyo,' I thought.

We went farther back the white Boola road, past Jer Long's farm, and Jack the Mason's cottage, and Delia Keane's mountain meadow. We turned left down the steep road to the mountain stream, up the rising ground again, past Shone Doody's cottage, and then took the right cutting into the heart of Nolan's bog.

In minutes Jack had unloaded and was sitting on a rock of bog deal with the sleán and a rasp in his hand. He was sharpening the blade of the spade-like implement with another cutting wing on the left side, and then honing it with a dry sharpening stone.

I stood there looking around me. The heather was blooming, purple and brown, and all around stretching on every side was a sea of white, myriads of small white-headed flowers of flax-like texture moving and waving and beckoning in the light morning breeze. Away on the horizon to the west was the stretch of the Glanaruddery mountains, reflecting colours of black and brown and green in the light of the eastern sun. I looked for the two peaks, each standing at over a thousand feet, Muinganaire (The Overgrown Swamp of Grass), and Knights Mountain (The Sheep Rancher's Hill). I looked to the south but could not make out the peak of Knockachur (The Hill of the Twist). Everywhere around, in fields and on rising ground, far into the distance, I could see cattle browsing in the morning sun. I knew I was standing in a place which eons of time and changing seasons had fashioned, and a small touch of a primeval and wondrous feeling passed inside my heart, like the brush of a wing of something eternal.

Soon the men were at work. Jack was on the sleán, believing, perhaps, that only he had the skill such a task required. Beginning on the outside, he pushed the sleán down with his right foot on the small wooden shoulder. A push and the ten-inch sod fell forward. Tadhg, standing in front of him, speared it with his three-prong pike, and threw it as far as possible onto the bank. There the other man took it gently on his pike and threw it farther again, avoiding at all costs breaking the soft wet sod.

Jack decided to let me have a go at piking from the cut. I was doing fine until, as always happens, I nipped the front of my leg with a prong, and the blood was flowing.

Jack, full of resource, dragged me onto the bank, got down on his knees, and sucked all poisons from the small wound. It was a minor setback. At about half past eleven, Jack called to me to build a fire. I felt like one of the old pioneers, gathering sticks and dry bog deal, and lighting my red-headed match. A makeshift crane was fashioned, and in a short time my five-pint sweetgallon tin was bubbling over the fire and whispering to me that my friends, the tinkers, had nothing on me.

How sweet the meal in the sweet air. How sweet the tea, and the cold bacon, and the hard-boiled eggs. How sweet the white and brown cake and griddle bread. How sweet is everything around me, how sweet is life. I will ask for nothing more than this, wherever I go. Nothing that can ever happen to me again, can match this day. I hope and pray that somewhere, some time, I can feel again the touch of a passing angel's wing, even if it is an angel in the imagination of a small boy.

The work of the bogmen, and my looking and wondering, went on all day, until the sun had made a good part of its way down the sky to the west. The bank was covered with glistening black and brown sods like a dark wet sheet a couple of hundred feet long by twenty feet wide. Jack held the sleán over his head in triumph, and called across to me where I was examining the recesses of a wide boghole filled with brown water.

'The job is done,' he shouted, 'we'll make for home.'

But the job was not done, and little did I realize that sunny evening the heart-scalding and persecution that same bank of turf held in store for me in the weeks ahead. It was three weeks later, one late afternoon after school, that my father announced we were all going to the bog again.

'It's ready for a first footing now,' he said and the whole family piled into the blue Baby Ford and made for the bog.

By this time the sun and the drying breezes had drawn the water from the sods, and they were ready to be made into small stooks for further drying, four or five sods put standing against each other, with one on top. My father and mother, my older sister and myself. Each sod laboriously lifted up with small fingers, the upper body bent forward from the hips, always in the same position. In ten minutes the muscles of the lower back began to ache and then scream for relief. But my father had no pity in matters of this kind.

'Keep at it,' he said, looking sideways at me over his glasses, a smile on his face. 'Footing turf is good for you. It'll make a man of you yet.'

He was right in one way. For three evenings in a row we kept at it, until all the sods on the bank were standing up like soldiers on parade, saluting us in mocking postures. But we had the last laugh, for by then the pain was gone. We were seasoned children of the bog, and remained so for evermore.

We second-footed it after that, making big stooks of four or five of the smaller ones, and in a couple of weeks it was ready for drawing out, and the time was come for another pantomime involving my father and Jack and the Pissing Jennet.

Drawing out was the most hazardous of all bog operations, as it often involved an area of soft bog on which no ass or pony, with loaded car and rail of turf, could tread without some sort of disaster. After an intensive survey of the terrain, the best place to build a passage had to be found. My father or Jack, on their own, would have had enough skills to make a passage adequate for the job, but together they found it extraordinarily difficult to come to agreement.

My father, I felt, was the more level-headed and practical of the two. After all, he had already built a four-berth trailing caravan with his own hands, while Jack was more distinguished for his capacity to break things. Jack was probably aware of this too, but nevertheless felt there was a certain question of rights of ownership to be taken into account. While my father owned the bog and the turf, Jack owned the brown pony and the car and rail that was to bring the loads safely to the roadside. To his mind, this conferred on him the right of having the final say.

There was a certain amount of diplomacy in the opening propositions, but this inevitably degenerated into a wrangle. The rights and wrongs were debated with increasing heat, until Jack entered the final argument.

'Look here, Master,' he said, with hot intensity in his face, 'if we go your way, the pony will be up to her belly in ten seconds. If my pony goes down, she'll fight to free herself, because you know very well that's the kind of beast she is. If she fights, she'll break a hock. If that happens, you'll still have your bog and your turf, and I'll have no pony. I'll be going now for the branches and dry sods, and you can have your mind made up when I come back. If you go my way we'll make the passage. If it's your way, I'll be off home to Abbeyfeale.' And off he went.

My father sat down on a lump of bog deal, and smoked a Gold Flake cigarette, chuckling away to himself and swearing to God between laughs about the 'complete lunatic' that was gone down to Shone Doody's wood for the tree branches.

'Have it your way,' said my father when Jack came back. Jack nodded his head and said nothing. But there was a half smile of victory on his face, and he set about the work with great vigour. The Pissing Jennet, as if she sensed her master's victory, behaved herself grandly in support, and did not go into a single act of her six-part repertoire of misbehaviour for the rest of the day.

The mischievous charm and the drama that was in Jack displayed itself in all facets of life as I knew him over the years, always turning the world upside down, never doing the obvious, but giving enormous thought to inventing the most cross-grained and improbable ways of doing even quite simple things. He laughed and cackled his way through life, well aware of the discomfiture he induced in his victims with his disorderly conundrum of thoughts.

After his mother died in 1944, he spent the last forty-five years of his life living simply and alone in his cottage, until his death in 1989 at the age of seventy-nine.

– 22 –

Last Wonders

IN OUR HOUSE we waited in hope and expectation for the people of the road who might come past our doorstep. Tinker, tailor, travelling man or woman. A new smile, a new glint of an eye, of anger or contentment, a new story or a new way of telling it.

Nellie Mulcahy came in, touched, bedraggled, and wild-eyed, embattled with life. Ragged clothing hung on her frail body, and white limp hair hung uncombed about her pale unhappy face. Inside the door of the kitchen she stood defiantly: 'I'm here,' she said, 'and what about it?'

She sat stiff and upright on a timber chair and said in a loud voice: 'I'm martyred by those scholars, may God blast them and all their generations. "Nellie with the timber belly," they shouted after me when I passed the school, and then rained stones down on my head. May God wither the hands of those blackguards that flung them stones.'

'Will you have a cup of tea, Nellie?' my mother asked, trying to calm her.

'Yerra, I will, girl,' Nellie replied, a broken smile on her face. 'And I might have two cups, with plenty of sugar, and a couple of cuts of sweet bread.' She settled herself, and rubbed her dirty skirt with her hands.

'Do you want to know where I slept last night? I slept in the loft of Abbbeyfeale church, as God is my judge. I slept on a bench of papers, with dead people walking all round me. They didn't give me a wink of sleep until I got the better of them. I put the run on them with a few sprinkles of holy water from a bottle I carry in the pocket of my bib. On papers I slept, didn't I tell you? I had a couple of *Cork Examiners* under me, and a *Kerryman* over me. What do you think of that, girl?' She laughed out at her own joke, and rubbed the water out of her eyes.

'Do you know who I came across today on the road? That ould wan from Cork that's always walking the country, day and night. "Mary from Cork", they call her. She had the twenty-stone mail-bag on her back like always full of gibbols and rags. Her Thomasheen she calls it. She's as mad as a hare on the mountain in the month of March. She should be back in the madhouse in Killarney, I tell you, and I tell you no lie.'

Nellie went out to continue on her own sad way, to battle with her own ghosts and her own wild images in her head.

When Mousheen Keefe came up the pathway from the gate on one of his visits, the children in the kitchen jumped in jubilation. He was a small man with a cap set straight on his head, and he always wore a rough tweed suit and a waistcoat with pockets. He looked a bit like a leprechaun, with black eyes and a pointed face and a small stoop on his back.

The stoop was from carrying a long brown bag as big as a bolster, with double handles at the top and straps across. What he had in the bag was better than the gold of any leprechaun. When he came in he threw it on to the table and smiled at the pairs of round eyes looking up at him.

He opened the bag and the treasures of the earth were there to be seen. 'I'm Santa Claus, and I'm here again, and it isn't even Christmas.' He squealed in a small laugh at his humour. 'And I didn't come down the chimney either,' and he squealed again.

He took out the coloured handkerchiefs, bangles with clasps, brooches and tie-pins. He laid them on the table and thrust his hands again into the bag. Silk stockings for my mother, and packets of needles, and thimbles, and spools of coloured thread. Tiny bottles of perfume, and flapjacks of face powder. Ties for my father, and shirt studs and cuff-links. Light ankle socks, and bunches of fairy ribbons for my sister's hair.

He had nothing for me, nothing to delight the heart of a boy. No small football, or toy popgun, or handball to play against the gable of the house. He looked at me and could see my disappointment. 'I'll bring something for you the next time,' he said. But I did not care too much, such was the atmosphere of joy he had brought in. I knew there would be other times. My mother made her purchases for everyone, and made tea for him, with white scones and butter and jam.

I never knew where he had come from, or who had bestowed on him all those beautiful things. When he had repacked his carpet bag and departed on the road again, my mother secretly slipped a silver sixpence into my hand. I went outside to see him disappear along the road, and I looked with happiness at the small coin warm on my palm.

Davey the Weaver was a different class of person again. He went around with his head full of stories, and after he got a mug of tea and a bit of bread and meat, he'd tell you as many as you liked for as long as you liked.

The cows were milked and everything was secure outside when he came into Delia's kitchen on a winter's evening. The lamp was lit and the fire was burning and sparking with good timber. After he had eaten and drunk his tea, he settled himself on the súgán chair at the side of the hearth. They were all in, sitting warm around, and waiting to listen to his story.

'There was this widow woman and she lived with her only son on a nice snug farm back country. She was a sort of clever woman with a good understanding of her own worth, with a grasp for the money, and anything she could get. She was a good way strongheaded, and put little or no value on anybody's opinion but her own.

'Some people said she thought she knew as much as the priest of the parish himself, or in some way or another maybe more. The son, the only son that I mentioned already, was as good a man as you'd find, and he was so good-looking that half the women of the parish were after him. His mother set it before her that the woman he'd marry would not only have looks but would have a good dowry to boot.

'But like everything else, things don't always happen as one might want. The girl the son fell for had the looks all right, but she came from a small farm, and was short enough by way of a dowry. In fact one could say she didn't have as much as half a dowry, that would be warranted by the farm she was coming into.

'The mother fought it to the last, but the son wouldn't be put off, and the mother gave in in the end, but with very bad grace inside. In fact she had a resentment to the girl in her head that never left her.

'There was little happiness in the house, even though two children, a boy and a girl, were born. The widow was always criticizing and prodding at the young wife, and digging her about the place she came out of and the paupers that lived in it.

'But things might have carried on, on a half keel as they were, if a certain thing hadn't happened.

'Now in a place not too far from the house, there was a hilly field, and rising in the middle of it was a fairy fort from as far back as time was known. It took up a good bit of ground, and was a kind of obstruction to the work, like when a team of horses would be turning in the field. Nobody laid a spade on it, for everyone but an amadán knew that interfering with it could bring down curses on that person's head that would be terrible to think about.

'But that was not good enough for the old widow. Nothing would do her but that the fort should be levelled, and she was ever grumbling and knawvshawling about it, if it wasn't about something else. In the end she broke down the son and one day in a fit of temper he took out pickaxe and shovel, and an iron sledge, and levelled it to the ground.

'He and his young wife knew, and all the neighbours knew, that he had done wrong and a kind of fear settled over the place, and the waiting went on for something to happen. It didn't take long, I tell you. One day on the heel of the evening, before the dark had settled down, a strange music was heard coming down from the hilly field, and the son of the house, who had just sat down to his supper, was taken by a fearful strangling of the throat. The two women ran to his aid but despite everything they could do, he died just as the clock struck the hour of midnight.

'It did not end there, I tell you. When the son was buried the old widow, defiant to the last, gave the young wife the door, and sent them out into the world. The people around took this very badly, and had no wish to see her, not to mind talking to her.

'There was this one old woman who came to see her an odd time, out of pity. They were sitting at the fire one night of a storm, with heavy rain, talking away. All of a sudden the visiting woman looked round to the door, with a look of fear on her face.

'"Whist a minute, woman," she said, and they both listened. Coming faint enough over the sound of the storm, but clear and plain enough to hear, came this strange music.

'"The Lord and his Blessed Mother protect us," said the visiting woman. "They're coming again."

'The old widow never answered a word. She rose from her chair, her face a deadly white, took her shawl from a nail behind the door and faced out into the storm. It was the last that was ever seen of her alive. Her body was found next morning, stretched out on the ground where the fairy fort had stood, her eyes were open and staring, and her face was black all over, with the dint of the death struggle she went through.'

Davey the Weaver had his head down, and there was not a word or a movement round the fire. Then he laughed out. 'That was not the end of it,' he said, 'there was a good end to it. Against all the odds the young widow got back into the farm with her two children, and lived happy there for ever after. They say the fairies have many a good turn in them, after all.'

For a few moments nothing was said, as if all were thinking a bit about the lesson of the story. Then Davey made a movement to get up as if about to go.

'Yerra, stay where you are, Davey,' Mossie said, ''tis a cold old night and you'd have a long way to go to another billet in the dark. You can settle down there in the corner.'

'Why not indeed,' said Mary, ''tisn't that often you pay us a visit. You might tell us another story to shorten the night for us.' Davey did not need any further encouragement and shuffled himself right in the chair again.

'The wan I'm going to tell you now, you mightn't be inclined to believe it. But I had it from the mouth of a cousin of the man it happened to.

'It was back near Dingle, not far from a cluster of cottages, the home of fishermen's families, who had boats on the strand below. 'Twas often said a woman had been seen sitting on a rock at low tide and combing her long blonde hair. But if anybody came anyway near her, she'd pick up a sort of oily skin covering she had on the rock beside her, and disappear in the twinkling of an eye. They called her a mermaid, a member of an enchanted tribe, who took refuge in the sea after one of the invasions in ancient times.

'This particular evening a small group of fishermen were making their way home from the sea, when one of them delayed behind for some reason or another, while the others went on ahead. His name was Deny and he lived alone.

'Deny turned to come on again on the cliff path, and whatever look he gave back he spotted her. There she was sitting on the rock, the most beautiful woman he ever had seen, combing her fine golden hair down from her head with a white seashell rack, and close beside her, spread out, was her covering. He bent down and quiet as a stalking ferret he circled round and came up behind her. He had enough sense to know that if he could get hold of the covering, he had her armed forever. So it was it happened. He seized the covering and held it firm. As soon as she saw him she got greatly alarmed and disappeared into the water. Deny stood quiet, and it was not long till she appeared again. She pleaded, with her hand, to be given back the cloak, but Deny refused.

'Then she spoke to him in his own tongue, and cried out and implored of him to give her back her mysterious covering. But Deny would not be moved, for he had heard that without the covering a mermaid was no more than an ordinary woman. Finally she threatened to send a mighty wave that would sweep him into the ocean. But Deny ignored all this and turned to make his way home. In the end the distress went from her, and she followed him meekly back to his own house. He hid the covering in a secret place high up in a top clevvy in the kitchen wall that she could never reach.

'He took her as his wife. She was a woman of great beauty with skin as white and fair as peaches and new milk, and although she had the daintiness of a china doll, she went about the work of the house and the chores outside as if she had been doing it all her life. She gave him three beautiful children, and although she appeared as contented as a woman could be, she never laughed or smiled, from the day she entered the house.

'One day, it was seven years to the day from the day he brought her from the sea, she was sitting by the fire with her third child on her lap. Her husband came in, in a hurry, and climbed on a high stool to rummage in the clevvy on the wall. He knocked down an old piece of sacking, and with it, unknown to him, came the mysterious covering of the mermaid.

'She moved immediately, and stood the child by the side of her chair. Then she took the covering and was away with it before Deny could get down from the stool. She ran down for the shore, the sound of her laughter ringing over the strand. Then she disappeared into the sea, and was never seen again.

'Deny mourned her always. But he and his three children prospered, and their descendants are still to be found in places around the Dingle area. 'Twas said, till the day he died, Deny spent time each day looking out to sea, over the rock, where he first found her. 'Twas said, too, that he never again was known to laugh, apart from a faint smile that would come to his face.'

*

It was my mother who decided that I should become an altar boy.

'I'm saying it for your own good. It's right that you should be up there on the altar, with the other boys, serving the priest at Mass. You'll never be nearer to God than when you're kneeling there in front of the tabernacle.'

She could see the look on my face and decided to rub it in with a bit of a joke.

'Do you know if you got used to it you might like it, and decide to be a priest yourself. Then you'd have your own altar boys running around and serving you with this and that.'

An altar boy was the last thing I wanted to be. I had no wish to go around dressed like a girl, in long black dress and white blouse.

'I don't think 'twould be the right thing for me to do, Ma,' I said, 'and in any case I heard it was very dangerous.'

'Dangerous, dangerous how are you, how could it be dangerous, who said that?'

'Would it be dangerous, Ma,' I replied, 'if I drank the priest's wine and ate the hosts in the sacristy, and maybe got drunk or sick itself? I heard the altar boys drink the wine and nobody knows a thing about it.'

My mother angered visibly at the argument I was putting up. 'I'll tell you something,' my mother said, 'you are a right blackguard, with a mind as crooked as the horn of a ram. I'll tell you something else, I'll make an altar boy out of you if it's the last thing I do.'

Never being one to push my luck too far, I said nothing and slipped away when the opportunity came. The truth was I never heard that the altar boys drank the wine, but the pressure was too hard on me and I had to say something. In any case I knew I was right. What cause had anyone to put me up there to make a fool of myself, up there babbling away in a foreign language that nobody understood, and for the boys at school to snigger at me and make jokes behind my back.

I knew of course she'd wear me down. What was I anyway but a helpless boy with nobody to stand up for me, and my father saying nothing but smiling away to himself? Soon enough I found myself in front of the curate in the sacristy of the chapel, by special appointment, along with two other conscripts. He threw his eye over us and he appeared pleased with how we looked.

'You know, boys,' he said, 'this is a special privilege given to you, that is not bestowed on everybody. Taking part in the Holy

Mass with the priest is a very wonderful thing. You'll have to spend a few weeks learning the responses to the priest. They're in Latin, and you won't understand them, but that does not matter at all, the priest will know what you are saying.'

He gave each of us a small catechism, with a chapter at the back entitled 'The Manner of Serving a Priest at Mass'.

'We won't begin learning the Latin this evening,' he said, 'as I'm in a bit of a hurry. We'll make it every Tuesday and Thursday, here at half past four, for about one hour.'

With a heavy heart I told my mother, and on the next Saturday she was off to the town of Abbeyfeale on her bicycle to buy the cloth for the soutane and surplice that would make an altar boy out of me.

The following Sunday I went to Mass with my mother as usual. It was the last Mass, at eleven o'clock, and as usual we were late, struggling up the slope of Close Field to make up time, with the sharp heels of my mother's Sunday shoes foundering on the soft ground. She was no angel today with a lot of sniping at me for being so far ahead. I inveigled her to take another short cut, up Bilcan's boreen to the very door of the chapel yard. I had forgotten how rough it was, worse than a quarry road, with stones and mud.

'This is the last time we'll go your short cuts,' she said to me with venom as we came up the last steep cutting to the top. 'You'll be up in time every Sunday from this on. Your Uncle Jack is right, you're only a little caffler.'

I was considerably offended at this unjust attack, but after she straightened her clothes and patted her hat outside the church door, I was right behind her as she marched up the aisle with the walk of a queen. She always went up about halfway and turned in to the pews on the right where the women sat, and I went with her. From there there was a good sight of the dressed-up Sunday women, from their hats down, as they walked gracefully by, and not forgetting to glance at the seams of their stockings and the heels of their shoes. The highlight of the day was the passage of Babelle, a returned Yank of buxom proportions. She came back from America with a trunkful of long floral dresses and hats that were astonishing to see. And when she sailed by to her place right before the altar, she gave forth a fragrance of powders and scents which no other woman could match.

As my mother genuflected at the end of the pew, I made a quick decision. I turned back down the chapel and went up the stairs to the gallery where the organ was kept, and where the choir sang on special occasions. In any case I wanted to have a good look at the altar boy and his manoeuvrings. It was a grand place to see everything. On the left, row after row of men's polls, some with hair and more as bald as a plate. The right side was like a flower garden of ladies' hats and scarves, and here and there old women with black shawls drawn up over their heads. Way in front, the altar white as marble, and the golden tabernacle, and the priest in his coloured golden robes moving this way and that.

The chapel was a pleasant enough place for me, with the Stations of the Cross on the walls, and the stained-glass windows, the scent of incense rising from the burning charcoal during Benediction, and the Crib at Christmas, with the people moving slowly around in the half-light of candles and oil lamps. These occasions were warm and comforting. There were hymns too that I liked. There was a certain air of defiance about 'Faith of our Fathers living still, in spite of dungeon, fire and sword.' There was for me an attractive quality too in the lines from 'Hymn to Mary', when the organ played and the choir sang out 'So I'll be ever ready, Thy goodly help to claim, When wicked men blaspheme Thee, To love and bless Thy name.' I liked that line, 'When wicked men blaspheme Thee.'

What I saw of the altar boy that day brought me no comfort. The thought crossed my mind as well that, if my mother made me an altar boy, my next road would be into the choir. I gave it a lot of thought and a plan was forming in my mind.

I was half an hour late for the first altar boy lesson. The curate did not say too much about that.

'We'll go over again what I was telling them before you came in. The priest bows down at the foot of the altar, makes the sign of the cross from his forehead to his breast, and says: "In nomine Patris, et Filii, et Spiritus Sancti, Amen." Now you say nothing to that.'

I put up my hand. 'What does that mean, Father?' I asked. He looked at me for a bit, but then he told me: 'In the name of the Father, and of the Son, and of the Holy Ghost, Amen.' Then he added, 'As I told you before, it does not matter that you don't understand it. The priest understands it, that's what matters.' He went on: 'Next the priest says, "Introibo ad altare Dei," and you reply, "Ad Deum qui laetificat ad juventutem meam".'

He repeated this again and again, but my head was down and I couldn't learn it. 'My God,' he said, 'Why can't you learn it like the others. What's wrong with you at all?'

'I'll tell you what it is, Father, it's the way I'm made. I can't learn anything I don't understand, no matter how long I spend at it. I think I was never cut out to be an altar boy.'

He didn't pursue it further. He looked at me with a certain severity and said: 'I'm inclined to agree with you. The best thing you could do now is go home to your mother.'

That's how it was. My mother was more than a bit scandalized, and wanted to fight a rearguard action. But in the end my father intervened. 'For Goodness sake, woman,' he said, 'be rational, don't you see he doesn't want to be an altar boy, no matter what you think. Leave it at that.' She left it at that, and I never again laid eyes on the black and white cloth she bought that day in town.

*

I saw the moon was up, yellow and full, and it was bright as day outside. I found a worn black leather jacket of my father's, that zipped up the front, and an old hat with a wide brim. From a nail on the back of the front door I took a red headscarf of my mother's, and I was as near as I could manage it to being the cowboy I wished to be. I slipped across the road and into a large moonlit field, and took up my position near a big rick of straw, stacked after the autumn threshing. Romance filled my brain. The open countryside before me was my prairie, but I had no horse to stand beside me, and no six-gun on my thigh.

The high moon filled me with wonder; it was the same moon that shone over the great plains, from the Rio Grande on the Mexican border to the Dakotas in the north; the same moon that glanced across Red River in Texas and the Big Horn in the hills of Wyoming and Montana.

Carnegie, the rich American who wanted to do good, was the man responsible for my dreaming. It was his books that came to our house in a box twice a year, from a library in Tralee. Fifty-two books each time, all with hard covers, all painting pictures of life and people and places that had me driven demented.

These books were mine to distribute, they were in my charge. I held the file, and the small white cards for the names of the borrowers and the date of return. There was no charge for the books, because Carnegie would have it so. It was in these that I found my first love. It was in the American cowboy that I found my greatest captivation. How could it be otherwise? How could one not succumb to the charm of this tall slim figure with his broad Stetson hat, loose knotted red bandanna round his throat, his brown cartridge belt above his hips, this cowboy who lives and fights on horseback, armed with a six-gun, swift and deadly, gracious to ladies, reserved to strangers, generous to friends, and brutal to enemies?

I rode with him at roundup time, branded the steers, and

searched the culees and gulches for missing mavericks. I rode with him beside the trampling herd, riding point at the front, swingman at the side, or drag with the weakened and worn-out at the rear, through noxious dust and choking heat. When a breaking branch or a horse's whinny set them on wild stampede through the dark, I searched all night with him for the missing steers.

I marvelled with him at the Texas longhorn, tall, bony and coarse-headed, thin-flanked, narrow-backed and sway-backed, this almost mythical beast who could walk the roughest ground, cross the widest desert, enduring cold, hunger and thirst.

I rode with him and a herd of three thousand cattle, from Texas to the Kansas railhead at Abilene. It was a journey of sixty to ninety days, over a thousand miles along the Chisholm Trail, the never-ending track used by the buffalo and the Indians for countless years.

I did my stint with him on night guard beside the bedded-down herd, and sang gentle lullabies to soothe the restless cattle.

'Oh, slow up little dogies, quit moving around; you have wandered and trampled all over the ground; oh, graze along dogies and feed kind of slow; and don't be forever on the go; move slow little dogies, move slow.'

I slept beside him on the hard ground in a bed of two blankets and a wagon sheet for tarpaulin, and saddles and coats for pillows.

At the first white streak of dawn I awakened with the others at the cook's cry from the chuck wagon: 'Day's abreaking, come and git it.' I ate the flapjacks and washed them down with hot coffee.

I rode mustangs and roans and robbed banks and held up trains, at the side of Billy the Kid and Jesse James, and saw them draw their six-guns with speed that dazzled the eye. I travelled with Wild Bill Hickock and Buffalo Bill, and was at Tombstone at the shoot-out at the O.K. Corral, when Wyatt Earp and his two brothers, and Doc Holliday, killed the two brothers, Frank and Tom McLaury, and the rustler and highwayman Billy Clanton.

The age of the cowboy lasted less than thirty years after the Civil War ended. It was finished by 1890. It was ended mainly by the tens of thousands of settlers and farmers who fenced off and ploughed the land. There was no place now for the huge wide ranging herds, no place any more for the cowboy. The prairie, the romantic endless grassland, was fast disappearing. In the last ten years everything had changed. Seventy million buffalo had been slaughtered, for meat, hide and bone, and mere sport; the Indians were defeated and driven to their reservations.

Two great blizzards, in the winters of 1886 and 1887, devastated the great herds, and they never recovered. Over two thousand miles of the Great Plains the greatest ice storms ever known ravaged the land. The cattle in their tens of thousands were frozen to death, or died of hunger. Their bodies filled the ravines and gulches and their bodies floated in their hundreds down the swollen rivers.

The cowboys fought valiantly to save the herds. Before they rode out into the blizzards they donned garments of survival. Two sets of heavy underwear, two woollen shirts, wool pants, overalls, and leather chaps. Over these they wore blanket-lined overcoats, with woollen caps on their head. They had wool gloves under leather mittens. They wore two pairs of wool socks after walking in snow and drying their feet. They stood in water in their riding boots, then went outside until a thin protecting sheath of ice had formed.

They blackened their faces with lamp-black to prevent snow blindness, and cut holes in their neck bandannas and masked their faces. They rode out to fight a losing battle. Many died in ravines or flooded rivers. Others died of cold, and their frozen bodies were lashed to their saddles and brought back to be kept for long periods in snow drifts until the hard ground softened out. Within three years the cowboy years had slipped away for ever.

These were the cold hard facts that came out of Carnegie's books. But the Wild West writers wrote their fiction, and the romance of the cowboys' life went on. These were the stories that gladdened the heart, stories of the heroic cowpunchers, horse wranglers, lone strangers, gunslingers, cardsharps, moving on the trails, and in the cattle towns. There were wrongs to be righted, bad men to be challenged, acts of chivalry to be performed, fair ladies to be rescued and their hearts to be won.

There were many round me that yearned for the tales of the legendary West, and they came to our door week after week for new thrills and new dreaming, new means to turn their minds away, for a little while, from the drudgery of their days. A cobbler of shoes, who carried with him from birth the indignity of a crippled foot; a spinster alone, who found life so painful that one day she decided to end it; an old widow confined to her chair; an ancient white-faced old warrior who struggled up two miles of road for his book; and many others. All sought renewal from the strange fantasies that came from places that were far away, and from another time.

The fantasy stayed with me also. Many times after, the vision came back to me of the boy dressed in his father's old clothes, standing in the moonlight by the rick of yellow straw and looking out over the wide prairie he had fashioned for himself.

*

It was all so far away. It was a Sunday afternoon in early September 1939, and the sun was bright and warm. I should have felt sadness that the summer days were gone, and on the next morning I'd have to cross the fields and the river again for another year at school. But I was thinking of something else. That afternoon on the wireless the news came in. The war was on, and planes and tanks and troops were moving.

I felt it was going to happen, from the wireless and the papers and the talk, over the last couple of days. I knew that Chamberlain had gone to see Hitler for a last try, and I knew he had said: 'If at first you don't succeed, try, try and try again.' And I knew that he had returned and waved a paper in the air and said, 'There will be peace in our time.' But I knew *now* that Hitler had gone into Poland, and that at eleven o'clock that morning the real war was on.

All through Friday evening and Saturday, my father had kept close to the house to hear every piece of news. He listened with a solemn look on his face, and the anxiety he felt came to me as well.

He had spoken about it a good deal during the previous year or so. At times I thought he was making excuses for Hitler. 'They went too far,' he said, 'they made it too hard on Germany after the Great War.' He explained to me what he meant, as if he were teaching me history at school.

When German troops crossed into Austria the spring of the previous year, he said, 'It's hard to know what is happening. I don't know what's happening. They were all together once, they're very like each other still.' When Hitler was threatening to take over Czechoslovakia, he said, 'A lot of that country is German already.'

But Poland was the end. He knew it was coming. Only a week before, he said: 'Hitler has signed up with Russia, Poland is gone. If I'm right, we're all in trouble.'

I was in trouble, too. At night I dreamt of waves of German fighters and bombers coming over and machine-gunning and bombing our house. The sky darkened in storm, and banks of black cloud built up like giant battlements. I could see the scenes of battle, with shells bursting and tanks rolling through.

I was eleven years old. Childhood was over, and childish thoughts. But dreams were still there, and the dreaming went on.